HOME
AND
AWAY

MATS SUNDIN

WITH AMY STUART

Published by Simon & Schuster

New York • London • Toronto • Sydney • New Delhi

SIMON &
SCHUSTER
CANADA

A Division of Simon & Schuster, LLC
166 King Street East, Suite 300
Toronto, Ontario M5A 1J3

All photos courtesy of the author unless otherwise noted.

This Simon & Schuster Canada edition October 2024

SIMON & SCHUSTER CANADA and colophon are registered trademarks of
Simon & Schuster, LLC

Simon & Schuster: Celebrating 100 Years of Publishing in 2024

For information about special discounts for bulk purchases, please contact
Simon & Schuster Special Sales at 1-800-268-3216 or
CustomerService@simonandschuster.ca.

Interior design by Joy O'Meara

Manufactured in the United States of America

1   3   5   7   9   10   8   6   4   2

Library and Archives Canada Cataloguing in Publication
Title: Home and away / Mats Sundin ; written by Amy Stuart.
Names: Sundin, Mats, 1971– author. | Stuart, Amy, 1975– author.
Description: Simon & Schuster Canada edition.
Identifiers: Canadiana (print) 20240365828 | Canadiana (ebook) 20240365836 |
ISBN 9781668053539 (hardcover) | ISBN 9781668053591 (EPUB)
Subjects: LCSH: Sundin, Mats, 1971– | LCSH: Hockey players—Sweden—
Biography. | LCSH: Hockey players—Ontario—Toronto—Biography. | LCSH:
Toronto Maple Leafs (Hockey team)—Biography. | LCGFT: Autobiographies. |
LCGFT: Biographies.
Classification: LCC GV848.5.S96 A3 2024 | DDC 796.962092—dc23

ISBN 978-1-6680-5353-9
ISBN 978-1-6680-5359-1 (ebook)

For Josephine, Bonnie, Nathanael and Julian

We do not remember days, we remember moments.
—*Cesare Pavese (1908–1950)*

CONTENTS

CONTENTS

1

February 2009

I jolt up in bed. I'm sweating. I can't catch my breath.

Relax, Mats, I think.

I was standing in an empty dressing room with Brian Papineau, the Toronto Maple Leafs' equipment manager. Something was wrong. My skate laces kept breaking. Sweat dripped into my eyes. The damn laces wouldn't thread. This would never happen in real life—Brian is way too good at his job. I couldn't even tie my skates. We could hear the roar of the home crowd down the hall. We were losing the game and the clock was ticking. My teammates needed me, but I wasn't there. I was stuck in the dressing room.

For a team captain, there's no worse feeling. It's my perfect nightmare.

I turn on the bedside lamp. I need to get my bearings. Everything feels out of order on this cold February morning. I'm in Toronto, the city where I've lived since 1994. But I'm in a hotel room. My house on Dunvegan Road, three miles away, sits dark and empty.

For fourteen years, hundreds and hundreds of times, I've woken up in Toronto, ready to start my game-day routine. Breakfast. A short team skate down at our home rink, the Air Canada Centre. Home. Lunch. Nap. Pregame meal. Suit on. Pregame snack, coffee, water. Back to the rink.

Today is game day, so I'll still follow that same routine. But there's one big difference: tonight, I'll suit up for the Vancouver Canucks. My last game as a Maple Leaf was nearly a year ago. It's February 21, 2009. Toronto is enemy territory now.

The Canucks arrived last night after a sound 5–2 win over the Ottawa Senators. I'd forgotten just how freezing Toronto could be in February—the sort of cold that seeps into your bones, a damp cold that reminds me of Stockholm. A few guys on the plane asked me how I was feeling. They understood the significance; even the media in Ottawa were asking me about returning to Toronto. I played thirteen seasons as a Toronto Maple Leaf, eleven as the team's captain. I'm the franchise's all-time leader in points and goals. In the fall of 2008, after a complicated year, I signed to play the final stretch of my hockey career as a Vancouver Canuck.

Last night, the drive to the hotel felt surreal. I've taken my normal route eastward from Pearson Airport to my house on Dunvegan hundreds of times. When the team bus turned south instead, my muscle memory tweaked. Traffic was light. The CN Tower stood lit up among the skyscrapers.

My teammates gave me space on the bus. I checked into my room and fell asleep easily enough.

This morning, I don't turn on the news. I stick to my routine. My breakfast consists of oatmeal and berries, toast, boiled eggs, fruit, coffee and juice—the same thing I've eaten on more than 1,300 game days. Routine has always been crucial to me. I need it. It calms me and gets me ready to compete. At home or away, I keep things familiar and predictable. The rhythms of preparation help temper the knot in my stomach. Around 11 a.m., I get dressed and descend to the lobby to board the Vancouver team bus. We are headed to the Air Canada Centre for our morning skate. I sit next to a younger teammate.

"Nervous?" he asks.

"A little."

"Everyone will be happy to see you," he says. "They love you here."

"I'm not so sure about that," I say.

"It'll be fine."

This teammate has played professional hockey for a few years, but never in Toronto. I've tried many times to explain the Toronto Maple Leafs to outsiders, whether it's fellow pros from other teams or friends and family back in Sweden. The Maple Leafs' history is long and storied and complicated. Dozens of reporters make a living writing solely about the Leafs, covering everything from trade speculation, to performance, to where players ate dinner last night, to what brand of hockey sticks we use. Every game is sold out. Despite decades without a Stanley Cup, fans are die-hard and loyal. Even when we'd play games in cities like Tampa or Los Angeles, half the fans in the building would be sporting our hometown blue and white. Leafs Nation is bigger than hockey. It's its own universe.

Pulling on the Leafs jersey for every game was a great honor. This city became my home. Many of my friends live here. My fiancée, Josephine, moved here from Sweden to live with me. Strangers would call out, "Hey Mats!" on the street. As I said, Leafs Nation is hard to explain if you haven't lived it. So, on the bus, I just nod to my well-meaning teammate.

"Yeah," I say. "It'll be fine."

We pull into the arena. The knot builds in my stomach as I get off the bus. The first person I see is Bill, the longtime usher. He offers me a warm and familiar smile.

"Welcome back, Mats."

I shake his hand, relieved. I'm intercepted by other staff, all offering the same warmth. Everyone seems as happy to see me as I am to see them. I feel my shoulders relax.

The visitors' dressing room feels like a hidden domain I always knew existed but never crossed into. It's nice, but not nearly as nice as the home dressing room on the other side of the rink.

I'm not here to get lost in memories. I'm here to play hockey. I lock into the rhythms of getting ready for the morning skate. Equipment on, sticks taped, skates tied. As soon as I step on the ice, I feel loose. *This* is familiar.

It's game day, so the skate is short. The coaches give us a few notes and send us on our way. Once showered and dressed, I wander down the hall to find Brian "Pappy" Papineau and the rest of the training and equipment crew. The walls in the equipment area are covered with the signatures of Leafs old and new. This staff was always such an important part of our team. Pappy is glad to see me. We catch up for a few minutes.

"Everyone's excited," Brian says.

I laugh. "Maybe not everyone."

After so many years in Toronto, I know better than to subject myself to the media stories about my return. I'd done a few interviews over the past few days and the questions were all variations on a theme: Do you think you'll be welcomed back? What if the fans boo you?

Toronto fans may well boo me tonight. Eight months ago, I left Toronto after we failed to make the playoffs for the third straight year. There'd been a lot of tension after I refused a trade in mid-season and then departed at its end. When I signed with the Canucks three months ago, the Toronto media demolished me.

So, no, I wasn't about to read what they were writing about me today.

"We miss you, Mats," Brian says.

I feel a lump in my throat.

"I miss you guys, too."

"Good luck tonight."

I nod. Brian steps aside to let me pass.

Back at the hotel, I settle in, calmer. I always read a book and eat ice cream before my pregame nap. Today, my book is P. O. Enquist's autobiography, *A Different Life*. Like my mother, Enquist is from Sweden's far north. His memoir is about difficult life choices and regret, which is on point today.

I'm relaxed. I pull the hotel curtains shut, set my alarm and fall asleep.

When I wake up ninety minutes later, the knot in my stomach has tightened. I dress in my suit and tie and head downstairs to eat a snack before gathering at the bus.

By the time we pull into the rink's underground parking lot, I'm in game mode. Focused, but anxious. I can remember being this nervous in 2006 before the Olympic gold medal game in Turin, or in 1992 at the World Championships, or right before a big playoff matchup. But these nerves are out of whack for a regular-season game in the middle of February.

In the dressing room, I grab a coffee and my sticks. Cutting and taping my sticks is a big part of my pregame routine. Sometimes I do two, sometimes three. Fifteen years ago, I didn't need to warm up my body. But these days, at thirty-eight, I take twenty minutes on the stationary bike and a long sequence of stretches to ramp me up to game-ready.

The clock ticks. I put on my gear, listen to the coaches and chatter with my teammates. As we stand to walk down the tunnel for our warm-up skate, the knot in my stomach twists. When I step onto the ice, there's a small roar. It's thirty minutes to puck drop, and the stands are still half-empty. But the fans who are here aren't booing at all. They might even be cheering.

As I take my first lap, I hear someone call my name.

"Mats! We love you!"

I look up at a small boy standing by the glass. He's holding a sign with a blue maple leaf and three words in bubble writing: *Thank you, Mats.*

I catch myself smiling as I skate by.

Back in the dressing room, coach Alain Vigneault announces the starting lineup. My teammates are ready. It's been a good week for the Canucks; we're on a three-game winning streak. A trainer props the dressing room door open, and I can hear the fans getting louder. Everyone in the room is locked in. At the signal, the guys stand up. Some yell, while others stay quiet. We grab our sticks and vacate the room. I step onto the ice and remind myself to veer to the visitors' side.

The crowd cheers again. I see many of my former teammates on the home side. Guys I played with for years are my opponents now.

We stand for the pregame ceremony. I close my eyes when the anthem starts. *O Canada, our home and native land.* I hum along. I've long known the words by heart. Almost twenty years ago, when I moved to Canada as a nineteen-year-old kid, it never occurred to me that this country would slowly become my home, so much so that I'd sometimes feel more Canadian than Swedish.

The fans sing and sway. When the time comes to retire from hockey, this is what I'll miss the most—standing on the blue line, anticipating the next sixty minutes. In this sport, every single game plays out like an unscripted drama. All the fans and media can try to predict the result, but the beauty of hockey lies in the fact that anything can happen. Any guy on the ice could turn out to be the night's hero. The goose bumps start on my scalp and work downward to my feet.

The lights come on and the puck drops. These days, it takes a few shifts for my legs to adjust to the intensity. It's always been hard for me to anticipate whether I'll have a good showing on a given night. I might arrive at the rink nervous or tired and then play in top form, or arrive feeling great and then flub a play. The game is so fast and physical, with a small margin between a great play and a fatal mistake.

Coach Vigneault is giving me more ice time tonight than in our previous game. I pride myself on my focus, so it's disorienting to feel distracted. I hear a few distant boos when I first touch the puck. My arms and legs go numb for an instant. It feels like a parallel universe to be on the ice at the Air Canada Centre and trying to score against the Leafs.

There's a commercial break six or so minutes into the first period. While I'm on the Canucks bench, a highlight reel of my career as a Leaf starts to play on the scoreboard. The fans stand and cheer. The guys on the Leaf bench tap their sticks. Even the Leafs management staff, way up in their private box in the rafters, rise to their feet. I'm overwhelmed. I look down, but can't hold back the tears. When the ovation shows no signs of quieting, Coach Vigneault taps me on the back to send me on the ice.

I skate to the end zone and line up to take the face-off against Matt Stajan, my friend and teammate of five years. I want the play to resume, but Stajan and the linesman back away as the ovation continues.

"Let's go," I say finally.

Stajan says something to me, but I can't hear him.

The puck drops and he wins the draw. My blood starts pumping again.

The game ends in a 2–2 tie. After five minutes of overtime, the tie stands. This means we go to a shootout.

"Sundin!" Alain yells. "You're shooter three."

The knot in my stomach is back. Toronto shoots first and misses. Pavol Demitra scores for the Canucks. The Leafs miss again. The Canucks miss. Finally, the Leafs score and the stage is set.

The shootout is tied. I'm up. Shooter three. If I score, we win the game.

The announcer calls my name. I circle back to the Canucks net. Our goalie, Roberto Luongo, gives me a nod. The crowd is deafening. As soon as I take my first stride toward the puck, the noise disappears, like a mute button has been pressed. My nerves disappear, too. I skate to pick up the puck, like I've done thousands of times. At center ice, I collect it almost casually. I might as well be back in Sweden, playing street hockey with my brothers in our driveway. In our imaginary scenarios, we were always the heroes. We were always moving in on a goalie, about to score the winner in a tie game. There was always a roaring crowd and a game on the line. I feel at home now. This is my building, these are my fans.

I gain speed. I know my move before I even cross the blue line. My dad's voice is in my head: Fake the goalie. Just a little deke to throw him off. Leafs goalie Vesa Toskala was my teammate last season. He knows my tactics, but bites anyway when I fake a shot. I cut past him and switch to my backhand, pausing for a split second before firing the puck over his pads and under the crossbar.

The red light flips on. Goal.

The mute button releases, and the noise of the crowd hits me. The Leafs have just lost, but their home fans are cheering wildly. I'm happy, relieved. My Canucks teammates join me on the ice. When I glance at the Leafs bench, I catch Brian Papineau smiling. What a strange night.

"You won't forget that one," a teammate says as we skate off.

Only after I'm back in the dressing room does it sink in just how much I'd dreaded this day. Despite my stoicism with the media and my teammates, I've been worried. I'm relieved it's over.

A reporter, Elliotte Friedman, finds me in the hallway and pulls me aside for an interview.

"Did you go to the Leafs dressing room?" he jokes.

I laugh and choke out a no.

"What a storybook ending for you."

As I try to respond, there's a crack in my voice. I'm dripping with sweat. I admit to him that the past week had been challenging because of how much Toronto means to me. Over the years, I've become good at controlling my emotions during interviews. But at this moment, I'm barely hanging on.

The truth is, I spent fifteen years imagining my last game in Toronto, ever since I was traded here in 1994. In my dream version, my final game was playing for the Stanley Cup. We win the Cup in front of a home crowd, and an entire city unleashes before our eyes. Thousands and thousands of fans flood onto Yonge Street, honking horns, their flags hanging out every window. A sea of kids laugh and cheer with the blue maple leaf painted on their faces. The parade fills the streets for miles. Even in the dream version, I feel a remarkable sense of pride in giving millions of loyal Toronto fans what they've wanted for so long.

I did score the winning goal tonight, but it wasn't the dream ending. There's no Cup to hoist, only a flight to catch. As I head to the showers, I wonder if this will be the last game I'll ever play at the Air Canada Centre. After eighteen years, my time as an NHL player is nearing its end. Lately, I've caught myself looking back on it all. The long journey from my childhood in Sweden, to an NHL career full of ups and downs, to this unforgettable February game in Toronto. How would I begin to untangle it? I'd have to start at the beginning.

2

Building a House

Tommy Sundin will tell you that it was love at first sight.

One winter Saturday night in 1965, he dressed up and went to a dance at Bacchi Wapen, a bar tucked on a narrow cobblestone alley in the oldest part of Stockholm. It was an era when men still took turns asking women to dance. Tommy had only just removed his coat before he spotted a beautiful woman across the room.

He couldn't take his eyes off her. The problem was that this young woman already had a lineup of guys waiting to ask her to dance. Tommy waited and waited, working up the courage. When the band announced the final song, he knew his time was about to run out. He nervously approached and asked her to dance. She said yes.

Her name was Gunilla Hamstig. The band played Frank Sinatra's "Strangers in the Night." Tommy and Gunilla couldn't have guessed that this would become their song. That night, once Tommy had Gunilla to himself, he had no intention of letting her go. As the lights came up on the dance floor, he asked her on a date—not to dinner or a movie, but to a hockey game.

Gunilla seemed perfectly happy at this prospect. The following weekend, Tommy's favorite hockey team, Brynäs, was in Stockholm to play the local team, AIK. Hovet Arena would be stuffed to the rafters with fans. Tommy was thrilled that she'd accepted. They didn't exchange phone numbers, but settled on a meeting time and place and said their goodbyes.

A week later, at 7:30 p.m. sharp, Tommy Sundin stood at Gate 7 in his new shirt and shoes. He'd even sprung for a more expensive haircut. By 7:45, Gunilla was nowhere in sight. He waited a few more minutes, then a few more, trying to fight off a creeping sense of rejection. Where was she? The crowds at the gates were thinning out, most of the fans already inside the arena. The game started at eight o'clock.

I'll watch the game by myself, Tommy thought, heartbroken.

Before entering the arena, he took one last look around. And there she was, standing alone at Gate 8, scanning the crowd. He called her name. Gunilla heard it and looked around until she saw him. She seemed relieved, happy to see him. She'd simply gone to a different gate. Not the wrong one, she insisted. They'd agreed on Gate 8. Tommy could only laugh and take the blame. They entered the Hovet Arena to a sold-out crowd. There were no seats in the arena back then. Every section was standing room only, thousands of fans jammed into rows that today, with safety and capacity rules, might hold half as many.

Gunilla cheered more loudly than Tommy did. He was in love.

Two years later, Tommy and Gunilla Sundin were married, and my brother Patrick was born. The young family of three settled into a two-bedroom apartment in Ängby, a suburb west of central Stockholm. Tommy worked for the state-owned telecom company, Televerket, and Gunilla took a job as a nurse at Beckomberga Hospital, a large psychiatric hospital within walking distance of their apartment building.

I was born in 1971. According to my mom, from the moment I

was born, I was a chaser. I started chasing my older brother, Patrick, as soon as I could crawl. My earliest memories are of trailing him around the grass courts between the Ängby apartment buildings. There was a metal statue of a bear that scared me. I'd always take the widest berth around it that I could.

Patrick was a natural athlete. If he was outside, kicking a soccer ball, I wanted to be outside, too. No matter where he went, I followed. When he was about eight years old, I tagged along with him and a friend as they snuck up to a delivery truck behind our Ängby apartment and swiped a bag of sugar from the open door of the cargo bed. The delivery man caught us. He wasn't about to phone the police on a four-year-old and his older brother, so he took us instead to our parents. Tommy and Gunilla were never the type to get angry, but this crossed the line. I was only four, but my brother got an earful harsh enough to end our brief criminal careers.

The apartment was small, but the tight quarters never stopped my parents from hosting friends and family often. Even in the darker winters, the apartment was always warm with the smell of coffee and cinnamon buns and the voices of neighbors and friends.

With two active and growing boys, the Ängby apartment was starting to feel small. My mother dreamed of a house. She came home one day and told my father she'd found a lot in Sollentuna, former cottage country twenty minutes northwest of Stockholm that was being parceled off for residential development. The lot was on a steep incline, about two hundred yards uphill from a lake.

"The lake will freeze in the winter," Gunilla told my father.

Gunilla had a vision. They'd build a house and raise their family there. But to Tommy, their little apartment in Ängby was fine. The lot was expensive and interest rates were at 14 percent. In 1970s Sweden, it was common practice to raise your family in an apartment. The Social Democratic Party—Socialdemokraterna—

had held power since the Second World War, with working-class voters like my parents as its core supporters. The prime minister, Olof Palme, was a strong advocate of unionized labor, women's rights, universal health care and schooling. He was progressive in his focus on building schools and hospitals, housing and roads, even bike lanes and transit. Not many Swedes were rich, but with a strong welfare system of tax-funded education, health care and dentistry, the broad middle class lived comfortably. In the early 1970s, France's right-wing president, Georges Pompidou, described his perfect country as *"la Suède avec un peu plus de soleil"*—Sweden, but with more sun.

To Tommy, Gunilla's plan felt out of reach. Sure, Sollentuna seemed like it could be a wonderful place to raise a family. The area was beautiful, and the lake was visible from the lot. But aside from the money they didn't have to buy it, there was one other major problem: Gunilla's dream lot was empty.

"How are we going to build a house?" Tommy asked.

"We'll figure it out."

Tommy wasn't convinced.

"If you're not going to buy it with me," Gunilla told him, "then I'll buy it myself."

By then, Tommy understood one thing about Gunilla. While he had been raised three hours from Stockholm in the sizable town of Bollnäs, his wife had grown up in the farthest northern reaches of Sweden. Her childhood village of Kainulasjärvi was thirty miles north of the Arctic Circle and had fewer than 150 residents. It was a village of loggers and miners. The winter months were long and dark, and the summer mosquitoes were fierce.

Kainulasjärvi was the sort of place that built character and forced a certain level of hardiness among its locals. This quality lingered in Gunilla. Her friends who'd also moved to the city came over often for traditional *syjuntas*, gatherings where the women would sew and chat. Gunilla still spoke Meänkieli, a minority language specific to the Tornio Valley region of the north. Tommy didn't understand the words, but he could often catch her meaning by the animated way she spoke. Gunilla was good at getting her message across.

Tommy knew he had no choice but to get on board with the lot.

With some help from Tommy's brother-in-law, who worked at a bank, Tommy and Gunilla secured a loan of 300,000 kronor—roughly $70,000—and bought the lot in Sollentuna and a Volkswagen Beetle. By 1973, they had a car, a steep lot covered in pine trees, and a building fund with a very high interest rate.

But no house.

Tommy called on his dad, Sture Sundin, for help. The two of them spent many weeks cutting down trees, then found a local company willing to blast out the hill to make room for a foundation. By the end of summer, the lot was clear and ready. Tommy stood over the hole in the ground and scratched his head. They'd made much progress. But the same question remained: How was he supposed to build a house?

He found himself a house plan with drawings. Then he spotted an ad in the newspaper for a retired home builder and called the number. Days later, the man stood with him on the lot, scratching his head, too.

"Don't worry, Tommy," the man said. "I will help you. We will build you a house."

It took two years. Friends and family helped, particularly Tommy's dad and Gunilla's brother Rolf, but mostly Tommy labored on his own. He learned to put up walls and lay flooring. If he had to call a plumber or another trade, Tommy would shadow them on the job so that he might tackle any similar task himself next time. This continued for months, evenings and weekends, until Tommy had a home for his family—two stories and a second-floor balcony with a clear view of the lake. There was a small bedroom for each of the kids and one for Gunilla and him. In 1975, the year my younger brother, Per, was born, the five of us moved to our new home in Sollentuna.

My parents loved sports, and it rubbed off on us. Our TV only had two channels, SVT1 and SVT2, both state-owned. Anytime either was airing sports, we were watching. It didn't matter what sport—soccer, pole vaulting, cross-country skiing. The TV and radio were on around the clock during any of the Olympic Games. My dad's favorite sport had always been ice hockey. Growing up, he'd been a goaltender.

In many parts of rural Sweden, hockey was less popular than a sport called bandy. Bandy is like field hockey on skates, played on an ice sheet the size of a soccer pitch. In 1939, my grandfather Sture helped start the Warpen IK ice hockey team in Bollnäs, and my dad took up the game as soon as he was old enough to skate. Tommy even claimed he brought his goalie pads to a tryout camp for the Swedish junior national team as a teenager. My mother joked that she'd only believe him if he could prove it.

Just as my mother promised, the lake down the hill froze that first winter in Sollentuna. My dad set out with a shovel to clear snow off a rectangular patch big enough for us to skate on. It took him time to perfect his rink-building skills—clear the area, then use a bucket to flood it. He couldn't work fast enough. Up the hill, his sons were waiting impatiently. All they wanted to do was play hockey.

3

Chasing Patrick

"Please," I begged my mom. "Please, can I go, too?"

I was six, and Patrick was ten. It was 1977. Nearly every day after school, Patrick and his friends would gather for a hockey game down on the lake. I was desperate to join them, to play. To be included. At two, Per was still too young to feel left out. That would come later.

"Patrick," my mother would say, "let Mats play."

My brother was understandably irritated. Every day, he faced the same scene. He'd make plans with his friends and get ready, shovel in hand, skates over his shoulder, a few pucks in his pockets. I'd ask to join them, and when he answered no, I'd run to my mother and plead with her to override him.

"Patrick," she'd say.

"He can't even skate!" Patrick would respond.

At this, I'd start crying.

Patrick had every reason to be annoyed. He and his friends were all a head taller than me, and a lot faster. I knew I wasn't welcome, that I was a pest in their way, but I didn't care.

"Fine!" Patrick would eventually say, exasperated.

He relented every time, but drew the line at waiting for me or helping me get ready. My mom was the one who'd tie my skates, secure my helmet and make sure I had gloves and snow pants.

Down on the lake, Patrick's friends were tolerant at best. Patrick was right—I couldn't skate. I fell constantly, tripping over cracks in the ice, landing hard on my stomach, then popping back to my feet. They never passed to me. If I was going to touch the puck, I had to find a way to get to it first.

This went on for years, Patrick and his friends skating, biking, playing soccer, and me, desperate to keep up, always chasing.

Patrick started playing organized hockey in the local league in Sollentuna. Most of his games were played outdoors, no matter how cold the weather. I'd tag along to his games and practices with my dad, desperate for the day I'd be old enough to sign up.

Even in Sweden, winter doesn't last forever. By March, the days would grow long and the ice on the lake or at the local outdoor rink would melt. Our focus would turn to playing soccer and riding our bikes. It became obvious to my parents that I was going to compete hard in any sport I played. I hated losing. I hated it when my brother and his friends tried to leave me out.

My mother resigned herself to the fact that her three boys would come home most days covered in dirt, our shoes scuffed, holes in the knees of our pants that she'd have to mend. This was her fate. The best she could hope for was that we didn't break any bones or lose an eye or any teeth.

With the Sundin brothers, even that was wishful thinking.

My front baby teeth fell out early in the first grade. After a few months with a toothless smile, my adult pair grew in, white and shiny and far too big for my young face. Any jokes about their size were short-lived, because the spring after I turned seven, a battle on the soccer field at school sent me flying open-mouthed into an opponent's skull. We rolled to a stop, him holding his head and screaming, me with a hand to my mouth.

It was my first time tasting the distinct metallic flavor of a mouthful of blood. I lifted a hand to spit, catching the two perfect white rectangles in my palm. My front teeth.

The school called Gunilla at work and she arrived to collect me. I remember the look of horror on her face when I forced a smile to reveal the toothless grin I'd only just outgrown, this time with my adult teeth wrapped in a paper towel. This set off years of visits to dentists in an effort to put them back in place and keep them there. Bridges were installed, special toothpaste used to correct the discoloring. My parents were dutiful in taking me to every appointment. I learned to smile with my mouth closed. They might not have put in the effort if they'd known my future was in hockey, all but assuring this wouldn't be the last time my teeth were knocked from my face.

During school hours, Patrick was spared being harassed by his unrelenting younger brother. Given our age differences, the three Sundin brothers were always at different schools. As a newer suburb, Sollentuna was still figuring out its school configurations. After a few years of primary a short drive up the road, I graduated in the fourth grade to a bigger building that I could bike to on my own.

My childhood summers were always about traveling north to my mother's village of Kainulasjärvi, or to Bollnäs to visit my dad's side of the family. Tommy's parents, Marta and Sture Sundin, got divorced when he was ten years old. Even though Sweden has never been a very religious country, divorce in the 1950s was still rare. When I was growing up, my dad never talked about their split. Sture was a train driver who lived in Stockholm with his second wife, Anna, and they spent their summers at a cabin in the wilderness. Marta lived in Bollnäs, but often stayed with us in Sollentuna. In the absence of a clear explanation, I never bothered to compute the logistics. I was maybe eight before I figured out that Marta and Sture had once been married. When I brought up this obvious fact to Patrick, he looked at me as though I'd just told him the sun was in the sky.

I loved our summer trips to Sture and Anna's cabin a few hours from Bollnäs. For nearly a hundred years, logging companies used the Voxnan River to transport logs from the deep forest inland to the timber mills along the coast of the Baltic Sea. Loggers would sleep in the cabin overnight as their haul made its way downstream. When the cabin was decommissioned in the 1960s, Sture bought it, painted it, furnished it sparingly, and added a small kitchen with a gas cooktop and a few cots. There was no electricity or running water.

The route from Stockholm required special focus in the final stretch to avoid hitting a moose. My dad drove while my mom kept watch. The final three miles took us over a bumpy gravel road that hugged the banks of the river. We had to park five hundred yards from the cabin because the last bit of lane was impassable. Over time, Sture labored at moving rocks and filling holes to open that final stretch of lane, allowing arriving cars to inch closer and closer to the cabin every year. As soon as I tumbled from the back seat, the fresh air would hit me, the woodsy scent of the surrounding forest.

The cabin was red wood with a black tin roof and small white windows. Its porch sat so close to the river's edge that you could cast a fishing line from a chair next to the front door. Anna and Sture always greeted us happily, ready for a few weeks of adventure, the seven of us sharing two rooms and a vast expanse of wilderness.

To a boy like me, it was paradise.

The river became the source of many vivid memories. At night, we'd hear the rustle of moose crossing its stream. There was an old rowboat we used to cross it ourselves, or paddle against the current as we fished for pike and perch, trout and grayling. Sture built a floating dock out of old oil barrels and scrap wood and anchored it out from the bank. In the evenings, my dad and I would stand on the dock with a bar of soap to clean up.

Once, when I was about five, we stood together on that dock and I lost my footing. My dad's back was turned. I still remember the sensation of sitting on the bottom of the river, looking around, my arms floating white and fuzzy in front of me. Then, there was a tug at my hair. I broke through the surface and took a breath. My dad yanked me up onto the dock. He hadn't seen or heard me fall in, only turned around to find the space next to him empty, my blond hair glowing under the surface.

He checked me over, distressed. I was fine.

"We won't tell your mother," he said.

A few years later, I stood on that same dock as my brother Patrick wound up to cast his line. But the unsteady current knocked his aim off. His fishhook caught me above the right eye and jabbed itself in. I screamed. Patrick screamed. The adults came running, their peaceful evening meal interrupted.

The closest hospital was sixty miles away, in Ljusdal. With the hook's barbs tangled deep in my skin, it was decided that my dad would drive me, even though we wouldn't get there until nearly midnight. It was Swedish summer; despite the late hour, the sun was only just setting.

In the passenger seat, I sat on my hands to stop myself from tinkering with the fishhook hanging above my eye. At the end of the gravel road, we passed an abandoned house. A lone moose stood eating grass in its field. That memory is even clearer to me than our arrival at the hospital, the pain in removing the hook, the stitches, the drive back to the cabin where Sture, Anna and my mother stayed awake and waiting. Mostly, I remember the sight of that moose in the field, its head down, focused on its task. It didn't even look up as we passed.

4

The Devil's Underwear

The car was always packed up to its roof with pillows, duvets, a cooler, sandwiches with cheese and a thermos full of hot chocolate. The three of us boys had fresh haircuts. My parents were on vacation and school was out for summer break. We were about to drive overnight, setting off as soon as my parents returned from work for the long trip to Kainulasjärvi.

From Sollentuna, the route to Kainulasjärvi follows the Baltic Sea for 550 miles before cutting inland. The trees that line the road, mostly pine, birch and fir, get smaller and smaller the farther north you go.

By early the next morning, we'd be on the final stretch. Tommy would sometimes have to stop the car to allow herds of reindeer to cross the road. He'd flip on the wipers to dispel the onslaught of mosquitoes. We were above the Arctic Circle by then. My father's patience was worn out just in time for my brothers and me to be awake and silly with excitement. Tommy would grip his steering wheel to stretch an arm into the rear seat, the three of us laughing and leaning back as far as we could to avoid his reach.

Finally, after fifteen hours of driving, we'd come to a sign on the road: *Kainulasjärvi*.

This is where my mother grew up, a village of 150 people in the Tornio Valley, the northernmost part of Sweden that hugs the Finnish border. A few miles east of Kainulasjärvi, the untouched Kalix River cuts a path from Kebnekaise, Sweden's highest mountain, to the Baltic Sea. Some villagers were Laestadians, members of a branch of Lutheranism founded in the 1800s that practiced a rigid way of life. They had as many children as God granted them, and their homes were humble and spartan. Even in the 1970s, a handful of villagers were so devoutly religious that they called window curtains "the Devil's underwear"—a comfort one should live without. Kainulasjärvi was a safe and warm community, the sort of place where you left a broom leaning on your door to indicate that no one was home. This is the "Tornio Valley lock."

My grandparents Sven and Elsa raised their family with a gentler approach. Their home was like any other in Sweden: They enjoyed music and television. They had curtains. My mother was the second-oldest of six kids, so they still had two teenagers at home when their grandchildren started arriving in quick succession.

No matter what time we pulled up in the morning, Sven and Elsa would be awake and waiting for us. Soon enough, my aunts and uncles and cousins would arrive, too. By the time everyone was there, there were seven adults and nine kids sharing a small house. The five Sundins all slept in the same top-floor bedroom. At night, it got so hot that we'd all sleep in our underwear, the windows closed to keep the mosquitoes out. I still ask my parents today why they didn't install a screen so that the windows could stay open. They have no good answer.

Kainulasjärvi felt like home. I loved the vast stretches of forest and the slow pace of the village. I loved how happy my parents were up there, free from the stresses of their work and our busy school and sports schedules. I loved riding bikes and mopeds through the village with no one concerned for our safety or location. I loved the way everyone in Kainulasjärvi helped everyone else, whether it was harvesting hay, cutting firewood or painting a shed or barn.

In the middle of this world, my grandmother sat at the wheel. She had a chair in the kitchen that was her perch, her territory. Our perch was her lap or the seat at the table next to her. She played music on a black cassette player that sat on the corner of the kitchen counter—often spiritual music about God or the Tornio Valley. Even during our visits, my grandparents sometimes led prayer meetings in their kitchen. As the visiting son-in-law, Tommy's job was to find enough chairs so everyone would have a seat.

On the outskirts of the village was a gravel soccer field with two older nets marking each end. The Kainulasjärvi SK played in Sweden's sixth division, and their games against nearby villages marked the biggest social event of the week. Its players were pale and tough men who spent the summers working in the forest or the mines, leaving the field free for us kids to gather and play.

In a village of 150, there aren't enough local children to form teams, so kids like my brothers and cousins and me, whose parents had moved away and were home visiting, were folded in as locals. The soccer field became a meeting point nearly every day. We did drills and played little matches before organizing a game.

The games were serious stuff. The big leagues, thanks to a man named Tore.

A local to Kainulasjärvi, Tore was an adult living with a developmental disability. He was also the village's official soccer referee. Every afternoon, he would arrive at the pitch on his bicycle, wearing a FIFA-grade referee uniform his mother ordered for him from the thick department store catalog all homes had in the 1980s. A large man with black hair and a mustache that instilled respect, Tore looked so professional and took his role so seriously that, as far as we kids were concerned, he might as well have been referee for a World Cup match.

One sunny afternoon in Kainulasjärvi, we stood in formation as Tore decided the teams. This was a challenge when there was a ten-year age range and a two-foot height difference between the youngest and oldest kids on the field. Tore was incredibly careful in his selections. He knew who the best runners, kickers and scorers were, which kids were sensitive and which could be tough, who was local and who was only home for a visit. With many levers to balance, he made his selections with a fair eye. Sometimes he put Patrick, Per and me together; sometimes we were opponents. That day, Patrick was my opponent.

To me, there was no such thing as a casual game. No setting where having fun was more important than winning. Whether I was shooting pucks in the driveway or sprinting the length of a soccer pitch, I was always full on. Losing *any* game ate at me, especially when one or both of my brothers were on the other team. Losing is bad enough, but there's no fate worse than losing to one of your brothers.

The soccer games were always spirited. That afternoon, my team was quickly losing by a few goals. I received the ball on a throw-in and carried it up the field. As I ran, an older boy nudged me and knocked me off my track. I lost my balance and fell, rolling several times in the dirt before coming to a stop on my stomach, my knees scraped and bloody. I looked up at the boy now running with the ball, then jumped to my feet, overcome with rage.

"*Javla skit!*" I yelled. *Fucking shit!*

Immediately, the whistle screamed. Tore's face was bright red. He strode at me, almost in slow motion, digging at his breast pocket. I could feel the panic setting in. His red card popped out in a wicked flash.

"Red card!" Tore called, his voice deep and booming. "For swearing."

I looked around. The other kids, including my brothers, stood wide-eyed and silent. I'd dug my own grave, and they weren't about to risk their spot in the game by trying to help me out of it. What did it matter that my parents didn't mind when we swore? This was Kainulasjärvi, this was Tore's turf. He was a religious man, a Laestadian to his core, and the words I'd uttered were blasphemy.

"Go home, Mats," he said.

I left the field in tears. I couldn't bear the sounds of the game starting again without me. Within a minute I was on my grandmother's bicycle, my bloody knees peddling a ladies' bike with raised handlebars. The seat was too high for me. The bike wobbled as I tried to gain speed. Still, I pedaled furiously back to my grandparents' house, crying loudly on the empty road. Mosquitoes flew into my open mouth.

When I got home, I leapt off the bike and ran into the house. My parents sat at the kitchen table, drinking coffee. My dad saw the look on my face.

"What's wrong?" he asked.

Breathing hard from the bike ride, I was unable to talk between sobs.

"What happened?" my mother said.

Finally, I got the words out: I was tripped. It was a foul. There was no call, so I swore.

My father shot me a look. "What did you say?"

I repeated my slur.

"Then Tore kicked me out of the game," I continued. "He gave me a red card."

The sobs took over. My mother guided me to the table and

offered me some milk and a sandwich. Then she sat, too. Why weren't either of my parents saying anything? Why were their heads down?

I'm not sure which of them broke first. A smile, then full-blown laughter. Then apologies for their laughter. Could this get any worse? Kicked out of the soccer game, a mouth full of bugs, and now my parents found the whole thing *funny*?

"You'll go back tomorrow," my father said. "Tore will let you play."

They were right. He did let me play. The red card was never mentioned again. And, on that soccer field, I never swore again.

Leaving Kainulasjärvi after our summer visits was always hard, but I loved our Christmas visits, too. That far north lived in polar night from November to January; the sun only skirted under the horizon for a few hours a day, casting everything in a dusky blue light. The temperature sank well below 0 Fahrenheit, and there was always so much snow.

When my mother was a girl, a few Kainulasjärvi men got together to clear a local field for a hockey rink. The story goes that this rogue pack didn't ask permission, but instead met up at random times to cut down trees and clear the oval. As more villagers found out, they joked that the men might get arrested. Eventually, the village invested in boards and lights for the rink. The Kainulasjärvi SK hockey team was formed from the handful of locals who owned skates. The ice stayed frozen well into the spring months.

The best thing about sports is that anyone can dream of being the best. Even in the farthest north of Sweden, you had the freedom to imagine that, one day, you might get to pull on the blue-and-yellow jersey and play for your country's national team. It didn't hurt that northern Swedes had a local hero who'd reached the highest levels of hockey. National superstar Börje Salming was from Kiruna, a mining town of fifteen thousand people two to three hours northwest of Kainulasjärvi along a bumpy mining and logging highway. Salming's father died in the local mine when Börje was only five years old. Kiruna was one of the only northern spots with an indoor arena.

My dad loved Börje Salming. The whole country did. But even in Stockholm, it was rare to get news of his games, let alone see footage of him playing. We only really saw him in action when he played for Team Sweden on the world stage. I loved hockey to my core, but the NHL was still mostly a foreign world to me. All I knew was that a man who grew up a hundred miles from my mother now played for a faraway team called the Toronto Maple Leafs.

5

Red Net

By 1980, my parents were running a two-person taxi business servicing three boys and their sports. I'd started playing organized hockey in Sollentuna. The Sundin brothers played hockey and bandy in the winter, and soccer in the summer. Patrick graduated from our local hockey league to the more competitive Djurgårdens organization in south Stockholm, a thirty-minute drive from home. On a Saturday, my dad might drive to three different practices, then arrive home, only to shuttle one of us up the road for a game of bandy.

My mom ran a tight ship. Meals were always cooked and eaten at home. We never went to restaurants. We were always on time for everything. But as organized as they were, sometimes even my parents slipped up. One night, my dad and I arrived home from a practice twenty minutes away and walked into the kitchen. My dad sat at the table, famished and exhausted. Busy preparing dinner, my mother didn't take immediate stock of us. Finally, she turned around.

"Where's Per?" she asked.

Where *was* Per? Sometimes the family logistics required bringing my younger brother along to one of our practices. He didn't mind. Per loved the arenas. He'd find lost pucks along the boards or gather other younger siblings to form a game. He could roam the rink and entertain himself for hours. Once I was off the ice, my dad would have to go in search of him so we could go home.

"Where is Per?" my mom repeated.

Without a word, my dad stood up, put on his coat and left.

Twenty minutes of driving home and neither my dad nor I had registered that Per wasn't with us. Tommy got back to the rink and found him on top of the snow pile made by the Zamboni. His own ice mountain. He never even clued in that he'd been left behind.

When my dad got home again, this time with all his kids accounted for, my mom only had to shoot him a look. It would never happen again. Per bounded into the kitchen, looking for dinner, never the wiser.

In December, the sun is only up for five midday hours. Morning and evening drives to the arena were almost always in the dark. But Swedes work hard to make the most of this darkness. Nearly every downtown street is crisscrossed with warm strings of light. Stores and restaurants line their doorways with oil lanterns. People survive by adopting the idea of *mysigt*—filling spaces with comfort and light. And they stay active. Even on the shortest, coldest day of a Stockholm winter, the local hockey arena and bandy pad were always bustling.

The winter solstice in December was naturally followed by every kid's favorite holiday: Christmas. Sweden is one of the most secular countries in the world. But the Christmas season is still full of traditions. In my house, one such custom was opening a gift on Christmas Eve. Every year, Santa made a special appearance at our house, arriving suspiciously soon after my dad announced he was stepping out to get the newspaper. Sometimes, Santa looked a lot like my dad. Sometimes, he looked like a neighbor or one of my uncles. He always wore the full Santa outfit—red suit, white beard, hat, and gift sack slung over his shoulder. He always greeted us with a booming *Ho ho ho!* By the time Patrick and I were old enough to see through the ruse, we played along on behalf of a younger Per.

I was nine in 1980. That Christmas, our house was buzzing with nervous excitement, our whole family dressed in our best clothes: the five Sundins, plus aunts, uncles, cousins and grandparents. My mom worked all day to prepare a Christmas Eve feast of ham, meatballs, sausages, flavored herring, potatoes, gingerbread cookies and *Ris à la Malta*—rice pudding—for dessert. The adults drank mulled wine and beer.

My brothers and I sat through the meal with our dress shirts on as patiently as we could. We were distracted. For a few days, there'd been a large box under our tree with our three names on it, but the rule was that we couldn't open it until Santa arrived and gave us the go-ahead. He'd delivered it early because it was too big for the sleigh.

We were still at the table when there was a knock at the door. I flew out of my seat. My dad answered, and in stumbled Santa. He made his way to the chair by the fireplace, insisting he was already tired from his Christmas Eve travels. My mother made a show of getting him some gingerbread and a drink.

"I hear there are some nice boys in this house," he said.

The three brothers nodded. Santa handed us each a gift from his bag, and we ripped them open. Then he pointed to the box under the tree.

"I have to continue on my travels," he said, "but you can open that one now."

As soon as he left, my brothers and I attacked the box. Wrapping paper rained around the room. This was a gift from Santa, but my dad watched us with his arms crossed, a big smile on his face. He seemed to know how much we'd love it.

"A hockey net!" Patrick shouted.

Per and I jumped up and down. We couldn't believe it. We looked at the picture on the box. It wasn't a full-size net, but a smaller one perfect for our driveway. Red aluminum—a real hockey net. We pulled the parts out of the box and watched in agony as my dad worked to assemble it in the living room. By the time it was put together, it was too late for us to shoot. We couldn't wake the neighbors.

I could hardly sleep that night. All I cared about was our net and all the shots I would take. It was the best gift imaginable, one I understand now that my parents would have had to save up to buy for us.

On Christmas Day, my mother couldn't get us inside for meals. The three of us—five, nine and thirteen years old—played outside for the entire day, taking shots, figuring out the best angles, picking corners. Our driveway was on an upward incline, which made shooting that much more of a challenge. The biggest argument was always over whose turn it was to play goalie. None of the Sundin brothers had plans to follow in our dad's netminding footsteps.

After Christmas, there were always a few days when my parents returned to work but school was still on holiday. For those stretches, my grandmother Marta would stay in Sollentuna to look after us. She spent most of her day in our kitchen, preparing meals and freezing dinners for us to eat after she'd gone home to Bollnäs. Often, we were under her feet, looking for snacks or attention. But this year, Marta mostly had peace and quiet with us outside playing street hockey and shooting for hours on end. One day, when she called us in for lunch, the ongoing argument over goaltending followed us into the kitchen. Marta listened to us bicker. She tried to referee the discussion, but none of us would relent.

"What's the problem?" she asked.

"We need a goalie."

"You mean someone to stand in the net," she said.

We nodded. She knew the position. Her son Tommy had played it growing up.

As we finished our meal, Marta found her coat and put on her boots.

"Where are you going?" one of us asked.

Outside. She was coming outside with us.

"I'll be your goalie," she said.

She didn't even take off her apron. We followed her outside, wide-eyed. One of us handed her a stick. She had no equipment, so we decided we couldn't shoot actual rubber pucks at her. Only balls. One of us showed her the proper form: Bend your knees, hold the stick on the ground, lift your elbows. Hold your other arm up to catch. She didn't have a glove, but she took the position anyway. Marta was ready.

Game on.

We started shooting the balls at our *grandmother*. She did her best to stop them, jerking a shoulder or kicking out a leg, crouching to take up more net, laughing at our cheers when we scored on her. Marta's logic was simple: her grandsons needed a goalie. How hard could it be? She washed her hands at the kitchen sink and took up her spot in net.

As the months passed and spring came, the paint on the net started to chip, but it never lost its luster. I took thousands of shots on that net, deking imaginary opponents, scoring the winning goal against the Soviet Union or even Canada, two hockey superpowers, then lifting my wooden stick in celebration. Beyond our driveway, we always looked for ways to keep playing hockey. Patrick and his friends took it upon themselves to form a summer ball hockey league. This wasn't just kids collecting at an agreed-upon stretch of roadway to play; it quickly grew into an organized league with local teams, home surfaces and set game times.

The boundaries were established according to the smaller communities within Sollentuna—Viby, Rotebro, Häggvik and our home turf, Norrviken. You could bike a loop through all four neighborhoods in under fifteen minutes, but to the players, it was as good as different countries facing off in the Olympics. The home surfaces were asphalt tennis courts or schoolyards. We'd bring nets and goalie equipment and play with a tennis ball. By *we*, I mean my brother and his friends. As always, I was the unwanted appendage, the short blond brother offering to play goal just for the chance to take part.

6

Pelle's Mask

At ten years old, I was starting to outpace many of my teammates on the ice. The coaches in Sollentuna often allowed me to play with older kids, which suited me fine. As my game improved, even Patrick and his friends resisted my presence less at the lake. Like Patrick had at my age, I needed to graduate from our local hockey club to play somewhere more competitive.

For my parents, this meant more time and cost. With three growing boys at home, they were buying four gallons of milk a week. By then, it was clear that they were going to do everything they could to make sure we could play. All they wanted was for us to be healthy and active and to have fun. In the spring or summer, when the schedule was lighter, they both took on overtime, extra shifts and even extra jobs to help pay for their kids' sports. My dad would source used hockey equipment for Patrick that would eventually be handed down to me, and finally to Per. He brought home electrical tape from his work to tape our sticks.

They never complained or pushed us. In the Sundin house, the line was drawn at having to convince us to play or train. There was a lot of sacrifice involved in getting us to games and practices, so we had to want it. And we did. We loved games and practices, and the three of us would go to bed at night, our legs like noodles from a day full of sport.

Aside from our travels to visit family, my parents had to work through the summer while we were on school break, so a schedule was cobbled together for us that included time with our grandparents and camps here and there. My favorite week of the summer was a hockey camp in Furudal, a small inland village ninety minutes from Bollnäs.

It was not a fancy setup, but to me, it was heaven. Two long sessions of hockey every day, then soccer and other games, and barbecues every night. Kids traveled from all over Sweden to attend. There were no cabins, so the campers slept on inflatable mattresses spread across the classroom floors of the local elementary school. We swam and water-skied in the nearby lake.

The highlight for everyone was always the surprise guest at the end of the week. Every year, the organizers would bring in a famous Swedish player, a guy who'd played in the Olympics or the Swedish Elite League. We'd skate around with him, then take turns lining up for photos and autographs. In 1982, on the last day of camp, they brought us all onto the ice, making a big show of it. There were rumors about who it might be this year, but no one had a solid guess.

The door at the far end of the ice opened, and out stepped Pelle Lindbergh. He wore his white goalie mask and his NHL Philadelphia Flyers jersey. Most of us knew Lindbergh from his time in the SEL and on the Olympic team. At the Lake Placid Olympics in 1980, he'd almost secured Sweden a win against the eventual champions, Team USA, but a late goal allowed for a tie. Even if none of us could find Philadelphia on a map, we understood the significance of a real NHL jersey in our midst. The kids went wild.

Lindbergh was smaller in stature than some of the young players. He lifted his mask to reveal a mop of dark brown hair. We crowded around him, full of questions. He answered them dutifully, laughing at many. Finally, he pulled down his goalie mask.

"Who wants to take a penalty shot on me?"

We couldn't believe our luck. When my turn came, I could feel my heart beating in my chest. I lined up at center to pick up the puck, then gained as much speed as possible. I took the hardest shot I could muster, but Lindbergh made an easy glove save.

There were no second chances if we missed, as we all did. In the locker room, some kids calculated their prospects as we undressed. If we made it to the NHL within ten years, we might play against Lindbergh and score on him in a real game. He was only twenty-three, so it was entirely possible he'd play for another decade. All we had to do was make the NHL.

That fall, Lindbergh returned to Philadelphia and played forty games for the Flyers. He was their starter for two more years. In 1985, he carried them to the Stanley Cup Final, where they lost to the Edmonton Oilers. He was the first European to win the Vézina Trophy as the league's best goaltender.

I did make it to the NHL less than ten years later. But I never got to play against Lindbergh. In the late days of 1985, he was killed in a car crash while driving home from a team party. When the news of his death was reported in Sweden, they wrote about his family traveling to the USA to bring his body on the long journey home. His number, 31, was never officially retired, but no Flyer player has worn it since.

That same summer, Patrick attended a training camp with his team from Djurgården. The coach running the camp was named Mats Hamnarbäck. Tommy loved his style of running practices and engaging the kids. When we learned that Coach Mats was a volunteer with Djurgården and planned to coach my 1971 age group the following season, I insisted that my dad let me try out.

I wanted to play for the same club as Patrick did. Even at ten, I was chasing my older brother.

Luckily, Coach Mats knew me. The previous spring, my Sollentuna team mounted an upset for the ages by beating Djurgården in the Stockholm city finals. This was the youth hockey equivalent of David beating Goliath. I'd done well in that game, so Coach Mats offered me a spot on his team.

My dad's driving time essentially doubled. Back then, it wasn't common for kids to play for teams far from home. Even today, the Swedish hockey system is built heavily on kids playing close to home. Organizations in the Swedish Elite League, Djurgårdens IF, had development programs meant to nurture talent and keep kids playing in the same group for as long as possible. As if he weren't busy enough with his day job, my dad even offered to act as manager for Coach Mats's team, handling the finances and planning.

Before my first season started, Coach Mats asked my new teammates and me to write our dreams on paper. I could see my teammates struggling to come up with their answers, but not me. I knew my dream.

To be the best, I wrote. *To play on the Swedish national team.*

These were lofty goals. Brash, for a player who'd just arrived from a small suburban league to play on the best team in the city. But I didn't care. I had no idea what my teammates wrote. When Coach Mats got to my piece of paper, he looked at me. He could have laughed, but he didn't. He nodded. Once the season started, he made it clear to me that my dreams were possible, and he was willing to help me make them happen.

"He's very talented," Mats told my father as our season began. "Is he?"

Tommy wasn't being naive, or sarcastic. He understood that I was a good player. Yet he knew that being noticeable on the ice in the small sample of Sollentuna was one thing. Whether that talent would manifest as the competition got harder remained to be seen.

For my dad, the best part of having two kids playing within the Djurgårdens organization was that players were offered free tickets to watch the SEL games. Busy as my family was, we somehow made it to almost every home game at Hovet Arena, the location of my parents' first date so many years earlier.

I played with Coach Mats on Djurgården for five years. As I got older and faster, he pushed and encouraged me more and more. He taught me that, while my talent was evident, many kids were talented. Talent alone wasn't enough. What mattered more was a willingness to work hard, to listen, to push myself, to bounce back when a shift or a game didn't go my way. He taught me that the players who had both the talent and that willingness to work hard would be the ones who'd go far. I wanted that to be me.

Every year in Stockholm, the minor hockey season culminated with all the top teams competing in the Sankt Erikscupen tournament. The final games were held at the Hovet Arena and covered by some of the local media. I was fourteen the first time we made it to the finals. After I scored, my photo was printed in the newspaper, hands in the air in celebration. I couldn't believe the feeling of seeing my name and picture in print. My mom clipped it out and put it in a brand-new photo album, the rest of its pages waiting to be filled.

7

Olof Palme

By the time I was fifteen, hockey was starting to take me places. One Christmas break, my Djurgården team traveled to an international tournament in Finland that brought together Europe's hockey powerhouses: the Soviet Union, Sweden, Finland and Czechoslovakia. We stayed in Helsinki and rang in the new year in a different city from home. While our team struggled at that tournament, I did well. I began to feel this sense of possibility. It was also becoming clear to my parents and coaches that my level of play was beyond that of most kids my age, that I was eclipsing even kids older than me. I needed more of a challenge.

In 1984, when Sweden won the bronze medal at the Olympics in Sarajevo, I watched the games with my parents and brought up the possibility of one day playing for a gold medal myself. I'd been dreaming of it for years, but it was around then that my parents recognized it as a real possibility, too. When the USSR trounced Sweden, 10–1, in the Sarajevo round-robin, the Russian player Viacheslav Fetisov—a towering, high-scoring defenseman—secured himself as the opponent of my dreams, the guy I conjured while taking shots in the driveway.

For a young hockey player, the USSR was an enemy as good as they come. My parents would have argued that as Swedes, we were lucky not to have many real political enemies, foreign or domestic. We'd stayed neutral in both world wars. While local politics could be contentious, acts of violence or protest were rare in our country. Sweden wasn't perfect. The ruling Socialdemokraterna party had been in power for a long time, and not everyone loved our politicians and their policies. Still, with communism still heavily in place, peeks into the troubles of our neighbors made Swedes feel secure in their country's safety and peace.

On the morning of March 1, 1986, that all changed.

It was a Saturday, so of course I had hockey practice. My mom opened my bedroom door to nudge me awake before sunrise. My bedroom still had the same green wallpaper with white circles they'd put up when I was small. Sitting up, I could tell something was wrong. My mother sat on the edge of my bed, frowning.

"Olof Palme is dead," she said.

I shook my head, confused.

"He was shot on Sveavägen last night."

It took a split second to register who she was talking about: Olof Palme. Sweden's prime minister.

"What?" I said.

"You need to get up. Breakfast is ready."

My bedroom was just off the kitchen. I got up in a daze. My dad stood over the radio at the counter while my mom served us breakfast. Per joined us, rubbing his eyes.

The announcer repeated the bulletin. Late the night before, Olof Palme had been walking home from a movie with his wife when a man approached them and shot him in the back. Lisbeth Palme was grazed by a second bullet. The shooter escaped into the darkness of a Stockholm alley. As of this hour, the killer was still on the loose.

"Where were his bodyguards?" my mother asked.

It turns out Olof Palme didn't have any bodyguards with him that night. In 1986, Sweden was the kind of place where our prime minister and his wife could meet their son and his girlfriend at a movie theater on a Friday night, then window-shop along the twenty-minute stroll home. There was no official residence for the leader of our country. He lived in an apartment in the city's old town and felt assured enough in his safety to waive his security detail once he was off the clock. That night, many passersby or fellow moviegoers would have recognized Palme, their own prime minister, sitting a few rows in front of them at the cinema, but few would have said anything. Swedes tend to leave even their most famous residents alone.

The radio reports cycled back to the start every few minutes. Palme had been declared dead five minutes after midnight, only fifteen minutes after taking the bullet. His wife was injured, but not badly. In the depth of the night, as most of the country slept, the deputy prime minister was sworn in as Sweden's interim leader. A manhunt was taking shape.

Even as a teenager, you study your parents in moments like this, judging how worried you should be. That morning, my mother worked to keep things normal for my brothers and me. She set down a breakfast of oatmeal and milk, hot chocolate and toast. My dad went outside to warm up the Volvo. I ate breakfast in silence, then collected my gear and threw it in the back of our car. It was a frigid morning.

We pulled out of the driveway. My dad had this peculiar way of fiddling with the car radio. He'd stay leaned back on the car seat and reach out with two fingers in a peace sign to pinch the knob, twisting it. For some reason, it drove me nuts. That morning, I studied his hand until he landed on the news station.

After a few minutes on the highway, Tommy took an off-ramp

that would direct us through the center of Stockholm. Normally, we stayed on the highway to get to my practices. I didn't need to ask why we were taking the city route.

Sveavägen is a busy road that takes you to the city's center from the north. Four lanes across, it's lined with a colorful mix of old and new buildings. Stores, restaurants, hotels. Movie theaters. Small parks. Cobblestone lanes. Churches.

On most drives to hockey, my dad and I would chat. But this morning, we were quiet. There was more traffic than usual for an early Saturday, people like us driving by the scene of the crime. First, we passed the Grand Theatre, its marquee unlit. There was a poster for *The Mozart Brothers*, the movie Olof Palme had watched the night before.

We continued one block south and came to the corner of Sveavägen and Tunnelgatan, a cobblestone footpath that led east to a long staircase. There were police officers, cameras, dozens of people. A metal fence had been put up. What I remember most are the flowers. So many flowers lined the brick wall of the furniture store where Lisbeth Palme had been window-shopping as her husband's assassin approached.

"Roses," my father observed.

Thousands of flowers piled almost as tall as the police officers guarding the scene: red roses, the symbol of the Social Democratic Party that Palme had led for many years. Eight hours before, the leader of our country lay bleeding on this cold sidewalk as his injured wife screamed for help. Bystanders stepped in and tried to revive him. The police arrived quickly, as did an ambulance. No one understood the significance of the scene until Lisbeth pleaded with a police officer.

"My husband is Olof Palme," she said.

My dad pointed to the Tunnelgatan laneway and staircase. "The killer ran up those stairs."

I narrowed my eyes. Maybe the killer might appear out of a darkened doorway if I looked closely enough. No doubt the manhunt was massive in scope, but he still hadn't been caught. Later, I'd see pictures in the newspaper of the large bloodstain that would coat the sidewalk for days after the assassination.

We drove the remaining ten minutes to the arena in silence. The mood at the rink was somber, too. On the ice, Coach Mats directed us through the drills with little enthusiasm.

Hockey has a way of bookmarking most of my memories. Even the death of Olof Palme is shaped by that morning drive to the rink. In the weeks that followed, the killer remained on the loose, and my teammates and I hashed it out in the locker room. We talked about whether bodyguards could have saved his life.

As we tied our skates or taped our sticks, the group ran through the various conspiracy theories making the news. Unlike most Swedish politicians, Olof Palme had tended to take sides on contentious international issues. Many Swedes loved him, and many didn't. He had no shortage of political foes. The killer could have been an operative from a foreign country. Or it could have been your neighbor. That was the scariest part.

Shortly after his death, Olof Palme was buried at the Adolf Fredriks cemetery on that same stretch of Sveavägen, exactly halfway between the movie theater and the storefront where he was killed. His funeral procession wound through Stockholm's streets as tens of thousands of Swedes stood on the sidelines. Hundreds of foreign dignitaries came to pay their respects, some of them from the countries mentioned in the conspiracy theories.

Nowadays, I pass the intersection often enough. The storefront is a deli now. There's a plaque laid flush with the sidewalk that marks the spot where our prime minister was shot. His wife, Lisbeth, outlived him by thirty-two years.

On the night of February 28, 1986, Olof Palme was unlikely to have taken much notice of the church and cemetery as he walked by after leaving the theater. Fifteen days later, his family would gather there privately to watch his coffin lowered into the ground. Every time I drive down Sveavägen, I think about how fate came for Palme that night, and he never saw it coming.

For months, Palme's death was the topic of most conversations, the story on the front page of the newspapers. Eventually, they arrested a man who lived one train stop from our home. But two trials later, he was acquitted. Conspiracy theories took firmer shape and included every possibility from the CIA to communist operatives. To this day, Palme's murder has never been solved. I understand now that my lifelong interest in history was triggered around this time.

The summer after the assassination put Sweden in the international news cycle, I was preparing to leave my home continent for the first time. My new team would be flying over the Atlantic Ocean and halfway across North America to play in a youth tournament in Winnipeg, Canada. To raise money for the trip, we sold raffle tickets and hot dogs at the arena and went door-to-door in our neighborhoods asking for contributions. We left Sweden that September and flew a circuitous route to get to the Canadian prairies. As the plane neared the airport, the farm fields out the window looked like patches on a quilt.

Each player on my team was billeted with a local family. After going through customs, we boarded a bus to a suburban arena where we were greeted by our hosts. My family was kind and welcoming; they had a son a bit older than me. In Sweden, you learn British English, but you still have an accent that alerts people to your foreignness. Here, everyone sounded like the music we listened to or actors in movies we watched back home. The kids on the host team all wore matching bomber jackets with the team logo.

I couldn't fall asleep that first night. The whir of the air conditioner kept me awake. AC was not a thing people had in Sweden. I lay in bed and thought of my parents and brothers almost 4,500 miles away, likely already awake because of a time change I couldn't quite compute. My house in Sollentuna felt like a figment of my imagination.

Winnipeg, and Canada, felt both different and the same as home. The weather was warm and the days were long. People were friendly, but far more outgoing. In Sweden, we couldn't drive until we turned eighteen, so it was a shock to see our fellow sixteen-year-olds behind the wheel. My host player drove me to a local mall, where we met up with groups of kids eating at the food court and shopping for clothes. I couldn't believe how sophisticated they seemed in comparison to us. My host family took good care of me.

At the tournament itself, the organizers had taken a wild guess on how to seed our Swedish team. We ended up winning every game by a large margin. We'd come so far to play hockey, but it wasn't hockey that formed the memories of the trip.

Once the shock of being so far from home wore off, it all felt so carefree. Everyone seemed to be enormous fans of their local sports teams and proud to talk to me about all the Swedes who played for the Winnipeg Jets. There was a lightheartedness in Canada that felt infectious. As we left for the airport to begin our journey home, I remember thinking: *If I ever do make it to the NHL, I hope I get to play in Canada.*

8

Broken Bone

At fifteen I was, at best, an average student. I didn't mind school, and I enjoyed reading and history. My parents were insistent that we maintain our grades and complete our homework. The end of ninth grade marked a turning point. The final years of school in Sweden are meant to help students prepare either for a vocation or for higher studies. I chose to study to be an electrician. I liked the idea of a trades career, of working with my hands.

To gain acceptance to the electrician program, my grades needed to be solidly average. Even though physical education was by far my best subject, for the past two years the teacher had given me a four, the equivalent of a B or B-plus. It bothered me. A five would bring my average up. As our grades were about to be tabulated, I found the PE teacher to plead my case. I excelled at almost everything we did. Floor hockey, soccer, team sports. Even in games like tennis, I thrived. But every year, we did a unit on gymnastics—*real* gymnastics, with the balance beam and uneven bars. When I approached him about my grade, the PE teacher reminded me just how much I'd struggled in the gymnastics part of the course.

"Not your best," he said.

No. Not my best. I was a gangly, inflexible hockey player, about as graceful in gymnastics as a baby giraffe. Still, I tried my best, didn't I? Couldn't my A be for effort?

He gave me the five. I knew it was a gift, and I accepted it gratefully.

In September 1986, I'd be moving on to *gymnasieskola*, the Swedish word for high school. I'd also be making the jump to Djurgårdens' elite team. That summer, the plan was to spend most of it in Stockholm to train with my new team and prepare for the following season. But first, the Sundin family would make our annual June trip to visit my grandparents in Kainulasjärvi. I didn't want to show up to summer training out of shape. I needed a plan for our time up north.

"You can train with the soccer team," my father said.

This was a daunting proposition. The Kainulasjärvi soccer team played in Sweden's Division 6 league. These were not professionals. The team was made up of local men who worked tough day jobs in forestry or mining. They were universally tall, pale and heavily muscled. My uncle Birger was on the team. The games were mostly against teams from other northern villages, played on local pitches that weren't all that well maintained. It was arranged that, on top of our own teams' summer training programs, Patrick and I would practice with them twice a week.

The teams' dressing rooms were two small sheds, one for the home side and one for the visitors. Patrick and I would ride our bikes from our grandparents' place, the stench of Tiger Balm hitting us as soon as we entered the shed. There was always beer tucked under the benches for afterward. With this team, practice didn't mean organized drills run by a coach. Practice was a scrimmage. Split the group in two, set a ball down and play.

During one scrimmage, I was sprinting upfield to catch a perfect pass from my uncle Birger. At the tail end of my first growth spurt, my body was taller than my brain computed it to be. I was about to break away cleanly with Birger's pass when one of the opposing defensemen tackled me. I stepped on the ball and flailed. Too gawky to properly brace for impact, I fell directly on my shoulder. There was a distinct crack. I heard it clearly.

I screamed.

By the time my teammates gathered at my feet, I was writhing in pain.

"Something broke," I said.

They stood over me, frowning.

"It's just his shoulder," my uncle Birger said. "It must be separated. We can pop it back into place."

I remember the sensation of my heart beating in my temples. The stabbing pain. They started discussing options. One of them had seen it done before. You pull the arm away from the body, then bend it to ninety degrees and lift. Or do you straighten it? They couldn't agree on the technique. When my uncle leaned forward to touch me, I must have hissed at him like a demon possessed, because he shot back up to standing.

"Maybe we take him to the hospital instead," he said.

Someone went to fetch my dad. Ten minutes later, I was lying flat in the rear of a Volvo station wagon, making the sixty-mile drive to the hospital in Gällivare. The pain was excruciating, every bump in the road like a knife in my shoulder. I cried the entire drive while my dad tried to soothe me from the front seat. At the hospital, I was given something for the pain and taken for an X-ray. The doctor came to find us around midnight.

"You have a break," he said. "It's pinching a muscle. You need surgery."

"When?" my father asked.

"Now."

They discussed the procedure: Sedation. Incision. Surgery to stabilize the shoulder joint. My heart wouldn't stop racing. Tommy must have been distressed, too, but he hid it well on my behalf.

"You'll be fine, Mats," my father said. "You won't feel a thing."

Within an hour, I was wheeled away. When I woke up the next morning, my left arm was bandaged and secured to my chest. The long incision on my shoulder left a scar bigger than any hockey injury ever would. My dad sat in a chair and laughed with the guy lying on the bed next to me. It was Alf Tillberg. He was my uncle by marriage and played forward on the Kainulasjärvi soccer team.

"Nice of you to come visit, Mats!" Alf joked.

His leg was in a full cast. A few days before we arrived to visit my grandparents, Alf had collided with the opposing goalie on a rush and tumbled hard, breaking his leg so badly that his bone popped out of his skin. The same doctor who had operated on me had treated him, too. When that doctor came in later that day to check on us, he asked the obvious question.

"Two breaks in one week. What kind of soccer field do you have in Kainulasjärvi, anyway?"

After he checked me over, the doctor turned the conversation to my recovery timeline. My shoulder was broken. I was in a cast. I should have known the news wouldn't be good.

"What about hockey?" I asked.

It's summer, he said. Don't worry. You'll be fine by the fall.

The fall? I was expected back in Stockholm for training in a few weeks.

Enjoying some cake on my second birthday, 1973.

My father, Tommy, was a goalie. Patrick (left) and I loved playing with our dad's goalie pads but did not take up the position ourselves.

Patrick and me suiting up to skate on the lake in the mid-1970s. We couldn't have known then that a Bruins jersey wouldn't age well.

With Patrick (right) on the lake near our house in Sollentuna, Sweden, 1975.

Patrick and me at my younger brother Per's christening with my grandfather, Sture Sundin, and his wife, Anna, 1975.

With a hockey career in my future, this wasn't the only time I'd be missing my front teeth, 1977.

Winning the 1986 TV-pucken tournament gave me my first taste of playing hockey under the bright lights. *Imago/TT*

I played with the Djurgårdens IF organization for many years, right up until I left to join the NHL. At any age, it was an honor to wear the *C*.

With Bengt Lundholm in Massachusetts. Bengt traveled with my dad and me to the United States to meet my agent near Boston. We then all flew together to the 1989 draft in Minneapolis, Minnesota.

In June 1989, I was the first European player drafted to the NHL first overall. The Nordiques' director of scouting, Pierre Gauthier, made the announcement. As we shook hands, he suggested I should pull down my new baseball cap. *Bruce Bennett / Getty Images*

I wore number 19 for years. When I joined the Quebec Nordiques, Joe Sakic was 19 and I switched to 13. I was born on February 13, so the number never felt unlucky to me.

Lifting weights under the guidance of Leif Larsson at the Bosön training center outside Stockholm, 1990s. *Leif Larsson*

During my rookie season in the NHL, I had the honor of playing with Guy Lafleur (left) and Joe Sakic (right)—one Hall of Famer at the end of his career, and one at the beginning.

With Börje Salming in June 1994, after I learned I was traded to the Maple Leafs. Börje helped me navigate the heavy media attention that came with the announcement. A few years later, he'd be the one to convince me to accept the Leafs captaincy.

9

TV-pucken

I stepped onto the ice, helmet off, the *C* shining white on my red jersey. The crowd cheered. As I took my first lap, I noticed the TV cameras in the stands. These weren't small camcorders perched on a guy's shoulder, but cameras the size of a horse that swung side to side as they captured the length of the ice. I smiled, then picked up a puck and fired it at the net.

TV-pucken was an annual tournament where each of Sweden's twenty-one counties enlisted a team of their best fifteen-year-old players. After my shoulder healed from the break and surgery, I attended the tryouts and was named captain of Team Stockholm. The 1986 TV-pucken finals were held in Märsta, fifteen miles north of Sollentuna. The semifinal and final games were televised and widely watched. After an undefeated run, our team was set to play the county of Gästrikland in the championship game.

An announcer's voice boomed through the arena and instructed us to line up on the blue lines. The Stockholm players stood shoulder to shoulder as a camera panned past us one by one, introducing each of us by name and home team. At fifteen, some of us were taller than others, but we were all awkward. Most of the players' hair was styled in mullets—long in the back, short on top—of varying lengths. My mother insisted on a cleaner look, but did let me keep some flow out the back of my helmet. When the camera landed on me, I looked right into it and smiled. I was so nervous that I wanted to vomit.

"Captain Mats Sundin," the announcer said. "Djurgården."

Once the puck dropped, the nerves were gone. I felt loose. I sensed that my teammates could be split into two types of players: those who seemed sick with nerves on the bench, who saw the cameras and felt panic even as the game rolled on, and those of us who grew taller under the spotlight.

It was my first time playing on TV. I felt faster and more in control of the puck and the play. My drive to score was that much higher. I knew that my grandparents, friends and schoolmates were all watching. After a scoreless start, we went up, 1–0. Then I scored to make it 2–0. I scored again a few minutes later. In the end, the game wasn't close. We won, 7–1.

Team Stockholm celebrated the win by throwing our gloves in the air and gathering at the net to congratulate our goalie. Then we lined up to shake hands. Before the trophy presentation, someone collected me and pulled me over to a reporter holding a microphone. They wanted to interview me on TV.

Playing the game, I'd been fine. Better than fine. But talking with a mic to my face? *Now* I was nervous. Where were my gloves and my stick? I'd thrown them up in the air in celebration after the win. Unsure what to do with my arms, I crossed them awkwardly over my chest, hands tucked by my elbows.

The reporter asked me about my goals. I craned my neck to the microphone and described them plainly. I punctuated every answer with a nod, as if confirming what I'd just answered was coherent. He asked if I'd had fun.

"The most fun," I said.

The next question threw me off.

"Do you think you'll keep playing hockey after this?"

For many young players in 1980s Sweden, TV-pucken repre-sented the pinnacle of their hockey lives. With NHL games played in the middle of the night local time and only a tiny handful of Swedes in the league, it wasn't really on our radar as a meaning-ful possibility. In Sweden, hockey was not a business. Even at the highest levels, you couldn't make a long-term living or career out of it. Most players in the Swedish Elite League would earn the equivalent of a teacher's salary and go to school or have day jobs on the side. In a dream world, I might represent my country on the world stage in tournaments or at the Olympics. I might make it to the SEL, play for Djurgården for a few years, then settle into real life and real work as an electrician.

The reporter's question was fair. Most of my teammates and opponents would quit over the next few years. I didn't know my future, but I knew I wanted to keep playing.

"Definitely," I answered. "I'm definitely going to keep playing hockey."

He congratulated me. At the presentation, I was called to col-lect the trophy. It had a large, round puck mounted in a gold *V*, with *TV-pucken* etched plainly in white. I hoisted it over my head as my teammates huddled around me, the fans cheering, cameras following, photographers clicking.

On the drive home, my dad was happy. He tapped the steer-ing wheel. Across the country, from Bollnäs to Kainulasjärvi, my family had tuned in; likely our neighbors and his colleagues from work, too. My grandfather Sture would be thrilled by the win and my postgame interview. Our chatter about the game lasted about fifteen minutes before my dad's focus turned to other things. Had I finished my homework for the next day?

Homework? I'd just been on TV. At the time, it could annoy

me the way my parents enjoyed my success but never fixated on it. I'd just won a huge game aired nationally on TV. Sure, my dad was immensely proud, but he still wanted my homework done.

The next day, I arrived at school wearing my Team Stockholm tracksuit. I'm not sure what I was expecting. I figured some of my classmates had watched the game. Maybe even some of my teachers. Still, I was taken aback when I walked into class and everyone started clapping. Not just my classmates, but the teachers, too. I got stopped in the hallway. It seemed like everyone in the building knew my name. At one point, the principal came to shake my hand and congratulate me. It was my first taste of fame, and it went a long way to offset the insecurities that came with being a teen. Shortly after TV-pucken, I made the national under-sixteen team. That honor came with another tracksuit and a winter jacket with the famous yellow *tre kronor*—three crowns—Swedish emblem. I felt a lot of pride putting on that coat, and I wore it every day for the rest of the term.

10

The Iron Curtain

I heard the sirens before I spotted the police car. The party was at a terraced house a five-minute bike ride from home. There were no parents or chaperones. It was a Saturday night, and I was in my best jeans and sneakers, dancing and drinking with my friends.

An hour earlier, a kid from school showed up to the party driving a random car. He wasn't a close friend, but I knew him. He made his way around the room until he got to me.

"Want to go for a ride?" he asked.

Luckily, I said no. I didn't ask him where or how he'd gotten the car, but I knew it wasn't his, and I knew he was too young to be driving it.

It didn't surprise me that I was the one he approached. Ever since TV-pucken, this small sheen of fame had followed me around Sollentuna. I was late to puberty but started growing fast that first year of high school. Just as my interest in girls was piqued, they started to pay some attention to me, too. Soon enough, I had a girlfriend and parties or dances to choose from every weekend. My electrician studies at school were an afterthought. Day to day, if I wasn't at hockey, my biggest concerns were making sure my hair was right or that my favorite jeans were clean in time for Friday night's social events. I was that perfect mix of confident and insecure that only a sixteen-year-old can be.

That kid who asked me if I wanted to go for a ride? Turns out he'd stolen the car. I was on the top floor of the house with a friend when the police cruiser appeared with that kid in the back seat. The officer stepped out and looked around. I recognized him at once. As if the party getting busted weren't bad enough, the cop was a good friend of my dad's and lived not far from us. I watched from a third-floor window as he walked up the stairs and into the house.

Panicked, I grabbed my friend and dragged him to hide in a bathroom. We huddled on the floor and listened as the music shut off downstairs. We could hear the officer asking questions. "Anyone know anything about this car?" No one confessed to having seen the boy earlier that night. With a stern warning to shut the party down, the officer left.

I got home late that night. I'd been getting home late a lot. It was becoming a problem.

When you're eight or ten or twelve years old, sports can easily keep you occupied. Your entire life can be built around playing hockey, soccer or bandy. In the years before a social world takes hold, you choose sports because you're still too young to be tempted or lured away by other things.

Then comes a tricky time. Just as our brains start to go haywire with hormones, those of us who show promise at a given sport will have to make a choice. When I joined Djurgårdens' elite team and then the national U16 team, my commitment jumped from three times a week to a few hours every day. I loved it, but I loved my social life, too. It's easy to understand why this is the time when a lot of kids quit. Many of my friends started quitting hockey and other sports. It's hard to wake up at 7 a.m.

for practice when you've been out until two in the morning the night before.

My dad must have sensed it. Not long after TV-pucken, he sat me down for what would turn out to be the only eye-to-eye conversation we'd have about my commitment to hockey. I couldn't get my driver's license for two more years, so it was still up to Tommy to shuttle me across town to every practice and game. If it was draining on him, he never showed it.

But lately, he'd been having a harder time getting me up in the morning for those Saturday practices. My parents had never pushed me. They'd never forced me to go to practice or try out for a more competitive team. Even though they recognized that I was talented, they weren't going to push me. It mattered to them that the passion and drive were coming from me.

When my dad prompted that talk, I was worried that I was in trouble. Maybe he'd found out about the party and the stolen car from his friend the police officer.

"Mats," he said, "you don't have to keep playing hockey. You can quit anytime."

I couldn't believe it. Why would I quit hockey?

"Listen," Tommy continued. "I will drive you anywhere you need to be. But if you're going to play, you need to make the full commitment. You need to get your homework done and go to bed in time to wake up properly the next morning."

My instinct was to answer him right away. Of course I wasn't going to quit. Of course I'd make the commitment. But Tommy told me I had to think about it and really contemplate what I'd have to give up. It meant fewer parties and dances. It meant being home and in bed at 10 p.m. on a Friday while my friends gathered at the park or the disco.

When I think about this conversation now, it strikes me that my dad never brought up my talent. Even at the elite level, I was scoring in almost every game. That never mattered to Tommy and Gunilla. My talent or prospects were never their guiding concern. All they cared about was my well-being and my character. If I made a commitment, I had to honor it. I also had to hold my own in school.

In the end, it wasn't hard for me to choose hockey. My passion for the game wasn't waning. If playing hockey meant scaling back on my social life, then that's what I was willing to do. The trade-off was the chance to experience things other kids my age weren't experiencing. I'd been to Finland and even Canada. In the winter of 1987, the U16 team was set to travel to the Four Nations Cup tournament in Olomouc, a city on the eastern edge of Czechoslovakia, behind the Iron Curtain.

I wasn't exactly a student of Cold War politics in 1987, but I understood the basics. Even though the four countries in the tournament were in the same general geographical region, the USSR and Czechoslovakia were part of the communist Eastern Bloc, and Finland and Sweden were part of the Western Bloc. Swedish residents could move freely around the world, while the USSR's citizens generally could not.

With no budget for flights, the plan was to take a bus. Everyone on the team needed passports and special visas. The bus would travel to the southern tip of Sweden, where we'd board a vehicle ferry and cross the Baltic Sea to West Germany. Then we'd drive east and cross over.

The Swedish portion of the bus ride took seven hours. Everyone was so happy to be heading on an adventure. We played card games and had pillow fights in the rear rows. It was February and the decks on the ferry were frigid, so we tried to sleep away most of the overnight crossing. Once we docked in West Germany, it took a few more hours of driving before we arrived at the East German border. The road bent to take us to a large checkpoint with low buildings and a watchtower, signs everywhere reading *Halt!* The mood on the bus shifted instantly when we noticed the military personnel out the window, leashed dogs at their feet, weapons in hand. This was a border very few crossed. We were ordered off the bus.

No one said a word as we filed out. We were brought into a stark building to have our visas and passports checked. The coaches whispered at us to stay quiet. You could see the alarm on their faces. Back outside, we found the guards surrounding the bus. Some held mirrors on long handles, checking its undercarriage.

It took two hours before we were released. On the bus, the quiet lingered as we pulled back onto the highway. The natural landscape was unchanged out the window, but instantly it felt like a different world. Nearly every car on the road was a Trabant, a model produced in East Germany that earned the nickname *Rennpappe*—"racing cardboard"—for its bare-bones construction. Just before crossing into Czechoslovakia, we stopped at a diner for lunch.

There are scenes in old Western movies where someone walks into a tavern and everyone stops to stare. This is what happened in 1987 when an entire team of Swedish kids and their coaches, dressed in their bright blue jackets, with jeans and new sneakers, walked into a roadside restaurant in the depths of East Germany. Everything stopped. Everyone stared. The coaches had a hard time convincing us to eat anything on the menu. To us, the meat and vegetables looked gray.

The city of Olomouc was old and stately. At the hotel, my teammates and I dug in on not wanting to eat the food. We sustained ourselves almost entirely on Coca-Cola and white bread for the duration of the tournament, which might be one of the reasons we lost badly to the Czechs in our first game. Their three superstars—Jaromír Jágr, Bobby Holík and Robert Reichel—made quick work of us. I didn't get much ice time. Everyone was so fast and skilled that I had to work hard to keep up. On the few shifts I did get, I was chasing.

The Soviet team wore the distinct *CCCP* lettering on its jerseys and had a superstar winger named Pavel Bure. When I scored an early goal against the Russians, our coach started giving me more ice time. His message was clear: earn your shifts, and you'll get them.

We lost to Finland in the semis, but we did get to stay in Olomouc to watch the Czechs battle the USSR in the championship game. In theory, these two countries were politically aligned. Czechoslovakia was a satellite of the USSR and a fellow communist state. But by 1987, the communist superpower was starting to wilt and Czechs were eyeing a different future, one where they were out from under the Soviet Union's thumb. The championship game in Olomouc was going to be spirited, because the Cold War had long had a way of playing out on the ice.

A few months before our tournament, a scandalous game between the Canadian and Soviet junior teams made headlines worldwide. It was played just two hours south of Olomouc, in the Slovak city of Piešťany. With six minutes left in the second period, a fight on the ice spread quickly into a bench-clearing brawl. It got so chaotic that the tournament organizers decided to turn off the arena lights. The game was nullified and both teams were disqualified. The Canadians were promptly escorted out of the country. Everyone involved faced bans from international play for several months. This didn't matter much to the Canadian boys returning home to prospective NHL careers, but the Soviet Hockey Federation, priding itself on discipline, vowed to strictly punish its young players who'd tarnished the game by fighting. For young Russians like Alexander Mogilny and Sergei Fedorov, not being allowed to play international games was a devastating consequence.

For the championship game in Olomouc, one end of the rink was filled entirely by soldiers in their CCCP army uniforms. The rest of the arena was filled with Czech fans. Our Swedish team watched from center ice. Any time the soldiers yelled, "*Shaybu!*"—puck!—they were drowned out by wild boos from the locals. The game wasn't even close. The Czechs pulled ahead quickly and won by more than five goals, silencing the end zone that held the USSR army. No one would go as far as to say that a hockey game mattered in a country's early fight for independence, but that night the Czech fans celebrated like it did.

I don't remember much about the bus ride home. Mostly, I remember the feeling of crossing the Baltic Sea to return home. I think everyone on our bus felt a sense of relief. As teenagers, we tend to focus on the things we don't have, like a nicer car or the newest clothes or shoes. But on that trip home, I felt nothing but gratitude for the relative safety and comfort of Sweden. We weren't rich, but we had everything we needed.

11

Scouts and Agents

Around 1988, a new word started popping up in arenas: scouts.

I began to hear stories of scouts attending not just tournaments, but games and even practices. Their job was to seek out the best hockey players in the world. The Swedish Elite League had scouts, but every team in the National Hockey League now had a representative or two making frequent trips across the Atlantic. The European talent pool was opening up, and scouts were the prospectors sent to pan for gold. At one Four Nations tournament, I was approached by a man holding an unlit cigar. He was tall, with a thick head of hair under his fedora. He handed me a Vancouver Canucks pin.

"You have a big future in hockey," he said.

I took the pin and thanked him. When I showed the pin to a teammate, he pointed out that the guy in the fedora was a big deal.

"That's Pat Quinn. The president of the Vancouver Canucks."

Early in 1988, I returned to Canada to play in the Esso Cup, an international under-seventeen hockey tournament held yearly in Quebec. Each of the Four Nations countries was represented, along with the USA. Canada was such a hockey powerhouse that its talent had to be divided into five separate teams: Atlantic, Pacific, Western, Ontario and Quebec.

Quebec was cold and snowy in the winter. Unlike my visit to Winnipeg, this time there was a strange air of prejudice I hadn't experienced before. It was clear that, for the players on the Canadian and American teams, an NHL career was the goal, and the influx of prospects from Sweden and other faraway countries was now a potential barrier to that goal. One afternoon, I was in an elevator with a handful of my Swedish teammates when a group of Canadians entered.

"Chicken Swedes," one of them said to us.

Some of the Canadian kids had full beards. They seemed big, confident and angry. My teammates and I kept our eyes cast down until the elevator reached our floor. A few days later, we beat those Canadians and I scored a hat trick. We finished second in the tournament only to Russia.

For me, the obvious question started to swirl: If I could play well against the NHL prospect Canadian kids, didn't that make me a prospect, too? The following fall, when I was seventeen, I moved up again to play for Nacka HK, the farm team for Djurgårdens' SEL team. Scouts were regularly at those games. One night, I even heard that Pat Quinn was in the stands, but that he'd fallen asleep in his seat because of jet lag. It was my final year of high school. I was eligible to be selected for the 1989 NHL draft to be held in June in Bloomington, Minnesota. As late as that March, it still seemed so far-fetched. There were very few stories about the NHL in Swedish news; even my idols like Mats Naslund and Kent Nilsson were rarely featured in the media. As my season continued into the playoffs and more scouts showed up to our games, it was suggested to my dad that we should consider finding an agent.

My parents and I were learning how it worked on the fly. Behind each NHL team was a complex network of farm teams, executives, scouts, trainers, coaches and owners. Sports agents acted as the link between players and teams, betting on young hockey talent the same way a music producer might bet on young songwriters. They seek out talent to represent in the hopes that a handful will go on to have long and profitable careers.

When the World Championships descended on Stockholm in April 1989, many powerful hockey people landed close to our home. North American agents started calling us directly. They wanted to meet the Sundins while they were in town for the tournament.

The first agent I met was a Canadian named Don Meehan. He took me to the Hard Rock Cafe on Sveavägen, only a few blocks north of where Olof Palme had been shot three years earlier. I had no idea whether Meehan knew anything about Palme, or about Sweden in general.

My family never went to restaurants. As Stockholm restaurants went, the Hard Rock Cafe felt high-flying. The front featured a neon sign that read "No drugs or nuclear weapons allowed."

Don was friendly and welcoming. My English was pretty good, but with the restaurant loud and bustling around us, I had to pay close attention to catch his words.

At the table, the server handed me a huge trifold menu.

"Order whatever you want," Meehan said.

We talked about the World Championships starting that very week. I didn't let on that my parents couldn't afford game tickets. We ran through the Swedish team's lineup until the food arrived. Don asked me who my favorite player was.

"Kent Nilsson," I said.

I had Nilsson's poster in my bedroom. He was a Swede who'd played eight seasons in the NHL and two more in the World Hockey Association. Don Meehan suggested I might play with Nilsson, or other Swedish greats, one day. I loved that idea. The meal was delicious. A burger, fries and milkshake were rare treats for me, an amazing taste of North American culture. On our way out, we passed a merchandise display wall.

"Pick whatever you want," Meehan said.

Was he serious? I couldn't believe my luck. I chose a gray sweatshirt with the Hard Rock Cafe logo across the chest.

Over the next few days, Sweden got swept up in a hockey frenzy. The US and Canadian rosters held some of the biggest NHL stars, but the team to beat was the USSR. Every night, my family gathered around the TV at home in Sollentuna to watch whatever game was on. Little did I know the roles many of the players we were watching would play in my life over the next two decades. Börje Salming, Dave Ellett, Alex Mogilny, Dominik Hašek—a fellow Swede who would help me navigate the big moments of my career, a veteran who would welcome me into his home when I arrived in a new city, a supremely talented linemate who would beat me out for our team's scoring title, and an opponent whose goaltending feats would end my playoff dreams.

The hottest ticket in Stockholm was the round-robin game between Sweden and the USSR. Both teams went into the matchup undefeated, but the Soviets won, 3–2. Russia's Sergei Fedorov and Alex Mogilny were the youngest players in the tournament.

In the Nacka locker room, we debated the talents of these two young Russian stars. One teammate told us that while they were in Stockholm, the Soviet team had a KGB security detail everywhere they went.

"So they don't run," he said.

By "run," he meant defect. In 1989, you could only leave the USSR under strict conditions for specific reasons, like competing in the IIHF World Championship hockey tournament, as they were. Fedorov and Mogilny both played for Moscow's infamous Central Red Army club. We'd heard stories about the Red Army's training regimen: long weightlifting sessions in the mornings, six-mile runs in the evening, and hours on ice in between. Players were recruited as kids from the far corners of the USSR. There were rumors they were kept from seeing their families.

No Soviet hockey player had ever defected. Hockey players were generally proud to play for their team and their country. Yet most players in the tournament could be a patriot and still play in the NHL. There were already two dozen Swedes in the league. Soviet players faced different rules. They were only allowed to leave once they'd spent their best years playing hockey in their home country. No Soviet player had ever *started* his career in the NHL. That would require defection, and defection was treason.

The World Championships ended in early May with the USSR winning gold with a perfect 10–0 record. A few days later, it was all over the Swedish newspapers: *Young Soviet star missing in Stockholm.*

Mogilny hadn't shown up for his team's flight back to Moscow. He was defecting. The next few days played out like a thriller movie. The news cycle told stories of him ducking from hotel to hotel every few hours, with the KGB in hot pursuit. The Buffalo Sabres, who'd drafted him in 1988, were working to get him a US visa. Years later, I heard from teammate Dave Ellett that Mogilny hid for at least part of this time in the same hotel where Team Canada was staying.

A few weeks later, Mogilny made it to the States.

For me, life was not nearly as dramatic. The attention of the scouts and agents focused me and raised my level of play. When I knew they were in the stands, I pushed that much harder. One night, our Nacka team squared off against Tyresö HK, a team from south of Stockholm. Midway through the game, I slashed one of their veteran defense, Göran Lundqvist, hard on the arm. He was older than me by eight years or so. He didn't like being slashed by a kid and spent the rest of the game making that clear to me.

"That Lundqvist doesn't like you," one of my teammates said.

At eighteen, I sometimes played against men ten to fifteen years older than me, veterans with far more experience. To them, I was the kid doing whatever I could to keep up.

That spring, another agent, Mark Perrone, traveled to Stockholm to meet me. Perrone had a secret weapon in the form of Bengt Lundholm, a star former Swedish national team player who'd spent a handful of seasons with the NHL's Winnipeg Jets. My father organized a meeting at our house and then presented the plan to my mother.

Gunilla may not have understood much about the NHL or the draft, but she did understand what it meant to have important American visitors in our living room. The morning of their arrival, my mother cleaned frantically while her famous cinnamon buns baked in the oven.

Lundholm and Perrone arrived at our house in Sollentuna a little bent out of shape. They'd almost gotten in a car accident on the hill leading to our home. Mark was a short man with perfectly styled black hair and a dark suit to match. He wore a red tie and carried a briefcase. Bengt was dressed far more casually in jeans and a blue shirt, Swedish in his looks and manner.

My mother served her cinnamon buns and coffee. When I saw Bengt and my dad speaking animatedly in Swedish, I knew which agent we'd be signing with. It wasn't about Mark; it was about Bengt. Bengt recognized the bubble my parents lived in and how little they understood about the whole process. He knew they'd have questions that an agent used to dealing with players from North America might not think to answer. Things were moving quickly, and Bengt would be our lifeline.

"Your son is a top player in the world," Perrone told my father.

"Maybe," my father said.

Maybe? I rolled my eyes.

My dad couldn't wrap his head around the basic rule of the NHL draft: when a team drafts you, that's where you go to play. It might be Los Angeles, or Montreal, or anywhere in between. Essentially, you have little say in where you end up. That part seemed bizarre to my parents, but to them, all these NHL cities were still just dots on the map of a faraway place.

Bengt explained it as best he could, including the steps after the draft: the awarding of a contract, the financial possibilities. Even with big numbers being tossed around, it became clear to him that my parents' primary concern was my well-being. My mom cared more about what I'd eat than what arenas I'd be playing at. Bengt shifted his focus to discussing how he and Perrone would take care of me once I landed in North America, how they'd ensure that I found a comfortable place to live and ate the right foods, how they'd help me safeguard my earnings.

Through it all, my parents just listened and nodded.

Bengt became a vital bridge between my Swedish family and the NHL's workings. A plan was made. In early June, my father and I, along with Bengt, would travel from Stockholm to Minnesota via Mark Perrone's home in Boston. Unlike many European players before me, we would attend the draft in person with the expectation that I might be selected in the first round.

All I had to do was finish high school first. The rest of the spring was marked by my graduation and a busy hockey training schedule. I didn't worry much about the draft. In early June, I graduated as a certified electrician and got ready to fly across the ocean. I thought I was prepared, but I had no idea what was coming.

12

The NHL Draft

The flight from Boston crossed the Great Lakes before descending over the flatlands of Minnesota. I watched movies while the adults around me—Mark, Bengt and my dad—discussed what the week ahead might bring.

Minneapolis was very different from Stockholm, but there were hints of home. The Mississippi River cut right through its center, just like channels of the Baltic Sea did back in Sweden. It also shared longer June days, many bugs, and warm weather that cooled at night. The plan was to settle into the hotel and prepare for the team meetings that would start the next morning. The draft was a few days away. I'd also been promised a few rounds of golf.

All my dad did was ask questions. He'd helped me navigate all my decisions to that point, and he was a quick learner. Before we left for the United States, he'd even helped work out a verbal agreement with Djurgårdens IF that, should I be drafted, they'd release me to the NHL for a set fee if I played one or two seasons within their organization.

Still, the NHL draft was on a whole new level. My dad's English wasn't great. He'd left home with strict instructions from my mom: take care of Mats. Even in the NHL meetings that week, his primary focus wasn't on money or contracts. He wanted the logistical details from the teams' management groups. Where will Mats live in your city? Who will make sure Mats eats and sleeps? What happens if he gets injured? Bengt understood his concerns and patiently ensured all his questions were answered.

The biggest question remained: How did we know when, or if, I'd be drafted?

In 1989, the Quebec Nordiques had the first-overall draft pick, followed by the New York Islanders, Toronto Maple Leafs and Winnipeg Jets. Back then, the selection order depended mostly on where a team finished in the standings the previous season.

A few days after our arrival, my prospects seemed clearer.

"One of these first four teams will select Mats," Mark Perrone said. "Guaranteed."

In our meetings with Pierre Gauthier, the Nordiques' director of scouting, he told us they planned to pick me first overall. It would be historic if it happened. Very few European players had ever been drafted in the top ten, and none had been taken first overall. New York Islanders GM Bill Torrey invited me to a private meeting at his hotel. He was warm and curious about my life. He asked me tons of questions about my upbringing and schooling. I knew just how good he was at his job—from 1980 to 1983, he won four straight Stanley Cups with the Islanders.

"If you're available, you'll be our pick," he told me.

Despite these promises, Bengt was pragmatic and warned us not to get our hopes up. Hockey was a business, and the NHL Entry Draft was the league's biggest venue for wheeling and dealing. Draft picks could be traded just like players could, and trades and transactions could be made down to the wire. A team might change its mind about its pick right before walking to the stage to announce it.

The 1989 draft was held on June 17 at the Met Center, the North Stars' home arena, in a suburb of Minneapolis. It was the first morning of a heat wave. On the drive from the hotel, I sat in the car, sweating in my suit. We weren't prepared for the fanfare. The ice inside the arena had been taken out. The oval cement pad was lined with dozens of tables for the different teams and a stage at one end. Aside from all the guys in suits, it could have been a rock concert. There were cameras everywhere, reporters conducting interviews, staff running between team tables with last-minute offers. The lower bowl of the stands was nearly full. So many players and their families had made the trip, just like we did.

Mark, Bengt, my dad and I were guided to seats about ten rows from ice level.

"This is crazy," my dad said as we sat down.

I couldn't speak. I just looked around, taking it in. The scope of it all was a shock.

An announcer welcomed everyone and called for the proceedings to start. Would the Quebec Nordiques please take the stage for the first selection? When Pierre Gauthier approached the microphone, a silence fell over the crowd.

"Here we go," Bengt said.

My leg bounced. A camera was trained on me from the aisle, so I tried to hold a smile. Out of the corner of my eye, I could see my dad's leg bouncing, too.

Pierre Gauthier started talking.

"The Quebec Nordiques are extremely proud and happy to select . . . a young man with an exceptional future . . ."

Okay, I thought, he could be talking about me.

Gauthier let a thick pause hang in the air as he looked high into the stands. He was playing it up. Going for drama. When he opened his mouth to speak again, I leaned forward. But instead of calling a name, he switched to French.

"*Mesdames et messieurs,*" he said, "*le premier choix des Nordiques en mil neuf cent quatre-vingt neuf...*"

No pick yet. Back to English.

"Ladies and gentlemen, the Quebec Nordiques' first-round overall selection . . ."

Then, more French. Or was he speaking Swedish now? My dad muttered something.

". . . Mats Sundin!"

I looked directly into the camera, then stood up. Mark Perrone stood, too. He shook my hand and guided me to the aisle. The cameraman blocked my route. I could only descend a few steps before a reporter placed his hand on my chest to stop me.

He lifted a microphone to my face and dove right in.

"When do you expect to play in the NHL?" he asked. "I know you still have some commitments in Sweden."

"Uh," I said, "I think maybe . . . two years?"

He asked me about my dreams, about the Swedish players like Börje Salming who'd come before me. I fumbled through an answer.

"Is this going to be a huge deal back in Sweden?" he asked.

"I don't know," I said. "Maybe."

Maybe? I am my father's son.

As I spoke to the reporter, Bengt and my dad remained in their seats and stared at the floor. For weeks, we'd been told this was a possibility. Quebec had all but assured us that I'd be the first European player ever to be selected number one in the NHL draft. In the moment, with a microphone to my face, I couldn't absorb that I'd just made history. Bengt and my dad felt it. They kept their eyes down and didn't say a word. They both knew that if they looked up, if they made eye contact with each other or with me, there would be tears.

The reporter congratulated me again and stepped out of my way. I took the rest of the stairs, then weaved through the tables and media to the stage. By then, I was used to larger crowds. I'd already played with TV cameras in the stands and had reporters ask me questions. But I was used to being in my hockey gear while the camera tracked me. I'd always had on an armor of pads and a jersey, a coating of sweat and a game to talk about.

Here, I wore a red tie and pants my mom helped me pick out before I left home. I had a fresh haircut and a thick Swedish accent. Thousands of people were watching me. I made my way to the stage, where Pierre Gauthier awaited, a new Nordiques jersey draped over his arm. He handed me the jersey.

"You probably want to put this on."

"Yeah," I said, aware of the TV camera hovering so close. "Sure."

I pulled the jersey over my head and smoothed it out. The fit was good. Next, he handed me a baseball cap. I set it on top of my head, like a crown. When I turned back to Pierre, he looked up at it in disbelief.

"Pull the hat down," he whispered.

So, I did.

He maneuvered me so we were facing the media, posed in a handshake. Someone asked if I spoke any French.

"Ah," I said. *"Bonjour?"*

Laughter. I held my smile until my face hurt, trying not to look up to the crowd in search of my dad. Eventually, they cleared us off the stage to make room for the second pick. On the floor, I was approached and interviewed again and again.

Someone told me that Quebec City would remind me of Stockholm.

"Okay," I said.

There were a lot of questions about being the first European to be drafted first overall.

"It's a great honor," I repeated.

"What do you know about Quebec City?" another asked.

"I know it's a nice town and it has a lot of girls."

Oops. I hoped my mom wouldn't read that quote in the Swedish papers.

As I was passed around, the draft selections continued. My Team Sweden teammate at the World Juniors, Nicklas Lidström, was selected in the third round by Detroit. When it came to scouting and drafting European talent, the Red Wings were early adopters. That year, they drafted two future Hall of Famers, Lidström and Sergei Fedorov, chosen in the fourth round.

In the sixth round, a frenzy ensued at the 113th pick, when the Vancouver Canucks called out a well-known name: Pavel Bure. Bure and I were the same age, and I'd played against him many times since U16. The complexity of the draft rules involving the USSR had most teams believing he wasn't eligible until 1990, or else someone would have drafted him far earlier, likely in the top five overall. He was an incredibly speedy and skilled player—a Soviet phenom.

Immediately, several teams tried to object to Bure's selection. It turns out the Canucks' GM had done plenty of due diligence in Europe over the previous few years, finding the wiggle room in eligibility rules that might allow them to secure franchise players in late rounds. This particular GM was good at reading the fine print—years earlier, he'd earned his law degree on the side while making the transition from NHL player to coach. I'd already met him a few times in Sweden, and he'd found me earlier in the day to shake my hand after my selection. It was Pat Quinn.

We called my family as soon as we could. My brothers seemed to get the significance more than my mom did. They were excited and full of questions. That night, Mark Perrone treated us to a fancy dinner in Minneapolis. The Nordiques were arranging for all their draft picks to fly to Quebec City the following day. I'd take that trip solo, then reconnect with my dad, Bengt and Mark in Boston a few days later. At dinner, Bengt tried to coach me on handling the press I'd face in Quebec. He told me to be myself and keep my answers nice and short.

What I appreciated most about Bengt, especially in the chaos of the draft, was his laid-back, humble nature. He played five seasons in the NHL, but only really spoke about his career if I asked him. He must have been nervous on my behalf. He would have known what I was in for. In hindsight, the true significance of being a first pick was lost on me. I had no idea of the pressures and expectations that would take hold in the next few years. Bengt tried hard to both prepare me and shield me.

That short visit to Quebec was a blur. The city and the Nordiques staff offered us a warm welcome. I endured my first press conference. Many of the questions were asked in French and then translated for me to English—a language double whammy. One reporter asked me when I planned to learn French. Someone in management answered that the new players would take French lessons once they started with the team. I frowned.

When I landed back in Boston, I was surprised by how relieved I was to see my dad and Bengt again, as though I'd been holding my breath for three days without realizing it. Mark took us to a Red Sox baseball game and arranged to have *Congratulations Mats Sundin!* written on the scoreboard between innings. I wondered how many people reading that would know what it meant. Did people in Boston follow the NHL draft? It was a hot and sticky night at Fenway Park. My dad kept yawning. Baseball didn't move fast enough for him.

We returned to Stockholm a few days later. Per and Patrick wanted to know all about Quebec. Had I met any NHL players? My mom already had the news articles about the draft clipped and organized in her scrapbook album. A lot of the coverage took time to explain the NHL draft to Swedish readers and why it was a big deal that I had been chosen first overall. It was strange to see my face on the front pages. There was one picture of me with my dad, which made him very happy. But the photo they printed the most was the one of me sheepishly pulling down the Nordiques baseball cap.

13

Djurgårdens IF

The Djurgårdens IF team didn't need an August training camp, because they worked out every day for most of the summer. Most of their training was held at Bosön, a sports facility northeast of central Stockholm. Bosön's large campus sits on a point of land that juts out into a wide channel of the Baltic Sea. It has the same feel as a summer camp. There are buildings full of fitness centers and testing facilities, a pool, residences, and a large forest crisscrossed with trails.

But Bosön is far more than a camp. It's a world-class athletics facility, a research and training ground run by the Swedish Sports Federation and designed to push athletes to their limits. When I joined my Djurgården teammates after returning from North America, assistant coach Lasse Falk took one look at me.

"You look like a lamp cord," he said.

I didn't know what he meant.

"The cord you pull to turn on a lamp? That's you. Long and skinny."

He wasn't wrong. I was six foot three and weighed 175 pounds.

Djurgården's training regimen was designed to change that. We didn't spend a lot of time on the ice. We sprinted, lifted weights, did resistance and interval training. I gleaned pretty quickly that none of my coaches or teammates cared that I'd been drafted first overall by an NHL team. Djurgården was the undisputed top team in the Swedish Elite League, and its reigning champions. Even top draft picks sometimes turned out to be busts. The roster had several guys who'd already *played* in the NHL and proven themselves. My draft selection was a strong vote of confidence in my abilities, but I'd yet to prove anything.

In September 1989, Djurgårdens IF put together an exhibition schedule that included a trip to the Soviet Union to face off against the top teams from Moscow. I'd spent my entire childhood watching Russian superstars crush their Swedish opponents, and my respect for them was healthy. I was surprised by how short the flight from Stockholm to Moscow was—barely two hours. Russia was awfully close to home for a country that felt like another planet.

The Moscow airport was renovated in the late 1970s to accommodate the 1980 Summer Olympic Games. It looked like an industrial complex from the air. As we disembarked the plane, what struck me was the lack of color. Despite its long winter nights, Stockholm is a colorful city, even its oldest buildings washed in shades of orange, yellow, red and blue. Here, it was as if someone had changed the channel and everything was now in black and white. The floors and walls, the sky, even the soldiers' uniforms were of varying shades of gray. As we navigated through the arrivals terminal, small children approached with an outstretched hand and said a single word: *ruble.* Money.

We boarded a bus. When we arrived at our hotel, someone mentioned that, at five thousand rooms, it was the largest hotel in the world. Tourism wasn't all that prominent in Moscow, so the massive hotel was mostly vacant. If you took a wrong turn, you'd find yourself wandering a dark and empty corridor. The rooms were cold. Our coaches joked that it was impossible to find a staff member.

The city of Moscow was beautiful, with grand buildings and public squares filled with soldiers and citizens. The Soviet Union remained an invitation-only place, even if the Iron Curtain was fraying at its seams. Only two months after our team's trip to Moscow, the Berlin Wall fell and the Soviet Union began to break apart.

In those exhibition games in Moscow, it became clear the coaches did not see me as a top-line player. Lasse Falk handled the systems and tactics, and head coach Tommy Boustedt ran the bench. Despite their completely different personalities, they operated as a perfect coaching unit, and they seemed to be in agreement on my role. I was lucky to get seven minutes of ice time per game. First-overall NHL draft pick or not, I was the youngest player on the team and was not about to be given a free pass, much less a shift on the power play.

As we returned to Sweden and the regular season started, it was more of the same. I was playing on the third line, sitting out the power plays and penalty kills. I was even scratched completely a few times. My father was very diplomatic about it. I was a good player, he said, but my teammates were more experienced. Some were a decade older and had thirty pounds more muscle on their frames. I hadn't even finished growing. Those players already had our coaches' trust.

"The ice time isn't yours until you earn it," Tommy said.

It turns out that I was also expected to earn a living off the ice. My salary at Djurgården was in the range of five hundred dollars a month. The organization arranged a flexible part-time job that wouldn't interfere with my game or training schedule. I was hired by a company called Essve. They made things like screws and fasteners for construction projects, then bundled them for sale to regular homeowners in corner stores. My job was to drive around Stockholm and sell the bundles to these stores. I had a Ford Escort and a cell phone the size of a briefcase. I wasn't a natural salesperson, and despite having my picture in most Swedish newspapers after the NHL draft, no one ever recognized me. It wasn't glamorous work, but I did love the feeling of driving around in my own car, talking to my friends on my huge cell phone.

Just after Christmas 1989, I traveled to Finland to play in the World Juniors. Sweden did not fare well in the tournament, and neither did I. I couldn't find the net. The media in Sweden printed stories about my failure to live up to the hype. At every game, I faced questions about my performance. The story wrote itself: the NHL's first draft pick didn't even crack the top ten in scoring at the World Juniors. Czech centerman Robert Reichel, who'd been drafted far behind me at seventieth overall, instead led the tournament in scoring, including several points he racked up in Czechoslovakia's 7–2 win against us. Most of the attention was on the sixteen-year-old Canadian superstar Eric Lindros, by far one of the youngest players in the tournament. Before our game against Canada, I made a bold prediction.

"We will beat them," I told the media. "We will beat Canada because we are due for a big win."

I was lucky my team stepped up and we did beat them, handing Canada their only loss of the tournament. Canada went on to win gold as I watched the final games from the stands. It was a humbling nine days.

I had a choice. I could return to Stockholm and accept my spot on Djurgården's fourth line, and take everything said and written about me to heart—one reporter had actually used the word *dud*. Or I could work harder. Not just in games, but in practices, too. I could try to scramble my way onto the third line, and eventually the second line. My Djurgården teammates weren't going to make it easy on me. But that boy on the lake in Sollentuna? The one who was always chasing Patrick and his friends on the ice? At heart, I was still him. At eighteen, being the chaser still suited me. It drove me. If I was going to be successful, I needed to work that much harder.

By February, I was getting more ice time. As the regular season ended, Falk pulled me aside after a practice.

"Mats," he said, "you're going to be our secret weapon in these playoffs."

I smiled. This was music to my ears.

That spring, we won Djurgården's second championship in a row. I got more ice time in the playoffs than I had all season, scoring seven goals in eight games. I was on for the power play and the penalty kill. We hoisted the championship trophy, and I was back in everyone's favor.

The message was clear. If I'd listened to all the stories about me after the World Juniors, if I'd allowed myself to get discouraged by less ice time earlier in the season, I might have lost my nerve. By finding a way to ignore it, I'd been able to focus on working hard and earning a bigger role in the lineup. At just nineteen, I'd already learned a valuable lesson that I'd carry with me for my entire career. If I was going to survive at the top of this sport, I had to treat the stories about me as nothing more than noise.

14

Contract Troubles

In the summer of 1990, there were rumblings that the Nordiques wanted me to come play for them a year earlier than initially planned. Before the draft, my father and Bengt Lundholm had struck a verbal deal that Quebec could pay a set fee to have me released as early as the 1990–91 season. We were about to learn the hard way that verbal deals don't cut it at the top tier.

As I left for the 1990 World Championships and trained and played my way through the summer, the negotiations continued. Mark Perrone started making regular trips to Sweden and kept my father and Bengt closely involved. I could sense it was getting tense. With the NHL rabidly circling, European hockey associations were quickly realizing that they were about to lose their top players to North America—talent nurtured by their homegrown programs—with little to show for it.

In September, Pierre Gauthier traveled to Sweden to meet with us and try to broker a deal. He had a contract in hand for me to sign once an agreement with Djurgårdens IF was in place. We sat at my parents' kitchen table and I watched as my father reviewed it. In all those drives to the arena over the years, it had never occurred to my parents that playing hockey might one day be the way I'd earn a living. They lived paycheck to paycheck and gave up their weekends so the three of us could play sports and be active, not because they held some far-fetched dream of hockey greatness. Even as my prospects rose, even after the spectacle of the NHL draft in Minnesota, even as Mark Perrone made big promises about a long and lucrative career, it was clear that my dad hadn't absorbed the true significance until the contract was right in front of him.

It didn't matter that his English wasn't great. The numbers read the same in both languages: hundreds of thousands of dollars, millions of Swedish kronor. His teenage son was about to earn several years' worth of his Televerket salary for a single season of playing hockey.

"*Skitunge*," my father said. *You little brat.*

But he was smiling. Widely.

Meanwhile, in Quebec, the Nordiques training camp was underway. All we needed to do was settle things in Sweden, and I'd be free to sign on the dotted line. However, the negotiations were not progressing. It looked like the verbal agreement given to Tommy and me was not going to be honored, and Djurgårdens IF planned to assert its rights to me for the following season.

By then, I knew where I wanted to be. I told Gauthier I was ready to leave even if the negotiations weren't finalized. So, I did.

Perrone and I boarded a plane and made our way to his home in Ipswich, a small town about an hour north of Boston. The plan was for everyone else to stay behind and finish the negotiations. Traveling to the States was a totally different kind of culture shock from my fall trip to Moscow. Everything from the wide, weaving lanes of American highways, to fast food restaurants on every corner. Ipswich itself was a beautiful seaside town with warm sunshine. Mark's home had a lawn the size of a soccer field and a winding driveway. I'd never seen a house as big as his, with a bathroom for every bedroom. He had two dogs and a basketball net that kept me busy for hours.

Back in Sweden, my departure set off a bomb. It was on the front page of every newspaper. The tabloid paper *Expressen* chased down my father and Bengt Lundholm for comments. A member of Djurgårdens' board was quoted in the papers as saying that he would have me banned from ever playing for Sweden internationally if I did not return to honor my contract. A few interviews dutifully printed my father's insistence that a verbal agreement had been in place.

That past July, Russian star Sergei Fedorov had traveled to the US to play in the Goodwill Games. He disappeared from his team one Sunday afternoon, emerging days later in Detroit to sign a contract with the Red Wings. The NHL was being accused of stealing players. But wasn't my situation different? Sweden had celebrated proudly when the Nordiques drafted me first overall. I didn't understand why my desire to go play for them was now being treated as a betrayal.

Bengt took the brunt of it. To calm the storm, he agreed to be interviewed on TV. A shy and reserved man, he didn't think to ask for the questions in advance. Despite the uproar in Sweden, he didn't figure on hostility from the reporter. The video of the interview shows him shifting nervously from foot to foot, clearing his throat as he withstood the barrage about my lack of loyalty to my country, my broken promises to my Djurgården team and teammates.

The drama even found its way to Ipswich. One afternoon, I was playing basketball in front of Mark Perrone's house when a car sped up the long driveway. A man hung out the passenger window, holding a camera. The car stopped as the man took my picture. All I could do was look at him, then return to playing basketball after he drove away. The pictures would be printed in Swedish papers the next day. It felt bizarre that all this uproar was over me.

After a few weeks and countless hours of negotiations, a deal was struck that released me to the Nordiques. The contract was signed, and plans were made to dispatch me immediately from Ipswich to Quebec City to play in the next exhibition game. In hindsight, it made sense that Sweden and its hockey organizations wanted compensation agreements in place if the NHL was going to start drawing away its homegrown talent as soon as players were old enough to be drafted. I was just glad Bengt and my parents had survived the firestorm.

Two weeks after arriving in Massachusetts, I was finally able to pack my bags for Quebec City. All seemed quickly forgiven at home; I played internationally for Sweden less than a year later. If my teammates on Djurgården held any grudges about the whole affair, none of them ever said so directly. Although I did hear a rumor that one of the team trainers taped my picture to the back of a toilet bowl with the words *shoot here* written across it.

15

Shoot the Puck, Mats

The Nordiques locker room sat quiet and empty. Our exhibition game—my first with the team—didn't start for another three hours. But I couldn't shake the nervous energy, so I came to the rink to ensure that my equipment was in place and my sticks were cut and ready. Since I'd missed training camp, my agent asked Pierre Gauthier if there was any plan to get me up to game speed.

"There is no plan," Gauthier said. "He will play tomorrow night."

That night's game was at home against the Buffalo Sabres.

By NHL standards, the Colisée de Québec was nothing special. But to me, it was enormous, far bigger than the rink we played in back home. The Nordiques locker room was square and rimmed by one long blue bench separated by metal grates into cubbies. Each player's little nook was the same: skates, pants and helmets on hooks, shin guards and elbow pads tucked under the bench. Like the others, my space was identified by my white sweater hung name and numbers out, trimmed along the bottom with Quebec's symbolic blue fleurs-de-lis.

Sundin. 13.

The number 13 was new for me. For the past few years, my

number had been 19. But there was already a Nordique who wore that number: the captain, Joe Sakic. So, I switched. I'd worn 13 at certain points in my life. Because I was born on February 13, the number never struck me as unlucky. I wasn't superstitious, and I'd never felt all that attached to my jersey number. Still, the sight of that jersey in the stall gave me goose bumps. I wished my dad was standing next to me. There'd been talk of him flying over once the contract was finalized, but it was too short notice. He had to work.

It took me a minute to notice that one player's space was empty. Cleared out, the equipment gone. I walked over to inspect.

Lafleur, the name tag read.

Guy Lafleur. Even in Sweden, we knew about Lafleur. Bengt Lundholm talked about him. An NHL superstar and veteran of a career that spanned twenty seasons, Lafleur had won the league scoring title three times with the Montreal Canadiens. By hockey standards, he was old—he'd just turned thirty-nine. Reporters asked him about retirement daily. One more season, he kept saying. But now his equipment wasn't in the dressing room. Did he change his mind?

On my way to the equipment room, I heard someone clear their throat. I smelled the smoke before I saw him. At the center of the room, sitting on a folding chair, fully dressed, skates on and laced tight, was Guy Lafleur, a cigarette pinched between his lips. He was taping his stick.

"Hello, Mats," he said, focused on his tape job. "Welcome."

His English was fluent, but a Quebecois accent still poked through. Aside from one season with the New York Rangers, Lafleur had spent his entire life playing in the province where he was born. He won five Stanley Cups playing in an arena less than two hours' drive from his childhood home. With my family two flights away, that felt hard to imagine.

We talked about that night's matchup against the Buffalo Sabres. He asked me how I was settling in. I'd only gotten to Quebec the day before. At that point, I'd only been to the hotel and the arena.

"It's a nice city," he said. "An old city. It might remind you of home."

I nodded, then collected some tape and supplies. As I turned to leave, Lafleur called after me.

"Mats," he said. "You got here earlier than everyone else."

"Not earlier than you," I said.

He laughed. "You know what? That shows something. Getting here nice and early. Preparations and routine are important. You'll be ready. You'll have a long career because of it."

Back in the locker room, I started on my routine. My teammates began arriving, too, settling in. They greeted me warmly, shook my hand, welcomed me. The captain, Joe Sakic, shook my hand and leaned in to whisper something.

"I'm happy to have you to play with," he said.

I didn't understand. This was the NHL. Wasn't everyone talented? Yes. But I soon understood that what Sakic meant was that when that talent was split among twenty-one teams, some get a smaller share.

Eventually, Lafleur returned to the room and sat in his stall. You could see the way the younger players gravitated to him, listened any time he spoke. But I couldn't shake one thing. He'd already been dressed for at least an hour, and puck drop wasn't until 7 p.m. Even his skates were laced game tight. I couldn't work up the nerve to ask the burning question: Don't your feet hurt?

In those first few weeks, I was too busy to feel homesick. The team housed me in a hotel not far from the practice arena. Sometimes, I'd wake in the morning and imagine what my family was doing back in Stockholm, where it was already afternoon.

Per would be finishing his school day. My parents would be at work. Phone calls were expensive, so my dad bought a fax machine and put it in my bedroom at home. I'd write up messages for them, or for my brothers or grandparents, then ask the hotel desk or the Nordiques office staff to send them off for me or alert me when one arrived in response. There was always a pang when I saw my mother's familiar writing scrawled across the machine's silky paper.

The team took care of us. They did sign me up for French-language lessons that lasted about as long as the preseason. I don't remember much about those lessons, except that I was antsy and disinterested enough to wiggle my way out of them. My time at Djurgården had instilled good habits in me; I was never late for practice, and I was always prepared for games. Still, I was a nineteen-year-old living alone almost four thousand miles from Sollentuna. At home, the rhythm of each day—sleeping, eating, driving to the rink—had been enforced by my parents. My dad got me to the rink right up until I was drafted. My mom made sure I was fed, made sure I kept my room clean. In Quebec, I was left to my own devices. It wasn't always pretty.

Before our first regular-season game, my dad arrived in Quebec City. It wasn't easy for him to secure time off work, but he made it happen. I was at practice, so he planned to go to the hotel to nap off the jet lag and wait for me to return.

At the front desk, he secured his room, then asked for a key to mine.

"I could give you one," the attendant said, "but you won't be able to get into the room."

Tommy didn't understand. Why not? Wouldn't the key work?

"His clothes are everywhere," she said. "The cleaner can't even open his door."

I'm lucky I wasn't there to witness my dad's next moves. By

the time I arrived back at the hotel, he'd taken everything out of my room and put it in his, allowing the cleaners to do their work.

Tommy checked me over like a doctor might, likely according to my mother's instructions. Ensuring I wasn't too skinny, that I'd been taking care of myself, getting enough sleep. Answering his questions, I realized that, aside from our rare phone calls, I hadn't spoken Swedish in weeks.

"You cannot live like a pig, Mats. You need to clean up after yourself."

"Okay," I said.

He was serious, but I could only smile. I was happy he was there.

In our first game of the regular season, we went down 2–0 early against the Hartford Whalers. Lafleur scored early in the opening minute of the second period to get us on the board. Sakic scored on a power play a few minutes later. Three minutes after that, Sakic threw me a pass and I scored my first NHL goal. Even in the NHL, the best thing about hockey remained true: Momentum can change on a dime. Anything can happen.

The game ended in a 3–3 tie. In the locker room, I felt good. I'd scored a goal. Kept up. Played on the power play and penalty kill. I'd had no choice; there were thirty-two penalties and three fights. In one game.

That was the biggest adjustment from the game at home. The choppiness. If you got away from an opponent, they'd hook their sticks into your ribs and water-ski behind you as you tried to break up the ice. It's not like the referees ignored it, but they had to pick their battles. High sticks. Fights. Hooking. Tripping. Roughing. I knew better than to shy away. In the first period against the Whalers, as the first period ended, I went hard into a guy in the corner. My opponent punched me in response. The record shows that I got my first NHL penalty before I got my first goal.

In Sweden, hockey was a game of skill. The third and fourth

lines were reserved for developing younger talent. In the NHL, these lines were reserved for fighters, scrappy players who could make an entire career taking penalties to rouse their teammates out of a rut or protect the team's top talent.

Thankfully, I adjusted well. I liked the physical play, and my size helped me. After Hartford, we lost home-and-home games against the powerhouse Boston Bruins. Our first big win was in Toronto. I recorded four points and listened as the home fans booed their team off the ice.

"Tough crowd," Lafleur said in the room. "But Montreal is tougher."

The mood on the bus from Toronto to Buffalo was relaxed and happy. It was such an interesting mix of characters. There was Lafleur, still scoring highlight-reel goals in his final act. Our coach, Dave Chambers, was the first non–French Canadian to be hired by the Nordiques. His hiring was meant to mark a new era for this small-market team from Quebec City: a captain from the West Coast, a coach from Toronto, and a first-round draft pick from Sollentuna, Sweden.

We won our game in Buffalo, then tied two more. By our tenth game of the season, we'd only recorded three losses. It was a very good start. So, there was no reason to panic when we lost a close game to the Vancouver Canucks. Or when we lost the next game. Or even the next. Or the next. By the end of November, when we hadn't won in seventeen games, the panic was in full swing.

I hated losing, but as the fall wore on, I settled into life away from my family, into the rhythms of life with an NHL team. This feeling of grand adventure overshadowed the bouts of homesickness. With such a young team, it almost felt like we were kids taking the trip of a lifetime. Every city was new, so the traveling didn't feel like a grind. It wasn't kicking in that I'd moved away and lived in Canada now. It felt more like an adventure that would soon end and take me home to my friends and family.

Traveling all over the continent, I'd come back to Quebec City with a deepened sense that it was the city most like home. Like Stockholm, Quebec City's narrow cobblestone streets were lined with stone churches and buildings perched over the water. Like the Lake Mälaren outlet in Stockholm, the St. Lawrence River was a brackish mix of fresh and salt water. Europe is full of fortified cities and towns, but North America is so modern by comparison. The rampart walls of old Quebec City felt like a familiar exception.

Eventually, I checked out of the hotel and moved into a small apartment close to the practice arena. Ever the negotiator, my agent called the Ikea store in Montreal, and they agreed to furnish my new bachelor pad for free. Ikea must have immediately dispatched a loaded truck down the Trans-Canada Highway, because the apartment looked like something straight out of their catalog by the time I moved in. There were plates and bowls and cutlery in the kitchen, spare bedding in the dresser drawers. They'd even hung landscape art on the bare walls. It was small—only a bedroom, a living room, a kitchen and a washroom. But on my first night in that apartment, I truly felt like an adult.

Somewhere on the tail end of our losing streak, it was arranged that my grandfather Sture would come visit me. By then, he was seventy years old and retired. He'd sold the logging cabin a few years earlier. After enduring a stroke, Sture was on the mend and well enough to travel. He wasn't going to miss his chance to see his grandson play in the NHL. By the time I was let in on the plan, the plane ticket had already been bought.

"Where will he stay?" I asked my dad.

"With you," my dad said, as if the question made no sense.

I looked around my small apartment. *Where?*

Sture arrived in Quebec with only a small suitcase. As he

settled in, I announced that I'd secured him tickets for our two upcoming home games.

"Only two games?" he asked. "What about the rest?"

I'd never thought to ask how long my grandfather planned to stay.

"Three weeks," he said, looking around the apartment. "I'll be here for three weeks."

He was my grandfather, so of course he took the bedroom. Good thing the living room couch was a pullout. He loved coming to my games. It didn't matter that I was now playing in the NHL, he always had a comment for me on the drive home.

"Stop it with all the passing," he said. "You need to shoot the puck."

Funnily enough, Guy Lafleur had gotten into the habit of telling me the same thing. Sometimes, I'd return to the bench after a shift, and Guy would slide in next to me.

"*Tabernak*, Mats," he'd say. "Fuck. Too fancy. Just shoot the fucking puck."

Sture attended every home game during his stay. At the apartment, he also held on to the same routines that structured his days at home in Sweden. I liked to decompress at night by watching television. But Sture went straight to bed.

"Turn it down, Mats!" he'd yell at me from the bedroom.

I was nineteen. Sture was set in his ways, rigid in everything he did, from making oatmeal to brushing his teeth. Even his morning coffee was a precise concoction. It felt like I was ten again. I loved my grandfather, but I was soon counting the days until his flight home.

When I got back to my apartment after driving him to the airport, I turned on the TV and cranked up the volume. I was thrilled to have my bedroom back, to sleep in my actual bed. But when I woke up the next morning, the apartment felt empty. I'd grown used to the sounds of Sture in my kitchen. I lay in bed and studied one of the framed Ikea pictures on the wall. It was meant to be some kind of modern art, a bunch of wide strips of paint brushed up and down the canvas. It occurred to me that none of this stuff belonged to me. I had no pictures of my loved ones on the walls. My life was now here, but my family and friends weren't. Nothing in this apartment had come with me from home.

16

Standing Ovations

The seventeen-game winless streak ended in late November, but our season never turned around. By March, we'd only won fourteen games. The Nordiques were the youngest team in the NHL. A handful of us were still teenagers, and our co-captain, Joe Sakic, was only twenty-one years old. You could feel that youth in the room. Sakic was a quiet guy, but a natural leader with the poise of a veteran. He worked hardest in practice and was the first to hit the gym and the last to leave. Lafleur had enough veteran wisdom to spare.

But teenagers are teenagers. The Colisée was famous for its hot dogs, and a group of us would hit the snack bars nearly every day for lunch and eat several with no eye to the almost total lack of nutritional value. I couldn't keep my room clean. Owen Nolan, drafted first overall the year after me, was a gifted rookie, but like me, a kid. One day, after practice, the team emerged from the arena to two guys fighting in the snow. We rushed to pull them apart, only to see that it was Nolan and his dad. They stood up and dusted themselves off like it never happened, then got into the same car and drove away.

In true teenage fashion, the first thing I bought for my apartment was an oversized fish tank. I loved how it lit up the room, and I figured fish were low-maintenance company. At Christmas, the NHL only breaks for a couple of days, not enough time for me to return to Sweden. I wanted my family with me, so I used some of my newfound hockey money to fly my parents and brothers to Quebec City. There was never any discussion of a hotel. I had a small place, but they'd still all stay with me.

My mom couldn't be sure what supplies they'd have in Canada to prepare her Swedish Christmas feast. They decided to pack some items just in case. One such thing was blood pudding, a type of pork sausage not quite as gross as it sounds. Forget that it's probably illegal to carry into a country; blood pudding is extremely rich in iron, good for growing boys, even ones playing in the NHL. When the Sundins landed in Quebec City with a suitcase full of pork product, no one stopped them at customs.

I was so excited to show my brothers my apartment. When they arrived from the airport, my dad's gaze narrowed immediately to the fish tank.

"Mats," he said, "you can't have fish."

I was annoyed. "Why not?"

"You're away too much. Who will feed them?"

I argued my case, and eventually Tommy dropped it. Over the next few days, Gunilla worked to organize my kitchen so she could prepare a feast worthy of our Christmases in Sollentuna. I took my brothers to the rink to meet my teammates. We went out for dinners and visited the sights of the city. The Nordiques played two games at home while my family was there, even pulling out a 4–1 win against the Washington Capitals where I assisted on a few goals. I loved being on the bench, knowing my parents and Patrick and Per were in the stands. Even in Quebec, I was still conjuring up that kid in the driveway, only now I was chasing

NHL superstars. All along, I understood that I'd made it this far because of my parents and my brothers and the life we had back in Sollentuna. My success belonged to all of us, and it made me happy to think of the four of them savoring it, too. When it was time for them to leave, I felt a pit in my stomach. My dad said nothing more about the fish, but made sure I had extra food next to the tank.

With any playoff hopes dead by January, the talk became about building out the younger team. Veterans were traded away for draft picks. By late winter, the focus turned to the 1991 NHL draft and Eric Lindros, the young Canadian I'd played against a year earlier in Finland. The odds were good that Quebec would land the first-overall draft pick for the third year in a row.

This was management's focus, but we players kept our eyes on the ice. We wanted to close the season on a high note. In the final weeks, every away game was marked by a ceremony honoring Guy Lafleur. In places like Buffalo or Pittsburgh, they'd make an announcement and the ovation would last a minute or two, sometimes five.

As the season wound down, you could see Lafleur relishing his time in the dressing room. Arriving extra early and staying afterward to chat with the younger guys. Our final two games were a home-and-home against the Montreal Canadiens. To say that Guy Lafleur was a hero in Montreal is an understatement. The ovation before the Canadiens' home game lasted so long— seventeen minutes, I'm pretty sure—that as I stood on the blue line, my feet fell asleep in my skates. You could feel the emotion seeping out of Lafleur. Twenty years. Five Stanley Cups. Scoring titles. He scored a goal that night, pounding in a rebound on a power play. I'm pretty sure Montreal fans had never cheered that loudly for a player on a visiting team. We jumped off the bench to celebrate. Lafleur was one of the last NHL players to forgo wearing a helmet. His hair always looked good; he was famous for it. No one wanted to mess it up, but after that goal, the guys couldn't help but pat him on the head.

After a longer West Coast road trip in February, I came home to find several of my fish dead. I didn't admit defeat to Tommy, but I did give the fish tank away. In March, as our season wrapped up with the arrival of the playoffs, my phone rang. It was Conny Evensson, the coach of the Swedish national team. The World Championships were set to start a month later in Finland. My NHL season would already be over.

"We need a goal scorer," Evensson said. "Will you come play for Sweden?"

Of course I would.

I was thrilled to keep playing. Sakic planned to join the Canadian team, too. A few weeks later, I returned to Stockholm for the first time since the tense negotiations seven months earlier. Some of my former Djurgårdens IF teammates would be on the national team, too, so I was grateful that the bad blood seemed to have evaporated. The roster was very deep and included one of my favorite NHL veterans, Mats Näslund, and I was told I'd be playing on a line with veteran Swede superstar Bengt-Åke Gustafsson, who'd retired from the NHL after nine seasons with the Washington Capitals. I'd also be reunited with Nicklas Lidström, my former World Junior teammate, a defenseman drafted the same year as me by the Detroit Red Wings.

We arrived in Finland in early April, just as the snow was melting and the days were stretching long again. The tournament would be played in three cities that dotted the southern half of the country. Seven games in nine days, then a short playoff round.

In our first game, we routed Germany, 8–1. On the bench, Gustafsson's instructions to me were simple: skate and get open, and I'll get you the puck. The dressing room felt immediately different to me from the Nordiques. Lots of NHL veterans were on the team, including Håkan Loob, the only Swede to have scored fifty goals in the NHL, Kjell Samuelsson, Calle Johansson and fellow rookie Johan Garpenlöv, but the energy was positive. Confident. Before arriving in Quebec, I'd never experienced a losing season. The way it can grind on you. The tension that can build in the dressing room as guys anticipate getting traded. Or scratched. The way the pressures on the management trickle into the room. First-overall picks almost always get sent to teams that are rebuilding, and I was no exception. I loved my teammates and wanted to be part of that rebuild. But after a few games in Finland, I really grasped the cultural contrast between a winning and a losing team.

That contrast showed itself in our second game against the home Finnish team. With only a minute left in the third period, we were losing, 4–2. Our coach called a time-out, and our goalie was pulled. As we huddled to map out the play, we knew the game wasn't over. All we had to do was gain control of the play down low and put the puck on net. We scored with barely thirty seconds left. The Finns won the next face-off and pulled the puck back to their defenseman, who needed only fire it deep into our end to win the game. But Lidström skated from our blue line directly into the path of the puck. The defenseman's shot bounced hard off his leg and rebounded clear across the neutral zone, right onto my stick. Breakaway. I scored. With seconds on the clock, we'd tied the game. Just as we believed we could.

Not everyone had the same faith. Only forty miles south of the Finnish border, in Kainulasjärvi, my grandparents Sven and Elsa had been watching the game. Near the end of the third period, with the score still 4–2, my grandfather waved a frustrated hand at the TV and went to bed. When we scored our third goal, my grandmother didn't wake him. She didn't wake him when we scored again to tie it. The next morning, Sven woke up to the news of our comeback on the radio.

"Why didn't you wake me up?" he asked Elsa.

"Because you gave up on them," my grandmother answered.

Team Sweden went undefeated. Our final tournament game was in early May, on a cold and cloudy day in Turku, Finland. We were playing the mighty USSR, who'd won all their games except for a late tie with us. The Canadian team, including my Nordiques captain, Joe Sakic, were in the stands. With the final rankings decided by points instead of a single-elimination bracket, the game mattered as much to them as it did to us: the winner between Sweden and the USSR took gold, but if we tied, the gold medal went to Canada. By the halfway mark of the third period, it looked like the Canadians might prevail. The game was deadlocked at 1–1.

The Soviets were a juggernaut. Back-to-back world champions, they'd only lost one game in the last three tournaments combined. But that loss? It was to the Swedes. We'd beaten them before. We knew we could win. With nine minutes left, I jumped over the boards and circled low in our zone. The puck popped out of a scrum behind our net and bounced to me.

I looked up the ice. There was room. I had a lane.

For years, my brothers and I enacted this precise scene in our driveway in Sollentuna: Imagine wearing the Swedish blue-and-yellow jersey. Imagine a tie game. The gold medal on the line. The USSR in red, always the chosen opponent, defenseman Viacheslav Fetisov our favorite foe. I'd practiced scoring this goal so many times, programmed myself mentally and physically by taking thousands of shots on the red net, that it felt natural when it was finally playing out in real life.

I crossed into the neutral zone. Picking up speed, I stuck to the boards. There was no thinking required. No decision to make.

No fear. There I was: blue-and-yellow jersey on, tie game, gold on the line. And the defenseman closing the gap on me? Fetisov. Exactly as we'd dreamed of it.

One move, my dad always said. Just make one move.

I cut inside as if I planned to split the defense and try for the breakaway. Fetisov took the bait and couldn't adjust when I deked back toward the boards. By the time I reached the face-off circle, I had a clean shot. Fetisov whacked me with his stick, but the puck was already off mine. Low five-hole. Goal.

The crowd, mostly Swedes, went wild. As the final buzzer went, my teammates and I threw off our gloves and sticks and convened at the net. Some dropped to lie on the ice. As we stood on the blue line for the trophy presentation, I looked across at my opponents. Beating the Soviets was a dream come true. And just in time—with the collapse of the Soviet Union, the dreaded CCCP jersey was never worn at another World Championships.

Back in Sweden, a massive rally and parade were held in our honor. The streets of Stockholm filled with fans waving flags and screaming our names. At my parents' house, I could barely relax. My ears were ringing. I listened to my dad recount the goal over and over. They collected newspapers to add clippings to the scrapbook they'd started.

17

Enforcers

Because we finished dead last, the Nordiques were awarded the
first-overall pick in the 1991 NHL draft. There was little coverage of it in Sweden, aside from the fact that a centerman from
the northern coastal town of Örnsköldsvik, Peter Forsberg, was
expected to be drafted in the top ten. That June, the Nordiques
selected Eric Lindros, who quickly announced his refusal to play
for Quebec. Back then, without texting and the internet, my teammates and I had no real means to convene and discuss this news
or what it meant for the team.

In August 1991, the Swedish national team gathered again,
this time for a training camp in preparation for the Canada Cup,
a now-defunct six-country invitational tournament that used to
be held every few years. Unrestricted by NHL playoff schedules or
amateur status, it was the only time the best players in the world
collected in one place.

The Sweden team's training camp was held in Sunne, a lake
town four hours due west of Stockholm. The plan was to mix
dry-land workouts with some skates at the local rink. I was most
excited by the chance to play with Börje Salming. He'd retired from

the NHL the season before I joined it and was now playing in the Swedish Elite League. At forty, Salming was the oldest player on our team by nearly a decade.

The morning after settling into the hotel, the team met outside to head out for a run. We stretched and jumped to warm up while waiting for everyone to assemble. The last one out, and the only one opting to run shirtless, was Börje. As he greeted us with his friendly smile and raspy voice, everyone tried not to gawk. Forty or not, he was ripped, in better shape than the guys half his age.

The first of our games in the tournament were played in Toronto, where fans took to their feet to welcome Salming back. The games were incredibly fast. We finished in fourth place. In our game against Canada, Eric Lindros broke Ulf Samuelsson's collarbone with a body check. In the next game, he did the same to Czechoslovakia's Martin Ručinský. It was clear the talent Lindros would have added had he opted to join the Nordiques.

When the Canada Cup ended, each player headed directly to his NHL team to start training camp. In Quebec, we started the 1991 season with higher hopes. Sakic, Owen Nolan and I were all picking up points in nearly every game. But by Christmas, we'd only recorded nine wins. Pierre Pagé fired coach Dave Chambers and took the job himself. Remarkably, we went almost a full year—March 1991 to March 1992—without winning a game on the road. A few ties, but no wins. That's not exactly a statistic worth remembering. The drought finally ended on March 5, 1992, in Hartford. After finishing the first period tied, 3–3, we scored five unanswered goals in the second. I had five goals and two assists that night, the most goals and points I would record in a single game in my career. Nolan had a goal and five assists.

We only won twenty games that season. Here was this group of kids, earning an incredible living playing a game we loved. We were living our dream. But we were also learning about the business side of the game. The industry. The media. The responsibilities we carried to management, our teammates, the fans. Coming from Sweden, I'd had little idea what to expect. Maybe I figured I'd play a few years in the NHL, then go home. In theory, I knew that being drafted first overall was a big deal, but I hadn't fully grasped the implications. I was expected to be the best.

These expectations from the team and media were a shock to my system. I was young and naive with little wiggle room to grow up. Our team was still developing, still learning game by game. Our focus was on hockey, but we all understood on some level that the Nordiques organization was a mess and its financial troubles weren't about to magically go away. The NHL was growing, with talk of adding teams in Florida, California, Ottawa. Quebec City was small and French-speaking. TV coverage almost always favored the nearby Montreal Canadiens. Lindros had opted to sit the season out, and a deal to trade him was hanging over management.

To the players on the bench, it was only ever about each other, about the team. Sakic led the team with his actions. He worked hard, never complained, held himself accountable. If his shots weren't going in, he'd stay on the ice after practice to work on them. It set the tone for everyone else. Despite our record, winning felt within reach. We often lost by only one goal or squeezed out ties against top teams. We were playing against teams with far more veterans, guys who'd gone on long playoff runs. Guys who knew from experience what it took to win in the NHL. We were boys playing against men.

We didn't need a rebuild. We needed to mature, to learn exactly what it took to win in the NHL. Maybe the roster needed a few more pieces.

The season wrapped with a home-and-home series against Buffalo. Neither team had made the playoffs, but the wins felt symbolic to us. The first of the two games was at the Colisée. We won decisively, but a Nordiques fan jumped on the ice in the final seconds and approached the Sabres bench. He took a good twenty punches from Buffalo's enforcer, Rob Ray, before being dragged off by security. This set the scene for the next night in Buffalo. In the dressing room, my teammate Tony Twist warned us: "Could get messy tonight."

I'd played over 150 games in the NHL by then. I was used to the grind. I'd yet to drop the gloves in a fight, but I could handle the roughness. In Buffalo, with their season over, the fans were looking to be entertained. Any time two players tangled, they'd chant, "We want Ray." Rob Ray. They wanted a fight. Or fights.

I wasn't opposed to fighting, I'd just never played in a setting where it was not only tolerated, but expected and encouraged. Every NHL team had a couple of guys on their roster like Rob Ray or Tony Twist whose job title was "enforcer"—they were there to fight. A star player takes a hard hit? The enforcer fights. Losing a game and needing a boost? The enforcer fights. Need payback for dirty play in a previous game? The enforcer fights.

There was even a political angle to it. Every year, more and more European players were being drafted, almost always for their skill. To some, the refrain became that Europeans were soft or cowardly for not fighting, even if plenty of high-skill Canadian guys didn't fight either. The NHL was—and still is—the only league in any team sport where fist-fighting won't get you ejected from the game. At most levels of international play, fighting could lead to long and costly suspensions, even punishment from your home country's hockey federation. For the many players who didn't grow up in North America, fighting wasn't a hockey thing, it was an NHL thing.

Don Cherry, a former coach and player with a weekly TV segment on *Hockey Night in Canada* called "Coach's Corner," was vocal about his distaste for European players. He preferred guys who could drop the gloves. I knew little about him—Cherry was not popular in Quebec and rarely brought up the Nordiques in his segments. Besides, I liked the physicality of the NHL game and got a reasonable share of penalties myself. I had a lot of respect for the enforcers on my team. All it took was one fight for me to figure out that enforcer was the hardest job in hockey.

In that final game of the season against Buffalo, I opened the third period by taking a hooking penalty. When I returned to the ice two minutes later, the air felt electric. You could sense the trouble coming. I went into the corner behind my net to retrieve the puck and got knocked to the ice. While I was down, one of the Sabres threw a few punches. I yanked at him from the ice. My teammate Steven Finn arrived in support. Bodies started flying. Two guys were on top of me. Then four. Six. I was at the bottom of a pileup. My helmet came off. Skate blades whizzed too close to my face. The crowd kept chanting. By the time I got to my feet, the referees had already dragged a few guys to the box.

At the next face-off, the puck sailed into the corner again. There was another scramble along the glass and a lot of shoving. More guys arrived on scene. I was in the mix, my adrenaline still flowing from the last pileup. When Sabres player Dave Hannan called to me, I stepped away from the glass, skated toward him and dropped my gloves. Who cares that I hadn't fought anyone since tangling with my brothers in our driveway at home, I had eight inches in height and forty pounds on Hannan. If I was going to fight for the first time in my career, it might as well be against a guy a lot smaller than me.

Smaller or not, Hannan was no fighting rookie. He knew the strategy: grab hold of your opponent's chest at the logo with your weak arm, get your elbow up as a blocker, then swing furiously. All I could do was flail to free up an arm. My technique was terrible.

Hannan used my head as a speed bag for a good thirty seconds until I got a few punches in. Both our jerseys came over our heads and the referees pulled us apart.

I was headed to the box to serve my first-ever fighting major. I assessed the damage. My hands were fine, my head didn't hurt. It couldn't have been that bad. Maybe I'd held my own? When Tony Twist joined me a few minutes later after another scrum, he congratulated me on my first NHL fight. Then he laughed and shook his head.

"That was ugly," he said, tapping my gloves. "You might want to keep those on."

We won that home-and-home series, but our season was again over in April. Again I got a call from Conny Evensson, this time asking if I'd travel to Czechoslovakia for the 1992 World Championships. This time, one of my teammates would be a talented eighteen-year-old named Peter Forsberg, who'd been drafted sixth overall the year before by the Philadelphia Flyers. After a tough round robin, we were crowned world champions again. Victorious, I went back to Sweden to train and visit family. That June, the NHL draft became huge news in Europe when five of the top ten picks, including the first and second, were European players.

A few days after that draft, the Nordiques' management orchestrated a trade for Eric Lindros with the Philadelphia Flyers in exchange for money, two first-round draft picks and a long list of talent that included several veterans and one very familiar face: Peter Forsberg. When I saw this list of players Quebec would be adding to the roster, I couldn't believe it. The missing pieces were about to fall into place.

18

A Turnaround Season

By early 1993, the Quebec Nordiques were on track to set an NHL record for the biggest year-over-year turnaround in league history. We won more games in the fall alone than in the entire previous season. With the addition of guys like Steve Duchesne and Mike Ricci, our roster finally had depth and we rarely scored fewer than four goals per game. We'd yet to be shut out. We were scoring on the power play and even on the penalty kill. Our winning streaks were far longer than any losing stretches.

With this influx of talent, we were not only racking up wins, but goals and assists, too. In late October, a reporter asked me to comment on my points streak.

"It's at seven games," he said.

My default answer was always to redirect to comments on our group play. We had four lines of depth. I was happy to be contributing. Obviously, I knew how many goals and assists I had, but streaks weren't something I tracked. A few weeks later, when the streak reached fifteen games, I got asked about it almost every game night in Quebec. When it reached twenty, I got asked about it everywhere the team went. A few games later, when I cracked the list of the twenty longest scoring streaks in NHL history, reporters started asking my teammates about it. Then my opponents. During a road game against the LA Kings in mid-December, I registered an assist and hit a symbolic thirty games. I now held the only spot among the five longest streaks in NHL history not occupied by Mario Lemieux or Wayne Gretzky.

Two nights later, when I was pointless in the third period against the Sharks, my teammates were working hard to get me the puck. It knocked our game flow out of whack. We blew a 6–2 lead and ended regulation time tied at 7–7. After Scott Young secured the win with a late-overtime goal, I felt oddly relieved. It was a memorable run, but distracting. That game taught me the perils of the focus falling to one player and his accomplishments. I was happy to be headed back to Quebec with the attention back where it belonged.

It was a great team. We still had lots of youth, but with a good mix of veterans who knew how to lock in the group's focus and preparation. The personalities varied, too. The quiet leadership of Joe Sakic was offset by Ron Hextall, the goalie who arrived in the Lindros trade. I'd never played with a goaltender who racked up more penalty minutes than half the skaters on his team. His pregame routine was so dialed in, from ocular exercises to bending and lubricating his blocker and glove, that the rest of us knew it was game on when Hextall finally looked up from his stall, eyes ablaze, and yelled at us to go.

In late February, my parents called to say they planned to visit with my brother Per and my uncle Rolf during a run of home games in mid-March. They'd need four tickets to each game. And good seats, on account of this being Rolf's first visit. I considered asking where they planned to stay, but I knew the answer. One-bedroom apartment or not, they were all staying with me. How exactly does that work? My parents got the bedroom, and the rest of us shared the living room.

Uncle Rolf wasn't impressed when we lost the two home games he came to watch. The next game on our schedule was in Montreal. Rolf and Tommy studied a map of Quebec. It was a three-hour drive along the St. Lawrence River. No problem, they agreed. They weren't about to pass up a chance to watch a game in the fabled Montreal Forum to witness the Battle of Quebec in action. A plan was hatched. I'd travel to Montreal on the team bus, and they'd follow the afternoon of the game in my red Volvo 740, then drive back after the game ended.

The snow started before they left my apartment. No one was worried. It was almost nostalgic; my dad had a long history of driving through snow to get to my hockey games. As they worked their way to the city's edge, visibility dropped. Tommy, behind the wheel, noticed flashing lights behind them. He pulled over and waited for the police officer to approach. He rolled down the window and snow swirled into the car. The officer leaned in, shielding his face from the wind. He wanted to know where they were headed. Given the incoming storm, he said, they should probably turn around.

Tommy had a choice. He hated the idea of name-dropping, but he really wanted to get to Montreal.

"Do you know Mats Sundin?" he asked the officer.

The officer did. He described in detail one of my recent goals, the recent point streak.

"I'm his father," Tommy said.

Once it was established that this Volvo full of Swedes was my family headed to the Forum to cheer on the Nordiques, a police escort was offered. The squad car turned on its flashers and carved a path through the snowy Quebec City streets and across the Pierre Laporte Bridge to the Trans-Canada Highway.

It was a good thing the highway was mostly empty. Tommy had to fight the steering wheel to keep from fishtailing. It took six hours, but the Sundin clan were in their seats at the Forum before the opening face-off. We won, 5–2, and I scored the game's final goal on a breakaway. I was glad I got to make their troubles worth the effort.

By the time I was out of the locker room and we convened in the parking lot, my Volvo was completely buried in snow. Later, that March 1993 snowfall would be named the Storm of the Century for all the snow it dumped across the eastern continent from the Arctic Circle down to Florida. The Nordiques would not be returning to Quebec City that night. The roads were impassable, so there was no way my family could either. I found a team representative and told them our predicament. He called the hotel and arranged for the last two available rooms to be booked.

When we told my family the news, my parents both nodded.

"Two rooms?" my dad said in Swedish, raising two fingers.

The Nordiques rep looked worried.

"The hotel is sold out," he said. "Two rooms was the best we could do."

It meant that Per and Rolf would share one room and my parents would get the other. I had to explain to the representative that my parents weren't complaining—they were thrilled to be granted such a luxury. Left to their own devices, they'd only have booked one.

The Nordiques ended the season in fourth place overall. We'd broken the one-hundred-point barrier for the first time in franchise history and made the playoffs for the first time in seven years. Both Joe Sakic and I collected more than a hundred points. I led the team in scoring for the first time in my career. Momentum was on our side. We'd square off against the Montreal Canadiens in the first round, the Battle of Quebec extending into the playoffs. The matchup boded well for us; we'd won four of our seven games against Montreal in the regular season.

Things seemed even better when we won the series' first two games at home. But then we lost two games in Montreal by a goal each. Getting the puck past Canadiens goaltender Patrick Roy became harder with every shot. It took me a few games to find my playoff rhythm. By the fifth game, I'd adjusted to the tempo and scored two goals. But our team blew two leads and we lost in overtime.

Pierre Pagé wore his emotions on his sleeve. There's a well-known video of him yelling at us in the late stages of Game 6, after we fell behind, 4–2.

"We're getting outworked," he yelled. "All of you are getting outworked."

We lost that game, 6–2. It was disappointing, but the season didn't feel like a write-off. We were still building and gaining experience. Odds were that momentum would be on our side the following season.

Instead, we stalled. In early 1994, talk of the Nordiques relocating to a US city hit a fever pitch. The Minnesota North Stars had already been moved to Dallas. The league was expanding and changing; the markets and costs were growing. The team from a small francophone city like Quebec struggled to keep pace.

We traveled to New York City in February 1994 for back-to-back games against the Islanders and Rangers. Our chances of making a repeat trip to the playoffs were growing dimmer. After a morning skate at the Islanders' arena, a TV was set up so we could watch the 1994 Olympic gold medal game between Canada and Sweden. Well over half of the Nordiques roster was Canadian-born. We had a few Americans and Russians, but Tommy Sjödin and I were the only Swedes in the room. When

Sweden scored first, our cheers were drowned out by everyone else's groans.

In the third period, Canada roared back with two goals. Late in the game, a power play allowed Sweden to tie the score at 2–2. Overtime yielded nothing. The game would go to a shootout. Back then, shootouts weren't a thing in the NHL. It seemed ridiculous to the guys in the room that a gold medal could be decided by anything but playing the actual game.

The shootout seemed to go on forever, with the teams trading goals and saves back and forth. On the thirteenth shot, Peter Forsberg made a one-handed move on the Canadian goalie to score arguably the most famous goal in Sweden's history. There's a photograph taken overhead of Forsberg guiding the puck in after a reaching deke. That photograph was later issued on a postage stamp, cementing the goal's reputation. My Nordiques teammates took it well enough when Canada failed to score on the next attempt, awarding us the gold medal. Still, you can't exactly celebrate wildly when everyone else in the room is dejected.

There was one bright side. Two years after being drafted, Forsberg was finally set to cross the Atlantic and join the Nordiques the following season. I'd been the only full-time Swedish player on the Nordiques roster for four years. My English had improved a lot, and I even knew a handful of words in French. Sometimes, in the locker room, I'd get a sense of the camaraderie between the French Canadians, or the small cohort of Americans, or the guys raised not far from each other in Ontario or British Columbia. It's hard to pinpoint what's missing when you don't have that same connection with your teammates. So, I was excited at the prospect of a teammate from Örnsköldsvik, a town on the Baltic Sea that every summer marked the midway point of our drive from Sollentuna to Kainulasjärvi. I'd won gold with Peter at the 1992 World Championships and knew how good he could be.

But when our season ended without us making the playoffs, my agent, Mark Perrone, was already warning me that contract negotiations with the Nordiques were stalled, and I might be looking at a trade. My future in Quebec was in jeopardy.

19

You're a Maple Leaf Now

By May, I was back in Sweden, training daily and visiting family and friends. Mark Perrone was keeping in regular touch about trade talks and negotiations. More than once over my four seasons with the Nordiques, I'd watched veteran teammates with a wife and kids in school clean out their stalls after getting an early-morning call that they'd been traded to a team three thousand miles away. I was antsy, but I was twenty-three. It was easier for me to be casual about a trade. If need be, my small apartment full of Ikea furniture could be packed up in a day.

In June, I flew to Kiruna with my brothers, Patrick and Per, to go fishing with our cousins, Stefan and Thomas. Börje Salming was from Kiruna, a mining town two hours northwest of Kainulasjärvi, where my mother grew up. After retiring from the NHL and playing a few years in the Swedish Elite League, Börje now spent his summers in Kiruna running hockey camps and hunting and fishing. Salming was of indigenous Sámi heritage, and the Sámi culture's livelihood is focused on herding reindeer and fishing and hunting through the seasonal cycle. There is a saying in the Sámi language: *Ahki ii leat jagi viellja*—"No year is another year's brother." This speaks to the ever-changing climate and the need to learn the land and adapt to the constant change. His grandfather had been a reindeer herder. Despite living in North America for nearly two decades, Börje never lost his connection to the land. When I told him we planned to fish in the area, he connected us with a friend who would arrange for us to fish in the wilderness, just inland from the border of northern Norway.

I remember the date: Wednesday, June 29, 1994. The five of us packed our rods and tackle boxes, snacks, a few beers and the most important thing: Djungelolja—"Jungle Oil," the strongest mosquito repellent you could buy. It was a cool and clear morning. A helicopter picked us up in Kiruna and flew us to the shores of Ribasjaure, a lake full of trout and arctic char. This was true wilderness, the nearest road over forty miles away.

Even in early summer, the mountains of lower Lapland were still dusted with snow. My brothers and cousins were curious enough about my hockey life, but up here, we didn't really discuss it. They understood that this place was an off button for me, an escape from the pressures of the business and game of hockey. As we lit our fire to cook our catch or make coffee, we talked more about life in general. It was always so relaxed.

I didn't tell them that I'd talked to Mark Perrone right before we flew to Kiruna. As I fished on the shores of Ribasjaure, Mark—like every other hockey executive—was in Hartford, Connecticut, for the 1994 NHL Entry Draft. According to Mark, I was likely headed to the Toronto Maple Leafs in a trade for their captain, Wendel Clark. I knew Toronto was a huge market with sold-out games every night. Börje had only recently retired after playing sixteen seasons as a Maple Leaf.

We'd been fishing for a few hours when a distant noise caught our attention. We spotted a helicopter on the horizon. It approached and circled as close to us as it safely could, the wind from its rotors kicking up the dirt.

"He's not supposed to pick us up until ten o'clock," Patrick said.

"It's not our pilot," I said.

My brothers and cousins wondered who it could be. But I understood. This lake is hidden land. You'd have to know exactly where and how to find it. In other words, someone had been handsomely rewarded for alerting the media to my location. The helicopter doors opened and two men stepped out. One of them was carrying a large video camera.

"Did you invite them here?" Per asked me.

"No."

The pilot stayed in the helicopter even after the rotors stopped spinning. He wasn't about to look me in the eye when he, or someone he works for, had clearly sold me out.

The reporter approached.

"Per Nunstedt," he said, extending his hand. "*Expressen*."

Expressen, Scandinavia's largest daily newspaper.

"You've come a long way," I said.

"We want to talk about your trade to the Toronto Maple Leafs."

Per, Patrick and my cousins stood off to the side, absorbing it all. Of course they'd heard of the Maple Leafs, but we were still naive to the significance of the trade. Mark warned me it would be a big deal in the news. In Wendel Clark, the Maple Leafs' general manager, Cliff Fletcher, had traded away a Canadian fan favorite—for me. A Swede.

Nunstedt conferred with his cameraman, then lined up for the interview. You could see them both batting off the bugs. Patrick shot me a look as if to say, *Who are these guys?* The cameraman was in a white T-shirt. The mosquitoes were relentless; they would take chunks out of you if you showed up unprepared—say, wearing nothing but a white T-shirt.

Once they were set up, the questions started.

"How do you feel about this trade?" he asked.

"Of course, it's a bit tough to leave Quebec right now," I said. "But this is a new kick for me to come to a new team."

Then he asked me about Wendel Clark.

"I will do my best to show them I'm good as well and to be popular as well. I think Wendel's a very good player."

More questions. I still couldn't quite process what was happening. Here I was, on the shoreline of Ribasjaure, with a microphone in my face, being interviewed by *Expressen*. It was my first taste of how different life was when you played for the Toronto Maple Leafs.

At one point, they handed me a cell phone so I could speak to another reporter. They switched cameras to take photographs, then switched back to video. The questions kept coming. I talked about giving 110 percent effort, about my dream of winning the Stanley Cup. But it was getting hard to focus on the interview. Off to the side, Patrick and Per and my cousins had their heads down. They were trying not to laugh. Both the reporter and cameraman were being eaten alive. The cameraman's effort to keep his shot steady was honorable because, even from six feet away, I could see the army of mosquitoes drilling into his forehead. Sweat on his hairline mixed with his blood and streaked his face. The neckline of his T-shirt was red.

"Are you okay?" I asked him.

He nodded and wiped his brow. Talk about commitment. When the interview ended, I thought he might strip and run into the lake to escape the bugs. But they just thanked us, turned around and boarded the helicopter. The five of us watched as the helicopter lifted off and disappeared in the same direction from which it came.

A few days later, I was on the ice. My shot rang off the post with a *clang*. Bearing down on me was Börje Salming. As we lined up shoulder to shoulder along the boards and dug for the puck, he smiled at me.

"Come on, Mats," he said. "Let's put on a show."

So, we did, flying end to end to the roar of the crowd. Except this wasn't an NHL game, or an NHL crowd. We were playing an exhibition game in front of a few hundred people. After my fishing trip, I'd stayed in Kiruna as the special guest at Salming's summer hockey camp for local kids. The timing couldn't have been better. Börje knew the Toronto Maple Leafs better than anyone else in Sweden. No one was more poised to fill me in on what lay ahead.

When I arrived in Kiruna the evening before, Börje intercepted me at the hotel.

"Let's go," he said. "I've got to do a favor for a friend."

In no time, I was bartending at a brand-new restaurant owned by Börje's old friend. Word spread quickly that two Swedish NHLers were there, and soon there was a lineup out the door. A few years into my NHL career, it still felt strange when people went out of their way to meet me or asked me for an autograph. But Börje was a natural. He treated every person he encountered with his same welcoming disposition, whether it was a local from Kiruna or a reporter from Toronto. A competitive warrior on the ice, he was nothing but friendly and warm off of it.

Börje left Kiruna to go pro and broke into the NHL in 1973, when you could count the number of foreign players on one hand. He played over a thousand games as a Maple Leaf, then spent one last season with the Detroit Red Wings, then came home to Sweden, where he spent much of his summer in Kiruna, running camps for kids and doing favors like this one for his childhood friends.

We didn't speak much about the trade until the exhibition

game the next morning. In the locker room, I told Börje about the helicopter landing next to us as we fished in the middle of nowhere. He laughed.

"That's Toronto for you."

"There are Toronto reporters here today," I told him. "In Kiruna."

"Of course there are. You're a Maple Leaf now. They'll follow you around the world."

I laughed, not sure what was so funny. A knot was building in my stomach. It eased off, as always, when we hit the ice and took the opening face-off. Reporters watched from the sidelines. After the game, Börje skated to the boards to take questions alongside me.

"You came a long way," Börje joked to the Toronto journalist.

"Big story," he responded.

"Mats is spectacular. It's a great day for Toronto."

From there, Börje offered warm words about his former team-mate Wendel Clark. He said he understood why everyone was so upset about the trade. Every answer he gave danced on the razor's edge, a perfect balance of acknowledging the bad while steering toward the good. Right there, in his tiny hometown arena nearly four thousand miles from Maple Leaf Gardens, Börje offered me a master class on how to be a Maple Leaf. I could feel my cheeks redden as he talked about my skating and started comparing me to Mario Lemieux.

Lemieux? Way to keep expectations manageable.

"Just give Mats a chance," Börje said. "The fans in Toronto are going to love him."

Then, like a magician, he produced a blue Leafs jersey and waited for the cameras to be ready before making a show of pulling it over my head. The jersey was too small, and I had difficulty getting my elbows through the sleeves. But the cameras clicked away, so I followed Börje's lead and smiled.

The next morning, as I readied for a flight from Kiruna to Stockholm, someone handed me a thick stack of papers called the dailies. It was a printout of all the news articles about the trade. Right there on the front page of the *Toronto Star*'s sports section was a large black-and-white photograph of Wendel Clark wiping away a tear. Off to the side, another headline read, "Sundin eager to earn respect." Nearly every word Börje or I said had been taken down, filed and printed at the top of the page. At the center of the newspaper's front page was a picture of me on the shoreline of Ribasjaure, the cell phone to my ear. The headline read, "Leafs' newest player on top of the world."

Oh boy.

20

Fletcher and Burns

In August of 1994, I landed in Toronto. The Maple Leafs' GM, Cliff Fletcher, met me at the airport, which was a nice touch. In the car, Cliff laughed and told jokes to help me relax. I looked out the window to get a sense of my new home. Compared to Quebec City and Stockholm, Toronto was a sprawling city. Beyond the airport, the highway expanded to sixteen lanes. I could see the downtown skyline in the distance, the CN Tower twice as tall as the skyscrapers around it.

I was jet-lagged, but there was no time for rest. After half an hour, we arrived at Maple Leaf Gardens, one of hockey's oldest and most legendary arenas. I was anxious as we pulled in. Fletcher wanted to show me around before taking me to my hotel. He introduced me to every person we encountered, from the parking lot attendants to the trainers, equipment staff and security guards. He knew them all by name.

The final stop on Fletcher's tour was head coach Pat Burns's office. Burns was in his early forties, with dark hair, a mustache and an intense gaze. He stood up from his desk and gestured for me to close the door. His office looked like a private detective's.

The garbage can was overflowing with crumpled Styrofoam cups. There was a water cooler in the corner and a phone book and Rolodex open on his desk. I counted five pairs of reading glasses. The only sign of the team he coached was a Maple Leafs baseball cap on the shelf behind him.

He shook my hand and asked about my flight. We talked about the media interviews set up for the coming days.

"Just remember," Burns said. "They'll print everything you say. Keep your answers simple. Stick to hockey."

"I'll try," I said.

"I'll give you Doug's phone number," he said. "He wants to take you out to dinner."

He meant Doug Gilmour, the team's best player and the sure bet to replace Wendel Clark as team captain.

"How do you feel about centering the second line?" Burns asked. "Or playing on Doug's wing?"

"Whatever you think is best," I said.

"Maybe left wing," he added.

I didn't need to remind Burns that I was a right-hand-shooting center who'd arrived here in a blockbuster trade. He knew that. But looking at the papers scattered on his desk, I didn't get the sense that Burns was trying to assert himself or put me in my place. It was clear that he saw his players as chess pieces. He'd taken this team to the conference finals two years in a row, the closest the Leafs had come to the Stanley Cup in many seasons. His job was to move his players around the chessboard until he found the winning combination. I liked him immediately. If he'd asked me to, I'd have played defense.

"Whatever you want me to do, I'll do," I said.

Burns smiled. He reached for a blank sheet of paper and started drawing.

"What is that?" I asked.

"Directions to the weight room," he answered without looking up.

When he was done, he slid it across to me and smiled.

This was the Burns way. I was about to learn how good he was at setting expectations, sometimes without saying a word. Over the years, lots of coaches and trainers had stressed that I'd benefit from gaining some weight and muscle. But Pat Burns just drew me a map to the gym.

The days before my first Leafs training camp were a whirlwind. Everywhere I went as a Maple Leaf, reporters followed. After I took a few days to sleep off the jet lag, the Maple Leafs' public relations team introduced me to the Toronto media. There were dozens of cameras. It was clear that I wasn't in Quebec anymore. With a tiny number of English reporters and the smallest market in the league, the Nordiques had incredibly devoted fans, but didn't get a lot of airtime outside its city limits. Toronto was a very different story.

At the news conference, I was getting reworded versions of the same question: How do you feel about the Leafs trading Wendel Clark for you?

How could I answer? The significance of the trade was growing clearer to me by the minute. In Toronto, Wendel hadn't just been a captain; he'd been the face of the team and a beloved favorite among the fans and his teammates. But *I* hadn't made the trade; I was just a piece of it. I tried the channel to diplomacy Börje Salming taught me. My English still wasn't great. Finally, someone asked me how I felt about playing on the second line. A question purely about hockey. That, I could answer.

"I don't mind at all," I said. "Doug Gilmour is the team's best player. I think I can help the team on the second line."

Even Gilmour was still fielding questions about the Clark trade. He was a good friend of Wendel's, and the reporters poked to get him to say something controversial enough for the front page. But Gilmour knew firsthand how tough trades could be for everyone, and he was gracious no matter what they threw at him.

That week, my girlfriend at the time arrived from Stockholm for a visit, and Gilmour and his fiancée took us to see *Phantom of the Opera*. He talked and laughed throughout the show, which made me like him right away. I was a reserved guy, and Doug Gilmour was not.

In those first weeks in Toronto, I also got to know the training and equipment staff. Brian Papineau, the equipment manager who would work alongside me for the rest of my career as a Maple Leaf, approached me within my first few days to ask me about my routines. My equipment. My skates. How I liked things to be.

I told him everything. What kind of sticks I used, how I liked my skates sharpened. My helmet, gloves. Papineau took notes as if I were instructing him on how to perform heart surgery. When it comes to hockey equipment, every player has their preferences, and no matter what rink we were in across North America, home game or away, exhibition or playoffs, the equipment crew was going to make sure everything was perfectly set up for each player. No excuses. Not so much as a skate lace was out of place.

Hanging over the 1994 preseason was the threat of labor action within the NHL. The simple explanation was that the league and team executives wanted a salary cap, and the players didn't. The league wanted richer teams to share the wealth with smaller markets. For the first time in the NHL's history, there was talk of a lockout if an agreement wasn't reached by October 1. One of my new teammates, Mike Gartner, was the NHL Players Association rep for the Leafs and kept us updated on the negotiations.

NHL training camps could feel like a Roman gladiator tournament. In the 1990s, teams started out with more than sixty guys. Everyone knew that twenty-three would make the team, with another twenty relegated to the AHL farm team and the rest sent home.

Day by day, players got cut. You might show up for a skate and find the stall next to you cleaned and sanitized, your neighbor cut that morning, or traded, or put on waivers, or sent to the minors.

By the time the exhibition season started, I was ready to go. One of our first games was a Saturday night meeting against the Buffalo Sabres. Even for an exhibition game, Maple Leaf Gardens was sold out. The crowd sang along to both national anthems. As I stood on the blue line while they announced my name in the starting lineup, a handful of guys behind the Leafs bench started booing.

"Clark!" one of them called.

"Ignore them," the guy next to me said.

On the Sabres blue line stood Russian superstar Alex Mogilny. Five years after his remarkable defection in Stockholm, he'd already scored nearly two hundred goals as a Sabre. He scored their first goal that night.

The game ended in a 3–3 tie. I loved overtime. The tension of winner-takes-all stirring up memories of my years in our Sollentuna driveway, the moves and shots I'd practiced thousands of times. I stood on the bench as the puck dropped to start the five minutes of extra time. About thirty seconds in, Burns waved me onto the ice. I joined the play and picked up a pass from Gilmour on my backhand, firing the puck low on net. Goal. That got me my first real roar from the Gardens crowd. It was the greatest feeling.

The final roster was a mix of guys who'd played for the Leafs for years and new faces like mine. As the exhibition season wore on, the lockout still loomed. My agent, Mark Perrone, and Cliff Fletcher were locked in negotiations for my first contract as a Maple Leaf. Money was a complicated topic. On the one hand, we were facing a league shutdown because of it. The game we all loved was being dictated by dollars and cents. Things were even further complicated by the huge gap between what the players on each team were making.

Most of us would say we just wanted to play hockey and it was never about the money. But as my agent always reminded me, someone will make money off your talent, so it might as well be you.

Mark called me on a Thursday morning with the offer: eleven million dollars over five years.

Eleven million dollars. I thought of my dad reading over that first Nordiques contract. How bizarre it had been for him. That amount was a fraction of this one. When I called him to tell him, he did the math to convert the sum into Swedish kronor. It was an astronomical sum—too high to comprehend—for playing a sport.

I took the deal. The next day, the scrum of reporters asked me about it. I didn't have a strategy when answering their questions beyond being truthful but positive. I focused on my happiness at having the negotiations over with and my intentions to earn my keep. The next day, I was on the sports section's front page.

They printed every word I'd said, just like Burns said they would.

At the end of September, no one knew whether the season was going to start or not. Negotiations didn't seem to be going well. The team boarded a bus to spend a few days at a ranch an hour north of the city. With a hotel and a brand-new Olympic-sized ice surface, Burns told us this was the perfect place for team bonding. I'd been in Toronto for nearly two months, but still hadn't talked much to some of my new teammates.

On the bus, I was relaxed and happy. It was a cooler, rainy day. As we reached the outskirts, the trees along the highway were just starting to change colors. We were closing in on the resort when a teammate found me in my seat. He handed me a copy of the newspaper's morning edition and pointed to a small article at the bottom of the page.

"You see this?" he asked.

I took it from him. The entire article covered less than three inches of space: "At least 900 aboard as Stockholm-bound ferry sinks." The details were slim. Just after midnight local time, the MS *Estonia*, en route from Estonia's capital, Tallinn, to Stockholm, sank in a storm on the Baltic Sea. Rescue efforts were underway, with a coast guard member quoted as saying there were "lots of bodies in the sea."

It was common practice in Sweden for businesses to book trips across the Baltic Sea to hold retreats or conferences. I'd spoken to my older brother, Patrick, only a few days earlier. He was readying to board a ferry as part of such a work event. I racked my brain. Where had Patrick been going? Finland? Estonia? I couldn't remember.

For the rest of the bus ride, I sat in anxious silence. As soon as we arrived at the resort, I called my parents.

It wasn't Patrick's boat.

My parents shared the details they had. By that afternoon, it was all over the news in Canada, too. I watched it on TV in my hotel room. Halfway between Tallinn and Stockholm, the *Estonia* encountered a storm off the southern coast of Finland. With fifty-five-mile-an-hour winds, the boat's seals were compromised, and it sank before most passengers could reach the lifeboats. Other nearby ferries, including the one Patrick was on, were summoned to help. Nearly nine hundred people were presumed dead.

In 1994, there were still only a couple dozen Swedish players in the entire NHL and only one other on the Leafs, Kenny Jonsson. It didn't matter that Jonsson played defense, that he was a few years younger than me, or that he was from the south of Sweden and grew up playing nowhere near Stockholm. Our Swedishness alone connected us. We talked about the tragedy and shared the details we'd gotten from our families. In the coming days and months, everyone in Sweden would find themselves connected to the tragedy in some way. The entire country mourned and searched for ways to commemorate those who died, including placing a plaque ten minutes from my cottage on the Baltic Sea. But in Canada, an ocean away, the story would fade quickly to the back pages of the newspapers.

After a few days of training camp, news came that a lockout would begin on October 1. When we arrived back in Toronto, players lingered at the bus, unsure. Normally, the equipment staff handled our gear. They'd take it into the arena and ensure it was cleaned and put away in our stalls. That was one of the perks of being a professional. But that afternoon, even the equipment guys were at a loss. The lockout could last for months. No one wanted to be banned from the arena without access to his helmet and skates. Finally, Doug Gilmour waded into the pile of bags.

"I'm taking mine home," he said.

The rest of us followed suit. We said our goodbyes with no sense of what would come next. Little did we know it would be more than three months until we'd all be together again.

21

Too Many Europeans

With the season in question, I didn't know what to do. My family suggested I come home and play for Djurgårdens IF, but it wasn't that simple. The SEL season had already started, their rosters long ago decided. But after a few weeks of negotiation, the management found a spot for me in the lineup.

In late October, I flew to Stockholm. Even if they knew the lockout was a bad thing, my parents—my mom especially—were happy to have me back for a short while. That fall, I played a dozen games in the SEL and did my best to stay in shape.

News came at Christmas that the lockout would end in early January. I was thrilled to be flying back to Canada. My first stop back at the Gardens was Pat Burns's office. He suggested that, since the season would officially be starting, it was time for me to get settled in Toronto. No more hotels.

"You can move in with Ellett," he said.

He meant Dave Ellett, one of the team's star defensemen.

It's a common tradition in the NHL for veteran players to take in new guys when they first land in a city after the draft or a trade. At thirty, Dave Ellett was considered a veteran. But he and Wendel Clark had been longtime teammates and great friends. He was the guy who threw Clark a going-away party. Ellett was welcoming and friendly in our few conversations at training camp. But living together? That had the potential to be awkward.

I guess Burns didn't give Ellett the choice. It was a convenient option, and with Burns, *option* didn't always mean "optional." Some of the guys on the Leafs lived with their families outside the city and commuted an hour to the rink. But Dave lived alone a few blocks away and had a spare room. Like the rest of us, Ellett knew better than to say no to Pat.

Dave was nothing but gracious. If he resented me for the trade, it never showed.

I learned Ellett's routines quickly. Even on the coldest January days, he walked to work. Practice day or game night, he walked. So, I walked, too. I learned the route: out the door, a left to cut over to Yonge Street, then south down the city's busiest strip. Finally, left again to the arena's rear entrance. On game days, we'd nap, get up, dress in our suits, throw on our coats and walk. The two of us, heads lowered against the wind.

In January, once the team had convened back in Toronto, we held a weeklong mini training camp. Burns and Gilmour set the tone early: We would have each other's backs. Never say a bad word about your teammate outside of the room. All disagreements were to be settled behind closed doors. Personal lives stay personal. Even ribbing and practical jokes stayed between teammates only. And many of my teammates loved their jokes. In locker rooms, joking is a way of life. Almost a form of torture.

Shortly after our arrival in Toronto, Mark Perrone called me to say he'd heard from a local Volvo dealership. Their manager was a Swede, and he wanted to meet me.

"They'll give you a free car," he said.

My dad loved a good Volvo, and I was still his son. I took the meeting. After some handshakes and photos, the manager presented me with a luxury C70 coupe. It was a beautiful car. Leather seats, modern sound system. And it was bright yellow.

"Yellow," the manager said, smiling. "For Sweden."

I thought the yellow looked sporty. And a free car is a free car. I drove it off the lot to the rink. As soon as my teammates saw it, it was game over. They harassed me relentlessly. The true team jokers were Doug Gilmour and Dave Andreychuk. They started calling it the Bananamobile, and the rest of the team gleefully joined in. It got so bad that I couldn't drive it anywhere, especially not to the rink. The mockery was too much. After a week or two, I returned the Bananamobile to the dealership and sourced myself a plain old black truck.

The Maple Leafs started the shortened season on a two-game West Coast road trip. Even though my trade was now months old, it resurfaced as a huge topic among Toronto fans and media. I was relieved to be dressing for my first regular-season game as a Maple Leaf in Los Angeles, about as far from Toronto as the team could get. The downside was that it meant we were playing against one of the greatest hockey players of all time, Wayne Gretzky.

On the second shift of the night, not even two minutes into the game, the Leafs were awarded a power play when Kings enforcer Marty McSorley threw a punch in a scrum. The puck came to me at the face-off, and I hooked it back to Ellett, who slid it along the blue line to his defense mate, Dmitri Mironov. One hard slap shot and the puck hit the back of the net, top shelf. We gathered at the blue line to celebrate. I felt a wash of relief. I'd just recorded my first point as a Maple Leaf. On the bench, Ellett said nothing. He just tapped my leg with his stick.

The next night was a Saturday. We traveled up the California coast to play the Sharks in San Jose. The game would air at 10 p.m. in Toronto. Every Saturday night, TV's *Hockey Night in Canada* aired a doubleheader; a 7 p.m. game, followed by a later one from the West. The most watched segment on *Hockey Night in Canada* was Don Cherry's "Coach's Corner." Wendel Clark was one of Cherry's favorite players. In his first show back after the lockout, he spent the entire segment talking about the trade.

"I'm not here to knock Sundin," Cherry said. "He's not a bad hockey player. He's got a little guts for a Swede. Now you're gonna ask me how the Leafs are gonna do . . . This year, they're not getting over the hump. Too many Europeans and too many visors."

Gone was the quiet market of Quebec City. I was playing for the Maple Leafs now, and Don Cherry was a big deal in Toronto. And in the rest of Canada, for that matter. His weekly five minutes of airtime had a way of shaping hockey culture. He'd coined the term I'd heard before: "chicken Swedes." If Cherry was telling millions of viewers that European players like me were soft, that belief was going to catch on and spread.

But in San Jose, I wasn't watching "Coach's Corner." I was preparing to play my second game of the season. After four years in the NHL, my pregame routine was well established: Grab a cup of coffee and set up my sticks. Two sticks per game, sometimes three. Cut them to a precise height, tap the blades, flex them. Pick which one to use as the starter. In the locker room, my teammates worked through their routines. Thirty minutes before warm-up, everyone would start to dress. For me, it was always the same: Right shin pad first, then left. Skates in the same order. Laced tight. Jersey on. The pregame knot in the stomach grew with every step of preparation. By the time I stood for the anthems, I was ready.

Ninety seconds into my second game, Gilmour fed me the puck and I roofed it over the Sharks' sprawling goalie. My first goal as a Toronto Maple Leaf. That's all I could do. Focus on my game. Don't worry about proving anyone right, or wrong. Just focus and drown out the noise. Play one shift at a time.

22

Tie

February 1995 was a frigid month even by Canadian standards, but I didn't mind. Ellett and I still walked to the rink. By mid-month, we'd played ten games in the shortened season. Despite a few bad losses, the team was in playoff contention and I was among the top fifteen point scorers in the league. I enjoyed my walks to the rink with Ellett, so I found an apartment in the same building.

During those early days in Toronto, I felt more unsettled and uncomfortable than I ever had in my first four years in the NHL. It was a different world. The media coverage was constant and intense. I understood that I had a hill to climb if I was going to gain acceptance, and it was a steep one. I caught myself calling home more frequently, working out schedules to arrange visits from my parents or brothers.

Sensing my troubles, Doug Gilmour introduced me to Mike Walton. Mike was a former NHL player who'd been on the Leafs when they last won the Stanley Cup in 1967. He played another ten years in the league, winning the Cup again with Boston in 1972. In retirement, Mike settled in Toronto and started working as a real estate agent. He also took it upon himself to help new Maple Leaf players adjust to the city. Mike was around my father's age, and he quickly took on a role I didn't even know I needed. He started calling me *Weedsy*—a derivative of Swede a few teammates had taken up. He had this way of finding the perfect story to tell in any situation. There's a word we use in Swedish—*ventil*—the literal translation is "valve," but it means a person who diffuses tension and makes you feel better. Mike Walton became a dear friend who helped me manage the stresses of the game. He was my *ventil*.

The last week of February, we were set to play the Winnipeg Jets. It didn't take long to figure out that the biggest ticket in Toronto was a Saturday night home game at Maple Leaf Gardens. Well before game time, fans would start streaming in, wearing Leaf jerseys from every era, many sporting painted faces and carrying hand-drawn signs.

Like us, the Jets were in a race to secure a playoff spot, and in a shortened season, every game mattered. And the Jets were a tough team. Not only did they have Finnish superstar Teemu Selänne, but Kris King, Keith Tkachuk and Tie Domi were all feared enforcers. Over a single season, the three of them could rack up nearly as many penalty minutes as the rest of their teammates combined.

I understood by then that unwritten rules about fighting in the NHL were guided by one core principle: enforcers protect talent. Some guys will score hundreds of goals over their careers without once dropping their gloves. The last thing a coach needed was their biggest goal scorer breaking a finger in a fight. So, essentially, those stars were assigned an on-ice bodyguard or two. In Winnipeg, Selänne had three. If anyone so much as glanced at him the wrong way, one of the Jets enforcers would immediately drop the gloves.

By the second period of the Jets game, we were up 3–0 when I took a knee from Winnipeg defenseman Stéphane Quintal. It pissed me off, so I got my elbow up, right to his head, gashing him and drawing blood. The whistle blew and Quintal came after me, but my teammate Jamie Macoun intervened and took a punch on my behalf. The two of them went at it while the ref dragged me to the penalty box to serve my time for the elbow.

I came out of the box two minutes later. Skating to take the next face-off, I caught something out of the corner of my eye: Tie Domi was glaring at me from the Jets' bench. I spent the rest of the game shaking him off. You could tell he was begging his coach to line us up on shifts, to put him on when I was on. I was seven inches taller than this Domi guy, but he didn't seem to care. I'd drawn his teammate's blood with my elbow, and now he had me in his sights. I could have been eight feet tall, and he would still have happily lined me up for a fight.

The Jets scored two goals to tighten the game, but halfway through the third period, I scored on a beautiful pass from Doug Gilmour to widen our lead again. On the bench, I pointed Domi out.

"That guy's been on my ass all game," I said. "He's fucking crazy."

Pat Burns heard me. He got a wistful look in his eye.

Burns must have started lobbying behind closed doors that very night, because a little over a month later, word came down to the locker room that our fourth-line center, Mike Eastwood, had been traded to the Winnipeg Jets.

For Tie Domi.

In early April, Tie joined the Leafs as we pushed to secure our playoff spot. The first time I met him, I expected him to bring up the February game and my elbow to Quintal's head. But Tie shook my hand like he'd never seen me before. That game in February was just a night's work for him.

Tie was born and raised in Ontario. His parents now lived in Toronto. He was drafted by the Leafs in 1988, then played two games for them before getting traded to the New York Rangers and then the Jets. You could tell he was thrilled to be home. He thrived under the glare of the Toronto spotlight. I figured out quickly that Tie's enthusiasm was unmatched. It didn't matter if we'd just finished a grueling practice, he'd still be full of energy.

"You think he'll fight a lot?" I asked Ellett one day.

He laughed. "Tie? Probably."

Probably? The joke was on me. A few weeks after he joined the squad, we headed out on a short road trip through St. Louis and Dallas. In the first game, I'd just settled onto the bench after my opening shift when I heard the St. Louis crowd go wild. Less than forty-five seconds into the game, Tie had already dropped his gloves to exchange blows with Blues enforcer Basil McRae.

The next night, in Dallas, he dropped the gloves against Jim Cummins six seconds into the first period. Six seconds. I wondered if that was an NHL record. Then Domi got another fighting major before the first period was over. Three fighting majors in two games. Pat Burns was giddy.

In the locker room after the Dallas game, Tie rubbed at his knuckles and nodded to the trainer to bring him a bucket of ice. Over the next few games, I figured out that, aside from fighting, Tie also took on the task of getting the team going. He quickly became the guy Burns sent out in the second period if we were idling and needed a foot on the gas.

During a late-April game in Calgary against the Flames, we were on our heels late in a 2–2 game when Tie hit the ice and picked a fight with Flames heavy Sandy McCarthy. That triggered the adrenaline in the rest of us, and we held on for the tie. Two nights later, we were on the verge of blowing a 4–1 lead against the Edmonton Oilers when Tie started acting up again. Gloves off, names called, penalties assessed.

The 1995 playoff season started off well, with two quick wins

When I arrived in Toronto in 1994, Dave Ellett (center) and Doug Gilmour (right) both greeted me warmly and helped me settle into my new city and team. *Graig Abel / Getty Images Sport*

Under a pileup against the Buffalo Sabres, January 7, 2006.

Pat Quinn (rear) was my head coach for seven seasons. This picture was taken during the 2002 Eastern Conference Finals against the Carolina Hurricanes. On the bench with me are (left to right) Robert Reichel, Tie Domi, Alexander Mogilny and Jonas Höglund. *Ken Faught* / Toronto Star

In September 2003, the Leafs traveled to my hometown of Stockholm for a pre-season exhibition series. Playing in my hometown was a career highlight for me. This photo was taken on the steps of the Globen Arena. *Dave Sandford / Getty Images Sport*

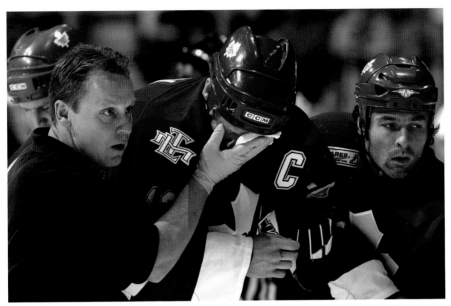

I had a few scary injuries over the years, but none scarier than breaking my orbital bone in October 2005. I had no vision in my eye, and trainer Kevin Wagner and teammate Darcy Tucker helped me off the ice for immediate medical attention. *Dave Sandford / Getty Images Sport Classic*

Sweden and Finland are longtime hockey rivals. The gold medal game during the 2006 Winter Olympics in Turin was the pinnacle of this rivalry. *Elsa / Getty Images Sport*

Winning the gold medal as captain of Team Sweden in 2006 was a career highlight for me, especially because I knew it would be my last time wearing the Swedish *tre kronor* uniform. *Damian Strohmeyer* / Sports Illustrated

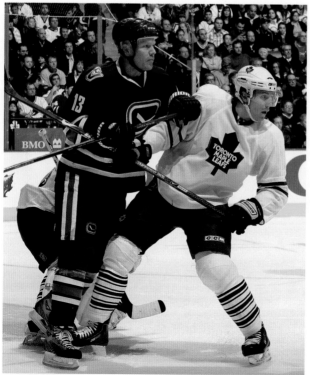

After fourteen years as a Toronto Maple Leaf, returning to the Air Canada Centre as a Vancouver Canuck in February 2009 was a surreal and emotional experience for me.
Dave Sandford / Getty Images Sport Classic

RIGHT: Josephine and I were married on August 29, 2009, in Stockholm. Many of my former teammates, trainers and friends from Toronto were in attendance.

All Over Press Sweden / Getty Images Entertainment

BELOW: In February 2012, Josephine and my parents, Tommy and Gunilla Sundin, came on the ice with me at the Air Canada Centre as my banner was raised to its rafters.

Claude Andersen / Getty Images Sport

Börje Salming was a dear friend and mentor to me for many years before his death from ALS in November 2022. In 1996, he became the first Swedish player inducted into the Hockey Hall of Fame. In 2012, I became the second.

Bruce Bennett / Getty Images Sport Classic

ABOVE: In November 2023, the Toronto Maple Leafs played two games in Stockholm as part of the NHL's Global Series. Before their game against the Minnesota Wild, I took to center ice with my children, Bonnie, Julian and Nate, to drop the ceremonial puck.

Mark Blinch / NHL

RIGHT: My kids, Julian, Nate and Bonnie, visiting my statue at Legends Row in Toronto.

My kids never got to watch me
play in the NHL, but we still
visit Toronto often.

Our eldest, Bonnie, was born
in 2012, followed by Nathanael
in 2014 and Julian in 2017.

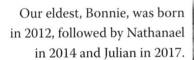

Celebrating life and family
with Josephine, 2023.

My parents, Gunilla and Tommy Sundin, standing in my childhood bedroom, with all my career memorabilia neatly organized. Sollentuna, Sweden, 2023.

Visiting Hovet Arena in 2023 with my childhood coach and friend Mats Hamnarbäck. Nearly forty years ago, I played in Stockholm's championship tournament at this arena with Mats as my coach.

Fishing on the shores of Ripasjaure in northern Sweden remains one of my favorite things to do. My brother Per took this photo. Fifteen years after moving back to Sweden, I'm still often sporting my Canada or Toronto apparel.

Per Sundin

in Chicago. It was my second chance at a playoff run, and I felt ready. I knew what to expect. But then we blew our series lead with two brutal losses at Maple Leaf Gardens. Chicago was out for blood after being ousted by the Leafs the previous year and having gone almost sixty years without beating us in a series. After crawling our way to an overtime win in Game 6, we lost Game 7 by a score of 5–2. In the dying seconds, the Chicago home crowd was deafening. We shook hands with our opponents and retreated to the room.

Pat Burns didn't yell at us for allowing three goals in the third period. His quiet was worse. For an NHL coach, Burns was a bit of an anomaly. He'd never played hockey professionally. He'd started as a part-time scout while working a day job as a police officer in Quebec. He drove a Harley-Davidson to practices and games. His toughness was bigger than hockey, and nothing was more imposing than his silence. It wasn't that Pat couldn't get enraged, but when he did, it was almost always to stick up for his players. He saved the worst of his temper for the referees. When we blew a 2–0 series lead and knocked ourselves out of the playoffs, Pat knew that the worst punishment he could afford us was to not say anything. To leave us to contemplate the first-round exit on our own. Silence was his best weapon.

In the days that followed, we packed up our gear, held meetings and figured out plans for a spring we'd hoped would include more hockey. The previous summer, after news of my Toronto trade, I'd traveled an hour north of Stockholm and bought a cottage on the Baltic Sea in an area called Norrtälje. My plan for the summer of 1995 was to rent a furnished apartment in downtown Stockholm and visit the cottage on weekends. Rest. Train hard. Head to the far north to fish with my cousins and brothers on what was becoming an annual trip.

Someone asked Tie Domi about his summer plans. With two

young babies at home and his parents and brother in Toronto, he wasn't going far.

"I'm playing professional soccer," he said. "Fletcher's given me the go-ahead."

Tie had been recruited by Kosova, a team in the Canadian International Soccer League, and he'd asked Leafs GM Cliff Fletcher for permission to play. As I left Maple Leaf Gardens for the last time that spring, I promised Tie that when I got back to Toronto in August, I'd be in the stands, cheering for Kosova.

23

Bosön and Leif

I stood on an oval running track, shaking out my legs. It was a bright summer morning with just a slight breeze off the water. Seven of us were lined up on the track behind a pair of Kenyan middle-distance runners. The runners were about to take off in a four-hundred-meter training sprint, completing a full lap in sixty seconds or less.

Our trainer had given us one simple instruction: keep up with them.

This outdoor track was at Bosön, an elite training facility in eastern Stockholm. I arrived back in Sweden with one goal in mind: to return to Toronto for my second season in the best shape of my life. When I landed in Stockholm that May, I was surprised by the sense of relief I felt. I hated that we'd been knocked out of the playoffs early, but with the trade and the lockout, it had been an intense year. Back in Sweden, I felt like I could breathe more freely. Think more clearly. It was good to be home.

I called Leif Larsson my trainer, but he was far more than that. Leif was an expert in athletic development and the head of the sports laboratory at Bosön. That summer, he agreed to design and oversee my summer workout program. Leif was not a hockey player, but he understood the toll of the game. He'd trained Swedish athletes in many different sports, from pro hockey players to Olympic champion skiers and runners. Though he'd once been a weight lifter, Leif was lean and wiry, always moving, the sort of person who would think, sometimes for a long minute, before answering your question.

"You need to build strength and speed," he told me.

Five years into my career and I was still hearing that. I needed strength.

Back then, Leif lived alone in an apartment on the Bosön campus. He was forty and a bachelor. His days were organized with the purpose and dedication of a monk, but his religion was training athletes like me.

Overload was Leif's favorite word. He loved the distinction between *overload* and *overreach*. Overreaching was bad. It meant you were training too hard or exercising without specific goals. Overloading meant putting your body under intense strain for a short period, replicating the strength and stamina needed for your sport, whether you played hockey, skied downhill or threw javelins.

Leif's life work was to seek out ways to create the specific kind of overload that would mimic the physical demands of each unique sport. He looked for inspiration everywhere. He kept a notepad next to his bed for the nights when he'd wake up with a new idea.

One day, he decided his hockey players needed to complete some of their cardio with the same striding motion we used on ice. But the Bosön campus did not have an arena.

"Your body needs to skate," Leif said. "You should be skating up a hill."

He found an uphill stretch in the forest and dug a trench a few feet deep and wide. It looked like a mountain creek run dry. Leif then demonstrated the exercise. We would jump left to right over the trench, replicating the bursting motion of skating, but while climbing a forested hill. It was a torturous version of a skater's stride.

In a basement storage area at Bosön, Leif found an old prize wheel for us to spin. One very narrow slot would win us an ice cream cone. The rest were things like three-mile runs through the forest or 100 push-ups on the grass.

Sometimes, if one of us questioned our ability to run a certain pace or squat a monstrously heavy weight, Leif would stand musing on the sidelines as we geared up to make the attempt. "Trying the impossible?" he'd say. "When? Why not now? Where? Why not here? Who? Why not you?" This was his version of poetry, and it was hard to argue with his logic.

No two training days were the same with Leif. Surprise was a big part of overload. That element of surprise was exactly how I ended up standing on the Bosön track, standing behind two world-class runners. A few hours earlier, the young Kenyans were directed to Leif's office in search of a scale to weigh themselves before their morning workout. As they took their measurements, he studied them.

"What *is* your morning workout?" he asked.

"Intervals on the track," one of them answered.

"What kind of intervals?"

The runners outlined it for Leif. They would complete a lap of the four-hundred-meter track at a sixty-second pace, then rest for another sixty seconds. They'd repeat that fifteen times to complete a thirty-minute workout.

"One minute lap, one minute rest," Leif repeated. "Times fifteen."

The runners nodded.

"Do you mind if we join you?"

By "we," Leif meant me and the rest of his trainees. A few

hockey players, a javelin thrower, and a downhill skier, Pernilla Wiberg, who was coming off back-to-back gold medals at the 1992 and 1994 Olympics. A treadmill was good, but to Leif, this was better. He was going to make us chase the fastest runners in the world. Before noon, we were at the track, lining up as Leif split us up into groups.

"You'll take turns running with them," he explained. "For every three laps they do, you will do one."

Okay, I thought. *That's doesn't sound horrible. One lap for every three.*

"But," Leif continued, "you must keep up."

I'm not sure any of us really understood what "keeping up" meant. A four-hundred-meter lap in a minute is about five seconds slower than the world record pace for a 1,500-meter race. For me, it was an all-out sprint.

We took off at full speed. The Kenyans looked relaxed in their strides. I was gasping by the halfway mark. We all collapsed as soon as we crossed the finish line. Meanwhile, the Kenyans casually stretched and jumped on the spot, steady and calm, readying to tackle their next lap in less than a minute.

Leif stood on the sidelines, pleased with himself. He knew that none of us would ever manage this pace on our own. But he also knew one fundamental truth about many elite athletes: They are chasers. They will turn any situation into a competition. If you want a group of elite athletes to run faster than they ever dreamed they could, line them up behind the fastest runners in the world.

Heavy training days at Bosön were balanced with time in nature and connecting with family and friends. I spent weekends at the cottage with my parents. A year after the reporters landed lakeside at news of the trade, my brothers, cousins and I returned to the far north to fish, a trip we still take every year to this day. Back in Toronto, Cliff Fletcher filled out the blue line by acquiring defensemen Larry Murphy and Dmitri Yushkevich, but otherwise the summer was quiet—no helicopters carrying reporters showed up.

When I got back to Toronto in August, Tie Domi called Ellett and me to alert us to an upcoming soccer game. Ellett and I walked the short stretch between our building and Varsity Stadium, the University of Toronto sports field that takes up a full block right in the center of the city. Ellett and I took our seats among the fifty or so other fans.

Tie waved at us as he warmed up on the sidelines. From the day we met, I understood that Tie and I were very different in many ways. He was vocal and freely shared his opinion; I was quieter. He fought more in his first week as a Maple Leaf than I would in my entire career. He was only two years older than me, but married with two small kids. His baby, Max, was born in Winnipeg that spring, just a few weeks before Tie was traded to Toronto. He visited his parents all the time, as they lived just up the road from his house, whereas mine were an ocean away. I considered myself a decent soccer player, but wouldn't have signed up to play in a league the way Tie had done.

Ellett and I figured out quickly that Tie played soccer the same way he played hockey. Scrappy. All over the field. His footwork was skilled. At some point in the second half, Tie had the ball and was carrying it downfield. Ellett and I rose to our feet to cheer him on. But then an opponent burst across the field and slide-tackled him. The referee blew his whistle and called for a free kick. As I watched Tie rise to his feet, I saw the look in his eyes. He'd only been my teammate for a handful of games at that point, but already, I knew that look. He wasn't interested in taking the free kick; he wanted to exact justice on the guy who tackled him. Someone took the kick in his place. As the game resumed, Tie started chasing the player in the opposite direction of the play. Tie was fast and agile, but so was his opponent. He did get him by the shirt eventually and the referee broke them up. No red cards were issued.

Tie's teammates were buzzing after that. Just like in hockey, he'd been the one to pump them up. They won the game, and it turned out to be a very entertaining night for Ellett and me. Afterward, the three of us went out for dinner. Tie talked a lot about his wife and kids and the happiness he felt at living close to his parents again. He told me that when he'd arrived in Toronto, Pat Burns had made it clear that his job on ice was to protect me. I couldn't have known then that Tie would become my longest-standing teammate and a lifelong friend. He taught me something about enforcers that I carried with me my entire career: their personalities off the ice often didn't align with their tough on-ice personas. Tie could be a sensitive guy. He had the hardest job in the game, and I was grateful to have him on my team.

24

Moving Trucks

Even after a full season, I was still struggling to feel settled in Toronto. Eventually, the city and its landscape grew familiar. I learned to navigate the way the streets and roads formed a grid that climbed north from Lake Ontario. I found favorite restaurants and coffee shops. The winter days were short, but not nearly as short as Stockholm's. My English was getting better by the day. But the spotlight on the team was intense, and it nagged at me that I'd never be considered good enough. Still, aside from sitting out a few weeks in November with a knee injury, my season was off to a strong start, and the Leafs made it to the short holiday break in December with a winning record.

By early January of 1996, we stood in fourth place in the Western Conference, comfortably in playoff contention with half the season to go. Burns pushed us hard, but it felt like he had full confidence in our play. In *my* play, too. I was getting time on the power play and penalty kill. His coaching style favored structure and discipline, but he was okay with his players taking creative liberties—if they worked. If they didn't, you had to answer to him.

A few weeks into 1996, I was invited to play in the NHL All-

Star Game for the first time in my career. That year's All-Star weekend was in Boston. I've played in a lot of international tournaments, but the All-Star Game is something else entirely. Back then, it put the stars of the league's Eastern Conference against the Western Conference stars, and the Leafs were in the West. I could look down the bench at Wayne Gretzky, Paul Kariya, Paul Coffey. Mario Lemieux, representing the East, would skate by. I got to reunite with my former Nordiques teammates Joe Sakic and Owen Nolan, who'd moved with the team when it transferred to Denver and became the Colorado Avalanche. Nolan was then traded to the San Jose Sharks, where he soon became team captain.

The weekend is meant to be fun and light—no one was chirping or tossing guys into the boards. Each lineup had a notable number of Europeans for the first time—my fellow Swedes Daniel Alfredsson, Nicklas Lidström and Peter Forsberg, but also many familiar faces from my days playing in the Four Nations tournaments: Jaromír Jágr, Sergei Fedorov, Teemu Selänne, Alex Mogilny. It felt like a few days of hockey camp with the best players in the world.

I arrived back in Toronto excited to play out the final two months of the regular season, to put together a strong finish and a long playoff run.

We'd lost three straight games in the stretch before the All-Star break, but the pause was meant to provide us with a good reset. In our first game back, we tied the Chicago Blackhawks at home—a result you can live with against a top team. But a few nights later, we tied the Ottawa Senators, who were in dead last with only eight wins the entire season. Then we lost a few more to stronger teams like Detroit and St. Louis. By early February, we left on a West Coast road trip on an eight-game winless streak. A month before, we'd been challenging for top spot in the Western Conference. Now, we were teetering, on the verge of falling out of playoff contention. When we lost the first game of the road trip to the bottom-dwelling San Jose Sharks on February 5, the dam broke. Cliff Fletcher left the NHL's general managers' meeting in Arizona to intercept us on our way to Anaheim. He called a team meeting at the hotel the afternoon before our game against the Ducks.

Cliff Fletcher had an intense presence. Always impeccably well dressed, he easily held the room when he spoke. In 1996, he was in his early sixties, forty years into a career in hockey management. Everyone knew he was capable of tough choices—he'd proven that when he traded Wendel Clark for me. Now we were on a bad skid, and he'd left an important meeting to catch a plane to see us. In my time with the Leafs, I wasn't sure Fletcher had ever addressed us directly as a group. He'd always left that up to Pat Burns.

We all knew it: this wasn't good.

The mood in the hotel conference room was somber. No coaches were present, which felt weird. Cliff walked in, sparing us any pleasantries as he took his position at the front of the room. You could tell he was angry by the red in his cheeks, but he didn't raise his voice. Like Burns, his low, quiet baritone was worse than yelling. He spoke about character, about his disappointment in our team play. It was no one's fault, he said; it was *everyone's* fault. He punctuated each sentence with a long pause. It was dramatic. Effective. The room was dead silent. He ended his speech on a more hopeful tone. He said he was confident that we'd figure it out and find our winning ways again.

He nodded at us. The speech seemed to be over. You could see everyone's shoulders relax. He turned to leave, then spun on his heel.

"But," he said.

He held a finger in the air. Another long pause.

"But . . . if you don't figure it out, if we don't get our shit together soon ... AMJ Campbell won't have enough moving trucks to ship all you guys out of town."

Then he left the room. The group of us sat in stunned silence. The moving truck line was a perfectly timed zinger, a pledge to spare no one. Surely, he'd come up with it beforehand. There's no way you'd think up a line that good on the spot.

We won that night, and then, after a bumpy few games, we beat the first-place Pittsburgh Penguins. It felt like we were back on track. Fletcher might have hoped that his speech worked. If only. Over the next four weeks, we managed to outdo ourselves with a ten-game winless streak. The team entered March with a losing record.

Sometimes, losing streaks make sense. They never happen because players don't care. If your team is rebuilding, you might face a few seasons in a talent deficit that makes winning hard on any night and renders losing stretches all but certain. The Nordiques had been a team on a rebuild. A stronger team might lose its best players to injury and go into a skid. Sometimes, a game or two might be lost to simple puck luck. Someone hits the crossbar in overtime or gets a bad bounce off the boards. Maybe there's tension in the dressing room, something off in the team chemistry that spills over to the bench. It might be a combination of some of the above.

Even now, years later, NHL team culture feels like a tricky thing to explain. There are so many variables at play. Teams are businesses, trying to earn profits. Players are assets of those businesses. Management weighs the value of those assets not just by their talent, but by their presence in the room. Their fit with potential teammates. Over the course of a season, a group needs to form a strong bond and find a way to bounce back from defeat. Even all the staff need to feel involved, included and respected. The NHL is so competitive that the organization best able to grow these bonds and culture will prevail. You don't need everyone in the room to be best friends, but a team's resilience is more about respect for each other and the bond between teammates than it is about talent.

In the winter of 1996, it was clear that we were losing games we should have been winning. We weren't young or rebuilding. For the most part, our roster was healthy and we all got along. But the losses got to our heads and as the streaks got longer, our resilience all but disappeared. Every mistake felt costly. Of course, you have to take responsibility. Your job is to win. You try to figure out what can be fixed, both as a player and as a team. Where the things to work on are. The power plays. Penalty kills. Tempo. Shots. Guys would do their best not to get spooked. We'd show up earlier to morning skates, take on extra workouts.

Pat Burns was frustrated. He knew that fundamentally, nothing had changed. The team that was losing night after night was made up of the same guys who'd held a strong winning record over the first half of the season. He fiddled with the lines, putting me on the wing, then back at center, trying to find the right combination. When one reporter asked him to explain his rationale, he joked that he didn't have one, that he was just drawing our names from a cup. If the team's performance was keeping Burns up at night, he wasn't about to admit that to the media.

At practice, Burns would remind us not to panic and just do the work. It was hard to know if he was panicking. He must have been exasperated and losing faith in us. Winless streaks are tough in any setting, but especially so in Toronto, where there's no grace period to get your act together. A few games into the slump, the crowds at Maple Leaf Gardens began to boo. It was quiet at first, almost polite. Just a small group of detractors quickly drowned out by the rest of the fans. But as the streak got longer, the boos got louder. As a player, you take each loss personally no matter where you play. But in Toronto, the millions of fans take it personally, too. It's the biggest hockey market in the world. Your losses are their losses. People do panic.

And for the Toronto media, the only thing that sells better than a story of victory is one about an epic losing streak. Panic is good for their business. There were endless angles the sportswriters could take. Endless ways they could break down the team's failings. They'd focus on leadership, then goaltending. Defense, then offense. Pick specific players to dissect. Then back to leadership, and repeat. Burns knew which of his players read the papers and would sometimes make comments to the press without naming names, dropping crumbs he knew certain guys would pick up. As a younger player on track for an eighty-point season, I was spared the worst of it from both Burns and the media, but that doesn't mean I didn't feel it. The pressure weighed on me. How does a team switch from winning to losing seemingly overnight? You feel responsible.

We all knew that our failure to win was going to cause collateral damage. As Fletcher promised a month earlier, the moving trucks would start showing up if something didn't change. Someone would be held responsible. We arrived to the dressing room one morning in early March to a message on the blackboard in Pat Burns's writing:

Good luck, boys.

He'd been fired while we were on the road, after two losses on the West Coast. As a gesture to Pat after so many good years, Fletcher agreed to wait until after we were back in Toronto to tell the media, so as to give Pat a head start out of town. The day we got home, Burns went to the arena after dark to pack up his office and write us a message. By the time we arrived for our morning skate, he'd already left Toronto.

His firing hit everyone hard, especially players like Gilmour, who'd gone to the conference finals twice with Burns, in 1993 and 1994. For all his intensity, Burns was a players' coach, and our failures were the reason he'd lost his job. In the locker room that morning, reading his note, I couldn't have predicted that I'd play in the NHL for another thirteen years under many different coaches, or that Burns would go on to win a Stanley Cup with New Jersey a few years later. I couldn't have known that I'd look back on my career nearly thirty years later and consider him the best NHL coach I ever had.

Fletcher replaced Burns with his director of player personnel, Nick Beverley. Nick couldn't have been more different from Burns. For one, where Burns never played professionally, Nick played five hundred games as a defenseman in the NHL. Burns had always been about systems and discipline. From our first practice, Nick made it clear he was going to take a more relaxed approach. His emphasis was less on discipline and more on raising the team morale. We were within inches of playoff contention. On ice, his plan was to cut us loose.

Fletcher made it clear that the moving trucks would indeed be coming for some of us. We broke the losing streak, but the players were still antsy. In mid-March, with just over a dozen games left in the season, Fletcher announced a blockbuster deal that saw my fellow Swede Kenny Jonsson traded for none other than Wendel Clark. And Fletcher wasn't done.

"There will be other moves," Cliff said. "Plural."

Plural is an ominous word. That night, as we readied to play the Jets, the media pressed me on how I felt about the Clark trade. They weren't about to pass up the chance to stir the pot. I'd learned not to take the bait.

"I'll see if I can keep my stall," I joked.

We tied the Jets, 3–3, that night on the effort of my frequent linemate, Dave Andreychuk, who scored two goals and assisted on the third. He was awarded the game's first star. As we collected in the room, it took him a few minutes to join us. We figured he was locked in media interviews about his performance. When he finally appeared, he was wide-eyed.

"Guess what, guys?" he said to the room. "I've been traded to Jersey."

By then, I'd been in the league for five years. Nothing shocked me anymore. Still, watching a guy you'd played hundreds of shifts with cleaning his gear out of his locker never got easier.

We ended the season on a winning note, defeating Edmonton, 6–3. When the season was over, only two points separated us, the fourth-place team in the West, from the ninth. It was such a tight race that winning our last game meant the difference between home-ice advantage in the first round of the playoffs and missing the postseason entirely. But in the opening round against St. Louis, we fell behind, three games to one.

In Game 5, which we won in overtime, a collision tore a ligament in my knee. The doctors told me I'd need six weeks to heal. Six weeks? No way. I put on a brace and played through it. Wendel Clark opened the scoring in Game 6, on assists from Doug Gilmour and me. But St. Louis answered with two goals in the third period and held on for the win. For the second year in a row, we were out in the first round.

Six weeks later, I was back in Sweden in time to follow many of my former teammates on the Nordiques, now the Colorado Avalanche, as they swept the Florida Panthers to win the Stanley Cup. I was happy to see Sakic hoisting the Cup, as he deserved to do.

After you retire from hockey and settle into life beyond it, stretches of your playing years become a blur. Entire seasons can roll into each other. You have specific memories, but can't always place them in the right time frame. Looking back, the stretch of my career after Pat Burns feels like that. The following season, Mike Murphy was hired as the coach. He had the toughest job in hockey. A not-great October was followed by a terrible November.

In early 1997, when it was clear the playoffs were out of reach, Dave Ellett and our captain, Doug Gilmour, were traded to the New Jersey Devils. That was a tough one. Cliff Fletcher was fired and eventually replaced by Ken Dryden. It could be hard to keep up with the trades, as well as to generate chemistry in the room when guys were coming and going.

We ended the season without making the playoffs. It was a time of transition for the Leafs, and a time of transition for the league, too. When I was drafted in 1989, European players made up about 10 percent of the rosters. By 1997, that share had more than doubled. Three of the league's best scorers—Jaromír Jágr, Peter Forsberg and Pavel Bure—were Czech, Swedish and Russian. It was a different landscape. One where a Swedish guy like me could be considered for the captaincy of a team as storied as the Toronto Maple Leafs.

25

Wearing the *C*

Over the summer of 1997, there was a ton of speculation over who would inherit the Leafs captaincy. The media tackled it from every angle, whether it would be me or whether the team would leave it vacant. To their credit, Leafs management did a great job of hiding the fact that they'd already asked me. The delay in announcing was that I'd requested a bit of time to consider it.

I wanted to be the captain. I'd been captain of many teams since the age of ten. Even as a professional player, I still believed that my performance improved when the coaches looked at me to be a leader. I was aware of the pressures and expectations, and felt ready to handle them. Yet something was holding me back. In the room, I wasn't a really vocal guy. Joe Sakic had been a quieter captain in my years with the Nordiques and had gone on to lead his team to a Cup win. There was one obvious person to seek out for a chat: Börje Salming.

Though he didn't talk about it much, Börje had twice been offered the captaincy in Toronto a decade earlier, and he'd turned it down both times. When I called to tell him they'd offered it to me, he was insistent.

"Mats," he said in his familiar raspy voice, "you have to say yes."

Börje told me that saying no to the Maple Leafs captaincy was the biggest regret of his career. As a guy from northern Sweden with a thick accent, he was worried people wouldn't accept him in the role. He'd heard it said that *C* stood not only for captain, but, symbolically, for Canadian. Every captain in the history of the Toronto Maple Leafs had hailed from Canada. Börje could have changed that, and regretted that he didn't. Now, it was up to me.

I knew all of this. And I *did* feel like a leader in the room and on the ice. When Doug was traded away, the role seemed to sway naturally in my direction.

"It's a huge honor," Börje said. "The biggest honor. You must do it."

Börje was adamant. If the role was being offered, it meant the team and management felt I was ready.

He was right. I called Ken Dryden to accept.

At the end of September 1997, Maple Leaf Sports & Entertainment held a dinner where former captain Darryl Sittler presented me with a jersey with the *C* sewn above the heart. It felt surreal to pull it over my head. After the dinner, I went home and called my family. It was 6 a.m. in Stockholm, but I couldn't wait to share the news. My parents were thrilled. They'd visited me in Toronto enough to understand the significance of my new role. It was big news here, but it would be big news back in Sweden, too.

I'd only been on the team for three years, but with so many changes, I was already one of the longest-tenured Leafs. The media asked me a lot of questions about the pressures of the role. I cracked jokes to deflect, but the truth was, the pressure didn't bother me. Eleven years earlier, as a fifteen-year-old standing under the camera's glare at the TV-pucken tournament, I'd learned that I played better on a bigger stage.

That turned out to be a good thing, because right off the bat, the pressures of the 1997–98 season were intense. In the first three weeks, we managed only two wins in nine games. The management were treating it as a rebuilding year, but that didn't make losing any easier. As captain, I had to answer for our failure to win. More than anything, I felt responsible to the younger guys navigating the pressures of Toronto for the first time. In a city that takes losing as personally as Toronto does, it's easy to fall into a trap of blaming yourself and letting your confidence spiral. It happened to all of us. At team meetings, I'd remind them to keep their focus where it belonged—on their game.

A bright spot that season was the agreement between the NHL and the International Olympic Committee that would allow professional ice hockey players to compete in the Winter Olympics for the first time. In 1988, I'd been too young to compete for Sweden at the Calgary Olympics. By 1992, I was playing in the NHL. I'd figured that by turning pro, I'd traded away any chance to play for Sweden in the Olympic Games. Heading to Nagano, Japan, for the 1998 tournament was a dream come true. As soon as the deal was announced, my family made plans to travel from Sweden to Nagano, by far the farthest from home any of the Sundins had ever been.

The league organized milk-run flights to Japan. Our flight from Toronto stopped in Vancouver to pick up more players before crossing the Pacific Ocean. At the Tokyo airport, we boarded buses for the three-and-a-half-hour drive west, inland to Nagano. I was jet-lagged and grateful for the chance to nap. With the cityscape rolling by, I fell into a deep sleep. When I woke up what felt like hours later, I was surprised to still see tall buildings out the bus window. On a map, the land between Tokyo and Nagano was green and rural. Had I slept the whole drive?

No. We were only just reaching the edges of Tokyo. By then,

I'd visited many cities that dwarfed Stockholm—New York, Los Angeles. Even Toronto could feel like it stretched on forever. But Tokyo was beyond my scope, a city with more people in it than all of Canada.

One of the best things about the games was that the NHL players got to stay in the Olympic Village with the rest of the athletes. The Swedish team's apartments were clustered together. Some of the people I trained with in the summers in Bosön were there, including downhill skier Pernilla Wiberg.

The tournament was tightly scheduled, so my family had to keep themselves busy while I attended practices and meals with the team. I was thrilled to be playing with legends like Ulf Samuelsson, but also newer guys like Daniel Alfredsson and Peter Forsberg. With professionals in the mix, this was truly the best hockey in the world. In the round-robin, we beat the USA but lost a close game to the powerhouse Canadian team, which included Wayne Gretzky and Joe Sakic. With a win against Belarus, we secured a quarterfinal matchup against our biggest rivals in sport, Finland. A tight 2–1 loss to the Finns bounced us from the tournament. I got a day or two to spend with my parents before we all returned to our respective homes. Per and Patrick were gracious. They'd had fun, even if we'd failed to advance to the medal round. Had my dad enjoyed himself?

"I hope I didn't bring you bad luck," he said.

In the end, a Czech goalie named Dominik Hašek stymied even the top scorers in the world, game after game. He led his team to an upset victory over Canada in the semifinals by stoning them in a shootout. Two days later, he shut out Russia to win gold. It was an admirable performance. I didn't know it then, but a year later, I'd come up against Hašek myself, deep in the Stanley Cup playoffs.

I got back to Canada in time to play out the final twenty games of the season. While Nagano was a disappointing result, it did teach me just how hard it is to win when the very best are playing the very best. Despite a final push in April, the Leafs failed to make the playoffs for the second year in a row. For four years, I'd led the team in goals and assists, sometimes by a margin of more than thirty points. At twenty-seven, I felt in peak form. But hockey is a team sport. Just as I'd been years earlier in Quebec, I was hopeful that the addition of a few missing pieces could tip us over the edge and back into contention.

As we were packing our bags in April for the second year in a row, coach Mike Murphy was taking the fall for our failure to make the playoffs.

The disappointment was tempered by my chance to go to Switzerland in May and play in the World Championships. Sweden went undefeated and won gold with a narrow 1–0 win over our rival Finland, an act of revenge for their ousting us in Nagano. I tied for the tournament's scoring with my teammate Peter Forsberg and Finland's Raimo Helminen. I loved winning at the international level, but seven years into my NHL career, my focus had shifted to the Stanley Cup.

At the end of June, Toronto reporters had no trouble tracking me down in Stockholm to tell me that the Leafs had hired Pat Quinn as the new head coach. They read back what he'd said to them in his first interviews after accepting the job.

"I will look at what we have," Quinn said, "and see how we can support Mats Sundin."

The reporters asked for my thoughts. I told them that Quinn's words made me hopeful. There was no doubt that we needed more depth. When the reporters asked me about Quinn, it was easy to be diplomatic: I was excited to work with him. The management team continued their work building our depth, securing winger Steve Thomas and goalie Curtis Joseph.

The earliest photo in the paper was of Quinn and Ken Dryden holding up a Leafs jersey. In his other hand, Quinn held a cigar. This was the man who'd approached me over ten years earlier at a Four Nations tournament to give me that Vancouver Canucks pin and assure me that I had a future in professional hockey. The man who'd stirred things up at the 1989 draft by selecting Pavel Bure when other teams were convinced he wasn't yet eligible. The man who'd sought me out to shake my hand when I was drafted first overall. By the time the Leafs hired him, Pat Quinn had already made a few brief appearances in my life. He was about to become a main character.

26

Quinn

The locker room door opened and in walked Pat Quinn. He circled us a few times without saying a word. Most players kept their gazes to the floor. No one wanted to make eye contact with the coach. It was so quiet that you could hear the guy across the room clear his throat. Still, Quinn circled, silent. He held a folded newspaper in one hand, as if he was readying to swat something dead.

It was October 1998. After starting the season with three straight wins, we'd lost on a Saturday night in Vancouver. We'd let our new coach down. Saturday's game had marked Quinn's first time back in Vancouver since being fired by the Canucks a year earlier. It was meant to be his triumphant return. After our big 7–3 Friday night win against Calgary, the media asked Quinn directly about going back. He got emotional talking about it. His kids grew up in Vancouver. He'd spent ten years of his life with the Canucks. It was odd for him to be taking up his perch on the visiting team's bench.

We knew what the game meant to him. Yet, despite registering forty shots, we only scored one goal. Trailing 3–1 halfway through the third period, we took back-to-back penalties and spent the dying minutes of the game playing shorthanded. The Canucks scored on the power play. At 4–1 with a handful of minutes on the clock, the game was all but over.

Reporters found me in the hallway right after the final buzzer. By then, I'd been captain of the Maple Leafs for a year. It was my job to answer for the team's failings.

"We gave up," I told the small media scrum.

The reporters looked surprised. It was unlike me to be blunt. They were used to my measured diplomacy, so they asked me to clarify what I meant.

"We couldn't score on a hot goalie, and then we took two penalties. We gave up."

The questions wrapped up and I joined my teammates. I can't remember if Quinn said much to us that night. But at the next team skate, he came into the room and started walking his laps.

Quinn was a tall man. Bigger than most of his players. He spent years in the NHL as a defenseman and enforcer. After retiring, he finished college and went to law school. Even at the arena, he often had a cigar in his mouth. Sometimes lit, sometimes not.

He circled the room for what felt like forever. Finally, he stopped in front of me. Quinn unrolled the newspaper he was holding and pointed at its pages.

"Our captain here says we gave up."

Everyone in the room looked at me.

"Gave up?" he repeated, this time as a question. "Isn't that the worst thing you can say about your teammates? That they gave up? You're the fucking team captain."

Silence. I met his gaze, keeping my expression steady.

"Why don't you explain what the fuck you meant by that?" he said, this time directly to me.

It felt almost funny. Ironic. The Toronto media often commented on the fact that I was less than forthcoming in interviews. That I was too reserved and stuck to platitudes. A quiet captain. And yet here I was, getting called out by my new coach for saying too much after a game.

"Mats?" Quinn continued. "You got something to say?"

There's an unwritten rule in hockey that you never throw your teammates under the bus when talking to the media. Even if a guy messes up horribly or your goalie gets shelled, even on nights where there's a specific player or play that lost you a game, you never call them out. Outwardly, you take each loss as a united front. Say what you need to say in the room. Hold each other accountable on the ice, at practice. But criticizing your teammates to the press was a mortal sin. He'd only been coaching us for a few weeks, but we already understood that no one took that team-first mentality more seriously than Pat Quinn, especially when it came to the media. As team captain and its highest-paid player, that rule applied doubly so to me.

But in that moment, something in the way Quinn hovered over me angered me. I resented him for calling me out. I was sweating and my heart was thumping in my chest. I had a choice. I could take it, or I could push back. I hadn't called any teammates out. I'd just spoken the truth.

I cleared my throat. The walls felt like they were closing in on me.

"Pat," I said, calm, "we had a shot in that game. But when you're down two goals in the third and you take two penalties, you're giving up. We had a chance to come back and tie it, and we gave that chance up."

Everyone stared at us nervously. Finally, Pat shrugged.

"You have a point," he said. Then he turned to the rest of the team. "Mats has a good point."

After that, Pat and I settled into an understanding, a dynamic we could both live with. I didn't speak up often, but when I did, he didn't ignore me, even when we disagreed. Sometimes, on a late flight home from a road trip, the guys would gather in the back of the plane and ask me to press Quinn for a day off. Maybe we'd been out of town for a week with a punishing schedule. Quinn liked to throw in Sunday skates. We all wanted to work hard, but sometimes, the guys needed a day to regroup. See their families. It was on me to ask for it. I'd walk up the aisle toward the front of the plane while my teammates peered at me over their seats.

"Pat?"

He'd look up from whatever he was reading.

"What do you think about a day off tomorrow?"

I'd state my rationale and he'd listen, thoughtful.

"Do *you* think the boys need it?" he'd ask.

"I do."

He'd nod, considering.

"Okay, Mats. Then you have the day off."

I'd head back to tell my teammates the news.

As a player, even as a captain, I generally tried to stay out of the management's business. If they asked my opinion, I'd give it, but they had their job and I had mine. In 1998–99, the Leafs had what team president Ken Dryden called a "management team." He was the GM, and Mike Smith was the associate GM. Bill Watters was an assistant GM. Anders Hedberg, a Swedish former player with the New York Rangers, was another assistant with a keen eye for the European talent pool. You could tell they were trying to build a team where all four lines were skilled skaters and capable goal scorers. They wanted a deep and balanced roster with the strongest possible goaltending. That model is standard now—they were a solid decade ahead of the times in this regard. Instead of investing in a few superstars, and then finding two more guys who could break forty points, they wanted *eight* guys to break forty points. They wanted their entire roster to dig in for at least ten points. Even goalie Curtis Joseph, aka Cujo, finished the season with five assists. There was also an emphasis on nurturing young talent instead of trading it. When eighth-round draft pick Tomáš Kaberle showed up to training camp in 1998 and caught fire, they opted to roster him as a key defenseman instead of sending him to the minors, as had been the original plan.

The management team had their vision. Pat Quinn had his. We players were buying in. By early 1999, we were well on the way to a strong turnaround. With thirty games to go, we'd already notched more wins than in either of our previous seasons. We'd sometimes go a few weeks without losing a game, and our winless streaks never got past three. We were on a good run. The playoffs were in sight.

Thanks to my friend and real estate agent Mike Walton, I'd bought a condo near Yorkville in midtown Toronto. It was a nice place—bigger than any place I'd ever lived on my own, and bright. All the other apartments I'd had in Quebec City and Toronto up to that point had felt transient. This felt like home to me. I soon had my favorite local coffee shops and restaurants.

The night before a home game, my evening routine was like clockwork. I was always in bed before 11 p.m. I'd always check the front door to make sure it was locked, then turn off all the lights. While brushing my teeth, I'd always get lost in thinking about the game the next day, the particular matchup. I still sometimes played on the wing then, but mostly at center. The current work-on was my defensive play. I was trying to improve my positioning in our end and find new ways to support my defense teammates as they worked to clear the zone.

One winter night, I'd moved through all these steps of my nighttime routine and gotten into bed. I lay in the dark, sleepy, when my bedroom lit up with the blue glow of my phone. I looked at the clock. It was 11 p.m. Who would be calling me now?

I answered it. It was a man's voice. Unfamiliar, gruff, calm.

"If you play tomorrow, you are dead."

I heard a click. My heart raced. I turned on the light and sat up in bed, hyperalert to the sounds around me, but all I could hear was the distant hum of Bloor Street below. I picked up my phone again and called Paul, the director of player security for the team. He didn't answer, so I left him a message. Paul was a retired police officer. I must have woken him up, because he sounded tired when he called me back two minutes later.

"Mats," he said. "Are you okay?"

"Someone just called my cell phone and threatened my life if I play in the game tomorrow."

Immediately, Paul took control. He asked me questions about the caller's tone, his exact words, whether I'd had any strange encounters recently, whether I knew of anyone who might want to threaten me. Paul had a British accent. His voice calmed me.

"Lock your doors and turn off your phone, Mats," he said. "I won't call you again until the morning, so don't answer any more calls. Get some sleep."

We hung up and I lay down. My head was spinning. I couldn't imagine falling asleep, but eventually I did. When my alarm went off at 7 a.m., I jumped out of bed like I'd been wide awake all night. I wondered briefly if it had just been a bad dream. Our morning skate was at ten o'clock, but I'd planned to be there two hours early. Antsy to hear from Paul, I turned on my phone, then went to the kitchen to make my breakfast. Twenty minutes later, my phone rang.

"Come to the rink, Mats," Paul said. "We'll make sure you're safe here. We'll be in touch with the league to figure out next steps."

I was relieved. Staying home would have been far more nerve-racking for me. At the rink, everything went on as normal. Quinn had clearly been informed, but he made a point of keeping the focus on the game that night. He surely understood that I didn't want to be thinking about it. After the skate, Paul found me in the locker room.

"You'll play tonight," he said. "We've evaluated with the NHL. There will be a lot of extra security on hand. Are you okay with that?"

I nodded. I wanted to play the game. I didn't want the space to replay that voice in my head, to ask myself how the caller got my number. The rest of the day, I was on high alert. Little sounds made me jump. As I stood on the blue line during the pregame ceremony, I scanned the fans. I'd never normally do that. Never in my life had I felt unsafe at the arena or worried about the crowd watching the game. I felt anxious for my first few shifts, but as the game wore on, I settled in. I played well, and we won.

After the game, I took questions from the media, as I almost always did. Paul had made it clear that this whole thing would be kept confidential. The reporters asked me about the game, about penalties we took and goals we scored. As I answered them, it struck me that, no matter how well the reporters did their jobs, they'd never have the full truth when it came to the players, and neither would the fans who got their information by reading these reporters' stories. They might know the basics about our families, but often they didn't know about sick relatives, or personal struggles, or in my case that day, of a death threat I'd gotten while lying at home in my bed the night before.

I never heard from the caller again, and I moved on along with our season. By February, there was a lot of fanfare in the air in Toronto. After nearly seventy years playing at Maple Leaf Gardens, the Leafs were moving to the brand-new Air Canada Centre at the end of the month. The ACC was right downtown, and purpose-built to house both the Leafs and the Raptors, Toronto's new NBA team that spent its first four seasons playing in a converted baseball stadium. There were events almost every day to mark the move, culminating in a parade down Yonge Street with the Stanley Cup.

A parade. With the Stanley Cup.

The guys found it weird. A parade is reserved for winning the Cup. It was hard not to feel like we were jinxing something. It had been over thirty years since Toronto had held an actual Stanley Cup parade. It felt awkward, offside even, to parade with the Cup for any reason other than winning it.

But the party was planned to the last detail, and we were assigned our roles. Our marching orders. Current players would be put in the back of convertibles with retired Leafs legends. When our goalie, Glenn Healy, was invited to walk and play the bagpipes with the 48th Highlanders Pipes and Drums, we joked about procuring earplugs to spare ourselves the agony. The route would take us about two miles south on Yonge Street, cutting right through the core of the city.

It snowed lightly the day of the parade, and then the sun came out. I was in a car with former captains George Armstrong and Sid Smith. Over twenty thousand fans lined Yonge Street. As the car inched southbound to our new rink, all I could think about was how much I loved this city and its fans. It was easy to imagine just how crazy they would go with an actual Stanley Cup parade.

We won our first game at the ACC. Maple Leaf Gardens had served the team very well for a long time, but this new arena was a beautiful place to call home—a fresh start. After two difficult losing years, it was amazing not only to be making the playoffs, but to be going in feeling like we really had a shot.

27

Playing to June

I set the puck on the center-ice circle. Less than a minute into the
third period against the Flyers, we were losing, 2–0. But I'd just
been awarded a penalty shot. I stared down the ice at Philadelphia
goalie John Vanbiesbrouck. He'd shut us out all game. There'd
been five or six plays where I was certain the puck was going in,
then it didn't.

I skated the length of the ice and shot. Save. Still 2–0. The
ACC crowd was muted. Not quite booing, but close. Three years
since the last playoff game in Toronto, the fans were hungry. They
wanted better from their team than this scoreless performance.
The pregame festivities had begun with a video of me in a pilot
suit in a cockpit, turning back to the camera.

"Prepare for takeoff," I said to the camera.

The fans loved it. But two hours later, the air was out of the
building. Two nights later, when we found ourselves trailing 1–0
late in the third period, the booing started. It's bad enough to
lose two playoff games in a row at home. Getting shut out both
times is indefensible.

But hockey games can turn in an instant. With two minutes

left in the game, Steve Thomas came flying up the right wing and fired the puck from a sharp angle. Somehow, it beat the so-far-unbeatable Vanbiesbrouck. The fans went wild. The bench went wild. Pat Quinn stayed completely composed, chewing his gum and barely registering a smile. It's not like we were winning, after all. We'd only managed to tie it. Fifty seconds later, when I picked up a rebound on my backhand and lifted it top corner, the crowd lost it. The bench, too. Again, Quinn was stoic. We'd go on to win, but now the series was tied, 1–1. It was Round 1. This was just the beginning.

In Philadelphia, we traded wins again. We won Game 5 at home to take a 3–2 series lead. Night after night, goals were hard to come by; almost every game belonged to the two goaltenders. In the third period of Game 6, we were locked in a 0–0 tie. In Games 5 and 6, Cujo allowed only one goal on sixty shots. He was stopping everything. All we needed to do was score. Once.

In the final three minutes of regulation time, the Flyers' John LeClair took an elbowing penalty against Mike Johnson. The Philadelphia bench flew into a rage. Usually, in the dying minutes of a key playoff game, the refs put their whistles away. But this time, a call was made, granting us a power play in a scoreless game.

With their season on the line, the Flyers defended desperately. It took us until the dying seconds of the power play to properly gain their zone. I stayed low, circling the crease; then, under the goal line, Sergei Berezin dove from the slot to fire the puck into the back of the net: 1–0.

This time, the bench celebration was muted. With fifty seconds on the clock, the game wasn't over. That final minute unfolded in an eternity, almost entirely in our end. At one point, Cujo literally stood on his head to make a save, flipping nearly upside down to keep the puck out of the net. The buzzer went, and we poured off the bench to celebrate.

For the first time in my NHL career, my team was on to the second round.

This time, our opponents were the Pittsburgh Penguins, who'd upset the first-place New Jersey Devils in the first round. Their star player was the league's top forward, Jaromír Jágr. Twice, the Penguins pulled ahead of us in the series, and twice we scrambled back to tie it. After a decisive win in Game 5, we returned to Pittsburgh with the series lead and the chance to clinch it.

It was in the sixth game of the second round of the playoffs, that our management's notion of four strong lines really came to light. We allowed two goals in the first period, but early in the second, I sent a pass up the middle to my linemate, who scored on a hard shot from the high slot. This linemate wasn't a roster regular—it was Lonny Bohonos, an AHL call-up who'd been playing a key role for us in the playoffs. Less than a minute later, Garry Valk weaved through their defense and goalie to tie the game. Two minutes into overtime, Valk took a diving dig at his own rebound and scored to win us the game and the series.

Only four teams remained. And we were one of them. Our opponent? The Buffalo Sabres and their star goalie, Dominik Hašek. It was mid-May and I was still in Canada. Still playing hockey. A reporter asked me what I wanted from the next series.

"I want to still be playing hockey in June," I said.

The weather in Toronto was warming by the day. The city took on a buzz. I'd long lost any real anonymity, but now everyone seemed to recognize me. Even at the worst of times, Toronto fans were always gracious in person. By the time the conference finals were set to start, they were positively elated. Joyful. The media scrum had also swollen to dozens and dozens of reporters. The Leafs were front-page news every day. We were eight wins away from the Stanley Cup.

With Hašek out due to a groin injury, we should have won the first two games. But Buffalo came at us hard, and we emerged tied 1–1 in the series. This deep in the playoffs, you start to see the lack of experience on the bench. Even as captain, it was new territory to me. Our inexperience, mixed with Buffalo's hot goalie, made it harder for us to reach the same level of play we'd found in the first two rounds. Our stamina was down, and that led to making more mistakes and taking more penalties.

Fourteen games into this playoff run, I'd learned more than I had in my entire NHL career to date. I understood just how much the game changed once the regular season ended. How different it was playing the same team night after night instead of traveling from rink to rink. How much harder it became to win. It was the end of May. I was hopeful that we'd make it into June.

But we were struggling to keep up the pace we'd held in the first two rounds. Buffalo was a disciplined, defensive team. After Buffalo scored an empty-netter in Game 3, Quinn opted to put out Domi and the fourth line for the final thirty seconds. When Domi was assessed a penalty for goaltender interference, Buffalo coach Lindy Ruff had some unfriendly words for Quinn. A reporter in the postgame scrum asked Domi about deliberately running Hašek, but Domi insisted he never touched him.

The next day, one Toronto columnist suggested that Quinn's fourth line wasn't helping our cause and should be scratched from the lineup, just as Buffalo had done with a few of their enforcers. That morning, Domi arrived at the skate in Buffalo as he always did—focused and ready to work. I knew he was more likely to read the news stories or listen to Leafs-related radio. For the depth of our friendship, it was another way we were so different. Domi was Torontonian through and through and he loved his city's fixation on hockey. After the skate, we hit the showers as a large media scrum gathered in the visitors' locker room. As the guys rinsed off, Domi got a look in his eyes. By then, I knew that look. I saw it on the bench all the time. Something was bothering him. There was an injustice he needed to correct.

"Listen to this, guys," Domi said to us. "He thinks I shouldn't play. He said Quinn should scratch me."

The guys tried to calm him, but we knew Tie was not about to let it go. The rest of us just nodded and let him talk.

"Like he's ever played hockey," Domi continued. "Like he's ever dropped his gloves."

The more he talked, the more it bothered him. For Tie, this was bigger than just him. If his role as enforcer was being devalued, then it was being devalued for every guy in the league who'd fought for their right to play. Every preseason, on every NHL team, a handful of guys showed up fully aware that their path to a roster spot was through their fists. Even at training camp, skating with prospective teammates, they were expected to fight—each other—to show their might. Tie had graduated beyond fighting for his roster spot years ago. He'd earned his right to be there.

I finished my shower first and got dressed. I'd just pulled on my shirt when Domi emerged from the shower, dripping wet, holding the towel around his waist with a tight fist. He walked right by me to the open area of the dressing room, where the media awaited.

"Where are you going?" I asked.

"To talk to that guy."

The gathered reporters all turned at once, shocked at the sight of him in a towel. Guys usually got dressed before emerging to face them.

"Where is he?" Domi said, naming the reporter. "I know he's here."

The crowd of journalists parted like the Red Sea, revealing at the rear of the room the columnist in Domi's crosshairs. Domi approached slowly. *Whatever he does*, I thought, *Tie had better keep a firm grip on that towel.*

"Where do you get off saying I shouldn't play?"

Flustered, the reporter tried to counter, to offer an explanation.

"I worked my ass off to get here," Tie continued. "I've played this game my entire life. This is my dream. I'm living my dream. What gives you the right to say I shouldn't play?"

At this point, many of the reporters were taking notes. A few turned their cameras on. Once Tie was done, he got dressed and the team boarded the bus to head back to the hotel. Tie took his seat next to me. You could see the relief in his shoulders. They were relaxed.

"I feel so much better," Tie said.

But in the end, the locker-room scene never made the papers. Reporters were too focused on the fact that we went out and lost Game 4 that night. Two days later, the Buffalo Sabres eliminated us from the playoffs, four games to one.

It was a terrible feeling. All I'd wanted was to keep playing. I'd wanted to play hockey into June. Our season ended on May 31.

28

Contraband

The Sundins' tradition of visiting Canada was well established by 1999, even as the brood got bigger. Patrick and Nina were married, and now had their little ones, Mikaela and Robert, in tow. My parents were still in the habit of packing food from home in their luggage. Their perfect record of smuggling contraband through customs might have made them a little too brazen about it.

The 1999–2000 season was off to a strong start. Even though I broke my ankle in early October and missed several weeks, we had a winning record. The lineup had the most depth we'd enjoyed in years. Over the summer, there was some upheaval in the front office. The management team that led us to a turnaround season and playoff wins had been dismantled in dramatic fashion. Mike Smith and Anders Hedberg, the brains behind building the group that had made it to the conference finals, were both gone. Ken Dryden remained president, and Quinn was now both the general manager and the head coach. As captain, I spoke to management as needed, and to the media, too. My focus was on the energy in the dressing room, and this season, it was excellent. My ankle injury healed remarkably quickly, and by the time I returned in early November, the team's record stood at 9–3–1. We only lost two games in December. At Christmas, my family was arriving to a team in great form.

I spoke to my parents before they left Sweden. They'd take a taxi from the airport, so we calculated when I could expect them at the condo. By the time they arrived on my doorstep, my dad was uncharacteristically out of sorts. He looked sweaty and exhausted. I wondered if the flight had been too turbulent. My brothers explained that as they made their way through arrivals to security, my dad was approached by a customs agent and a sniffer dog that seemed extremely focused on his bag. Tommy asserted vehemently that he had nothing illegal, like drugs.

"This dog is trained to identify prohibited food items," the officer said.

At the customs station, Tommy opened his luggage. The customs agent lifted the large blood sausage and examined it, then looked at Tommy.

"You can't travel with meat."

All these years later, it was still a struggle for Tommy to wield his name, but that blood sausage was full of iron, and iron made hockey players stronger. Bringing it to me in Canada was his annual holiday tradition. He felt he had no choice.

"It's for Mats Sundin," Tommy said. "I'm his father. We're his family."

The customs agent scowled at him. "I don't care who it's for, it's prohibited."

Tommy was about to plead his case further, but the agent turned and dropped the sausage into a bin to be destroyed.

The new year started out a bit bumpier, but after Toronto played host to the NHL All-Star Game in mid-February, the team managed to regain some traction. Even during the stretches where the games weren't going our way, the energy in the room stayed upbeat, focused and confident.

As the captain, it was obviously my job to be a leader in the room. But over the last few seasons, that role had shifted, too. Ten years into my career, I was now decidedly a veteran. It was up to me to take guys who were new to the team under my wing, just as Doug Gilmour and Dave Ellett had done for me. When defenseman Bryan Berard arrived in Toronto midway through the 1998–99 season, we arranged for him to get a condo in the same building where my girlfriend Tina and I were living. Over the course of that year, Bryan got into the habit of taking the elevator up to my place for pregame meals or dinners on nights off. On top of our friendship, I learned quickly that Berard was a great guy to have on the ice with me. By March 2000, he was leading the team's defensemen in points.

But hockey can be a cruel game. On March 11, we traveled to Ottawa to play the Senators. Late in the second period, Marián Hossa turned to fire a shot at Cujo from the face-off circle. The follow-through from Hossa's stick caught Berard in the eye. It happened almost in slow motion. Bryan dropped to the ice. Seeing the blood, Cujo approached and yelled for the trainers. Bryan was rushed off the ice and immediately brought to the hospital. After the game, the trainers who'd tended to him could barely speak. Someone asked them how Bryan had been as they prepped him for transport.

"Scared," one of the trainers said.

Scared. Berard knew something was wrong. By the time I was able to see him, we'd learned that he needed emergency surgery. I couldn't bear to look at the eye. It was possible he would permanently lose his vision.

Professional hockey players are generally good at compartmentalizing, at filing away our personal lives when we're on the ice. The next game, we beat the hot Detroit Red Wings in overtime. Then we lost three games, and I didn't score in any of them. A reporter asked me if Berard's injury was a distraction for the team or for me. A teammate was facing the end of his career at the age of just twenty-three because of an accident on the ice a few games earlier. He was a model defenseman with a fantastic sense of the ice, a great skater and passer, and such a key part of our lineup and locker room that his absence required a big adjustment. And he was a dear friend. Was it not human to feel shaken by it? I had to take a few deep breaths before I could answer the question.

"He was on our mind," I said. "But we are still focused on the game."

By the end of March, we had regained our footing and finished at the top of the Northeast Division. In the first round of the 2000 playoffs, we faced Ottawa and won in six games. The second round belonged to New Jersey's goalie, Martin Brodeur, who shut us out in two of the games and led his team past us in six. That year, New Jersey eventually went on to hoist the Stanley Cup.

After multiple surgeries, Berard declared that he hoped to play in the NHL again, and arrived at our training camp in August 2000 to spend time with the team and assess where he stood. Without full vision in his eye, he'd have to learn how to manage changes in his depth perception while playing at the game's top speed. It took him a year, and we never got to be teammates again because he opted to play closer to home in New York, but he did return to the NHL. It felt like a miracle, and I always loved seeing Bryan in action when we played against him.

In November 2000, eight months after Berard's accident, I ended up in the medical room at the Air Canada Centre. The Leafs' plastic surgeon, Dr. Leith Douglas, was working on me. Dr. Douglas was one of the city's top plastic surgeons. When

I first met him, he told me he'd done part of his training at the University of Uppsala, an hour north of Stockholm. As I lay on the table, Dr. Douglas's face was so close to mine that I could smell the mint in his gum.

"Ooof," Dr. Douglas said. "This is an ugly one, Mats. Nasty."

A few shifts into our home game against Chicago, Leafs defenseman Bryan McCabe tried to dump the puck into our zone. I was ahead of him and turned, thinking he might pass it up to me. McCabe has a strong shot. I learned just how strong when it hit me in the forehead.

There was a lot of blood. I skated off the ice as quickly as I could. Trainers Chris Broadhurst and Brent Smith guided me into the medical room and onto the table, then fetched Dr. Douglas. With all the blood, I couldn't see.

"Your eye's fine," Dr. Douglas assured me. "Just a cut. An ugly, ugly cut."

It was Remembrance Day. Dr. Douglas had a poppy—the red flower Canadians wear in November to commemorate fallen soldiers—on his lapel. He joined the Leafs shortly after they won their last Stanley Cup in 1967 and was as old-school as they come. But he took great care in his work.

"Just a cut," he repeated as he worked, "but a nasty one."

The word *nasty* was stressing me out. He froze my forehead and got to work, counting the stitches as he sewed them. Fifteen in total. At one point, he rooted around in the open flesh and pinched something out.

"Look at that," he said, amazed.

He held a sliver of something black up to the light.

"That's a piece of puck. Imagine that, Mats. A piece of puck jammed in your forehead." He looked for a spot to set it. "You should keep it."

I didn't keep it. I did wake up the next morning with two

black eyes and a swollen forehead. I'd have to wear a visor until Christmas. I hated wearing a visor. At twenty-eight, it was easy to be blasé about my eyes, even with well-documented injuries like Berard's a strong argument for mandating them. Over that November, in media scrums, the questions evolved from my eye injury to my use of the visor, to the visor impacting my play, to the scoring slump I was experiencing, and eventually my inclusion in a possible trade to Philadelphia for Eric Lindros.

This was year seven for me in Toronto. I was well trained in how the media worked and well practiced in staying level in my responses. Eric Lindros was currently sitting out the season, awaiting a trade instead of returning to the Flyers. In the first fifteen games of the season, I'd only scored four goals, far off my normal pace. For years, Pat Quinn had long made jokes about his love of Lindros, and Lindros had recently announced that Toronto was his preferred place to play. I'm pretty sure some Toronto reporters made a game out of trying to crack my diplomatic front.

"Does it bother you that management is talking to Lindros?"

"No," I said. "Not really."

Not really? They saw the crack.

"Does it worry you that these talks are happening while you're in a big slump?"

That was a direct hit.

"A bad coincidence, I guess," I said.

The questions bothered me, but not the workings of the team. I knew better than to worry about dry spells. I'd had slumps before and always emerged from them. Slumps, like streaks, eventually ended. All I had to do was stick to my game. Lindros was a top player in the league, and I wanted to win. Of course I'd be glad to have him on my team if a deal was possible.

Even in 2000, even as I was finding my place in Canada and Toronto, the baffling conversation around the grit of European players was showing no signs of dying down. It was still one of Don Cherry's favorite weekly topics, even if his talking points weren't well supported by facts. With back-to-back Stanley Cups in 1997 and 1998 and two more to follow in the coming years, the Detroit Red Wings were cementing themselves as a modern dynasty. Nearly half their roster hailed from Europe, including many guys in leadership roles. Season after season, they played a strong and tough team game that endured well into the playoff rounds.

While he made no secret of liking Lindros, Quinn was quick to shut down any whiff of it being about Eric's Canadian passport. We had a dozen Europeans on our team at the time. As a fellow history buff, Quinn sometimes liked to bug me about Sweden's neutrality during the two world wars. I'd respond that Sweden had fought the mighty Russia many times over the centuries, and that Finland beat back the Russians in the 1939–40 Winter War despite having 1 percent of the Russian tank and aircraft supply. Quinn raised an eyebrow at me, surprised. Despite ribbing me on my country's military prowess, Quinn had been a huge advocate of European talent from the beginning, even going on "Coach's Corner" once to rip into Don Cherry for insulting Pavel Bure.

Sometimes, it could feel like whiplash, how quickly things could turn in the media. Imagine a workplace where, one day, you're being celebrated for a game-winning goal, and the next, floated as trade bait. How do you learn to survive in a job where, on Monday, you're declared the most valuable employee and a hero for all your successes, then on Wednesday, someone calls you a heartless bum with no character? On Friday, you're given a gold star and Saturday, panned for a lazy effort. Fundamentally, I understood that this was the trade-off for the dream life of an NHL player, especially for the dream of playing in the biggest hockey market in the world. But I still needed a strategy to cope. I'd learned that, while good-news hockey stories sold well, bad-news hockey stories sold best, and the truth usually lay somewhere in the middle.

I needed to stay even-keeled. When I was on top, I needed to focus on the game and my effort. When I had a few shitty games in a row, I really need to do the same. I had to learn how to keep steady no matter what the weather around me. It was my job to speak openly about the team and my play. That didn't mean I had to read what they wrote. I had a good relationship with most of the media, and sometimes I'd poke them in return. When they'd ask me to comment on the specifics of a story circling about me, I admit that I took some pleasure in reminding them that I didn't read the news.

In the end, no one in the management group indicated that I was part of any Lindros trade talk. Within a few weeks, the visor did come off, and the slump ended.

We finished the 2000–01 season in seventh place in the Eastern Conference. For the second year in a row, we were set to square off against Ottawa in the first round. It was now dubbed the Battle of Ontario. The Senators had finished in second place and had set franchise records with forty-eight wins and 109 points. We had lost all five of our games against them. In early April, they nearly eliminated us from playoff contention.

But the playoffs are a fresh start. It took us five days to sweep the Senators, 4–0. In the second round, it took the defending champion Devils seven games to dispatch us. A decade into my career, I'd learned an important lesson about the NHL playoffs. Every April, they served as a reset. Rarely did the top two regular-season teams both make it to the Stanley Cup Final. There was almost always an underdog story. All you had to do was make the playoffs, and your chances would then be the same as every other team: 1 in 16. I'd carry this unwavering belief with me over the coming years.

In the days and weeks that follow a playoff exit, there was always a lot of analysis. The media break everything down. Management does the same. You hold team meetings before parting ways for the summer. As a player, you weigh everything, too. Your failings. The shifts where you were scored on. The shots you missed. In his deliberations, Pat Quinn talked to us about progress. We'd finished in seventh place, barely making the playoffs, then beaten the second-place team cleanly and pushed the top team to a seventh game. He was optimistic.

It's hard to look ahead when you're cleaning out your stall. Quinn had built a different team from his predecessors in Mike Smith and Anders Hedberg. In our contract talks, Quinn asked me what I felt the team needed. I believed a strong winger would help us gain more offensive ground. In my later years with the Leafs, a narrative I often heard was that, as captain, I didn't assert to management what I felt the team needed to win. That wasn't true. Quinn often asked me my opinion on possible signings or trades. I always gave my unvarnished take when asked, but in truth my thoughts didn't seem to get much weight. Ultimately, it was up to the GM to build the roster. As captain, I was going to respect that chain of command.

Even when we disagreed, Quinn and I always wanted the same thing: a winning team. A few weeks after our 2001 playoff exit, Quinn signed Mikael Renberg, Robert Reichel and Alexander Mogilny, three familiar faces dating back to my Four Nations Cup years. A few weeks after that, we agreed on a deal that would keep me wearing blue and white until my thirty-sixth birthday. Toronto was genuinely starting to feel like home. The deal even included a no-trade clause, a gesture of faith by Quinn and the rest of management that filled me with a sense of optimism. I believed in this team, in this city, and it seemed they believed in me, too.

29

Olympic Upset

The older I got, the harder I knew I had to train to keep up in the summers. I turned thirty in 2001 and would be arriving back in Toronto with a new contract signed and high expectations for my performance. I spent that summer training harder than I ever had. At the start of the 2001–02 season, Quinn put together a line that became known as the *Tre Kronors*—Three Crowns—made up of three Swedes: Mikael Renberg, Jonas Höglund and me. The season was off to a strong start.

Sometime around November, the Toronto media had figured out that ice time was a tender spot for some of the guys on the team. Ice time means everything to players; eighteen guys on the bench have to share sixty minutes between them. The top players—usually the highest paid, too—are able to produce because they get more ice time. The math has always been about the same—eighteen to twenty-three minutes a game for top forwards, and twenty-three to twenty-eight minutes for top defensemen. When Quinn suggested to a group of reporters that I played better when my ice time was under twenty minutes a game, they smelled blood. At my next media scrum, a reporter read Quinn's words back to me for comment.

I disagreed with that assessment. I felt my play improved the more time I got on the ice. But seeing the rabid look in the reporters' eyes, I held the line with Quinn. Our team had depth, and we were in first place. Every player on the team was willing to sacrifice to keep winning—end of story.

I wasn't lying into their microphones. I did feel that way. The team mattered far more to me than my individual success did. After years of playoff near misses, I understood going the distance required depth in the lineup. Still, I didn't feel like I had Quinn's full confidence. My role was to score goals and produce offense, and I needed ice time to do that. I didn't like that he was telling the media that my output waned if I played more than every third shift. In games, I sensed that he didn't trust me to handle specific matchups. He sometimes pulled me off the ice when his opposing coach put a big centerman on. He was very good in the locker room, but I often didn't agree with the choices he made as a bench coach. Quinn must have had his reasons, but I didn't know what they were. It took me two more seasons to bring it up with him. In 2002, I figured the only way to prove him wrong was on the ice.

By February, we were locked in a tight race for the top spot in the Eastern Conference with Boston and Philadelphia. The league was set to pause for twelve days for the 2002 Salt Lake City Olympics. Renberg and I set off to represent Sweden, arriving at the Olympic Village the night before our first game.

My parents and my brothers, Patrick and Per, along with Patrick's wife, Nina, and their kids, arrived at Salt Lake City at the same time as me, but security at the Games was so intense after 9/11 that I couldn't easily leave the athletes' bubble. Even with Peter Forsberg sitting out the Games to tend to injuries, Sweden had a strong team, but Canada was the undisputed favorite. The talent pool in Canada was so deep that they could arguably have put two or three separate teams together to compete for gold. Sweden was set to face Canada in our first game of the tournament's round-robin.

Canada's head coach? Pat Quinn.

As soon as the Olympic schedule was released, I circled that game on my calendar. This was my chance to show Quinn that I could play hard when matched up against the best players in the world. Against guys that Pat and Canada's GM, Wayne Gretzky, had handpicked for their roster. I'd been named captain of Team Sweden. I was glad we were being tossed straight into the fire by playing Team Canada first.

The crowd at the E Center in Salt Lake City was full of Canadians, with a few patches of Swedish fans in blue and yellow, including my parents and brothers. Our head coach was Hardy Nilsson. He used a system of play nicknamed "torpedo hockey" by the media. Torpedo hockey relied on a big ice surface, long lead passes and aggressive offense. In 2002, NHL rules still disallowed passes across the center red line from inside your own zone, and most teams played a tight neutral-zone trap system to account for that. This rule didn't exist in international play.

Rob Blake opened the scoring for Canada early in the first period. Minutes later, Daniel Alfredsson threaded a long pass to me up center ice, a pass that would be called offside in the NHL. A torpedo. On a breakaway, I scored on my Leafs teammate Curtis Joseph: 1–1.

Niklas Sundström scored to give us the lead, then I scored again on a low slap shot to make it 3–1. Back on the bench, I smiled. By the end of the second period, it was 5–1. The momentum was ours. We were in complete control of the game. We won the game, 5–2. For the Canadians, it was a major upset. It was one of the best games of my career, and remains one of the all-time best games Team Sweden has ever played.

In our second game, we beat the defending Olympic champions, the Czech Republic, 2–1, and then Germany, 7–1. We entered the playoff round in first place, with me as the tournament's leading scorer. Our opponent in the quarterfinals was Belarus, who had gone 0–3 in the first round.

We practiced the night before our quarterfinal game. Coach Nilsson wanted us to work on special teams. It was late by the time we got back to the Olympic Village, but I settled in easily to sleep.

The morning of February 20, 2002, was misty and cold in Salt Lake City. The drive from the Olympic Village to the rink cut right through the small downtown. The mountains, normally visible, were hidden by fog. All four quarterfinal matches were being played in one day, at three-hour intervals. They gave the early slots to European matchups so that the games would air in prime time in our home countries. Puck drop for Sweden–Belarus was at 11 a.m. local time.

In 2002, Team Belarus had exactly one player in the NHL, a journeyman defenseman from the Mighty Ducks of Anaheim named Ruslan Salei. The rest of the national team was playing in either Germany or Russia. Still, on our drive to the arena, everyone was dialed in. We were all professionals, and we understood that every game required focus and preparation. The media were anticipating a rematch with Team Canada in the semifinals. As far as they were concerned, a Swedish win against Belarus was a given. And even if our players would never say it out loud, we were confident we would win the game handily. Belarus had been outscored 22–6 in their three round-robin games, against Russia, Finland and the USA, and had suffered back-to-back 8–1 losses against the latter two. We were the favorites to win by a large margin. Anything but a Sweden win would take a miracle.

Compared to our game against Canada, the E Center crowd was muted. Not many Belarusians had made the trip to Salt Lake City. There was a large scattering of empty seats. Belarus took a penalty in the first two minutes, and Nicklas Lidström capitalized right away. Our bench felt relaxed. It was early in the game, and everything was going according to plan. Control the game and secure the lead.

But our plan ignored the fact that hockey is sometimes a game of fate. When your group is highly talented and hardworking, things will often go your way. You'll get those early goals. But sometimes, once in a rare while, everything that can go wrong, will go wrong.

Seven minutes into the first period, I took a roughing penalty, then watched from the box as Belarus scored. Ninety seconds later, Kenny Jonsson took a hooking penalty, and he watched from the box as Belarus scored again. Despite recording twenty-two shots on net, we ended the first period trailing, 2–1.

Coach Nilsson didn't press us hard in the room. We'd underestimated Belarus, but not anymore. In the second period, we would come out flying. No one was terribly worried. Yet.

In the second period, we outshot Belarus by double digits. But we could not get the puck past their goalie, a twenty-seven-year-old named Andrei Mezin who played for the Berlin Capitals in the Deutsche Eishockey Liga. He'd made all those saves in the first, and now he was playing like a man possessed. It took a power play for Michael Nylander to finally tie it up.

The worry was finally seeping in. By the third period, when Belarus scored to take the lead again, it was dawning on us: we could lose this game. Coach Nilsson started shortening the bench, and the guys getting all the ice time were tired. Mezin had stopped nearly forty shots in just two periods. With thirteen minutes on the clock, I took the ice on a power play and scored unassisted to tie it up, 3–3. If only we could score a couple more, we could wipe our brows and call the whole game a scary near miss, then regroup for the semifinals.

But fate was siding with Belarus that day. As the third period ticked away, they were closing in on their chance to make history. The whole team played with the guts of a group that had nothing to lose. They dove to block shots, forechecked hard, and fired on our net from everywhere on the ice.

In the dying minutes, one of their defensemen dumped the puck in from center ice, a play that happens dozens of times a game. You dump it in along the boards, then skate hard to chase it. But this time, he aimed for the net with a slap shot. The puck hit our goalie, Tommy Salo, in the mask, then bounced up and over his shoulder and landed on the ice. Salo shook off the blow, but couldn't see the puck as it crept behind him along the blue paint of the crease. Kenny Jonsson saw it from fifteen feet away and dove stick-first to swing at it, but not in time. The puck crossed the goal line. The buzzer rang. That defenseman leapt with joy and slid past our bench on his stomach. You couldn't blame him. This was his hockey miracle. His Stanley Cup.

We didn't recover. The game ended 4–3, Belarus.

As our opponents' bench cleared in celebration, I skated to center ice and dropped to my knees. Nothing else mattered in that moment—not my earlier success in the tournament, the captaincy, our win against Team Canada. When you lose a game like that, any success leading up to it is erased.

The silence in the dressing room was gutting. You could hear the Belarus team going wild on their side of the rink. My Swedish teammates were not the guys I played with every day, so I couldn't hash out the loss the way I might have with my regular NHL squad. I showered and readied to face the media. A large scrum awaited. Sweden's loss to Belarus was historic. It would become the main story of these Olympic Games.

"It hasn't sunk in yet," I said. "We should have put them away in the first period, and we didn't."

More questions followed about our play, about the disappointment we surely felt, about the disappointment our country would surely feel. Because he was selected for random drug testing, Tommy Salo was late leaving the dressing room. He eventually emerged to face the media and answered questions in Swedish and English for almost an hour.

The scrum turned back to me. The loss was in no way Tommy's fault. Unlucky bounces happen in hockey all the time. A good team needs to control the game so that the unlucky bounces don't decide your fate for you. Belarus's winning goal was only a memorable one because the entire team, every one of us, let the game get to 3–3 in the first place.

With my tournament over early, I spent a few days with my family. My dad always had opinions about my games, and would have been disappointed in his own right, but he understood that this one was touchy and left it alone. After our loss in Nagano, he did wonder aloud whether he was bad luck.

"I don't think Tommy Sundin being in the stands is the reason Sweden lost a hockey game," my brother Patrick said.

Even without social media, my family still caught wind of the storm brewing at home. The Swedish media was in a feeding frenzy. Headlines like "A day of shame" and "Guilty of treason: They betrayed their country" were splashed across the front pages of the major papers. One newspaper printed the players' faces in a row, like mug shots, with our NHL salaries underneath and suggested our passports be revoked. I was returning to Toronto, but my parents and brothers would be heading straight home to the aftermath.

Canada, the team we were set to meet in the semis, beat Belarus, 7–1, and won the gold medal. Four years after Nagano, it was another lesson in what it took to win in a best-on-best tournament. Looking back, I probably played my best international hockey in Salt Lake City. Despite playing fewer games than my counterparts, I still finished first in scoring. But my individual stats didn't matter. When you fail to make the medal round, nothing else matters.

On the flight back to Toronto, fellow Swede Mikael Renberg and I discussed our return to the Leafs' locker room. It would be easy to congratulate Cujo and Quinn on Canada's gold medal, and to commiserate with Tomáš Kaberle or Robert Reichel on the Czech Republic's 1–0 quarterfinal loss to Russia. But Tie Domi? Renberg kept nervously bringing him up on the plane. He knew Tie was going to have a field day with us.

Sure enough, for the next few days Tie broke into a "Belarus! Belarus!" chant every time he laid eyes on me. Tie told the Toronto media it was his job to keep us humble. Tie could make light of even the most heartbreaking losses. No one was spared. Insensitive? Not really. It was kind of admirable. He took it upon himself to get a laugh out of us and make sure we moved on.

Less than a week after The Loss, I was back in blue and white for a Tuesday night game against the Carolina Hurricanes at the Air Canada Centre. That's what I love most about hockey: you almost always get a shot at redemption. We won that game handily, and finished the rest of the season strong, breaking the symbolic hundred-point barrier by winning our final four games. I finished fourth in the NHL's scoring race with my best point tally in six years.

Quinn and I found our rhythm in those final months of the season. We were very different people, with different leadership styles and different visions of the game. But the mutual respect was strong, and those differences seemed to combine into one positive force; the team benefited from the balance we struck. You can put all the talent in the world on a team, but if the dynamic is off in the locker room, if guys don't get along or hold each other accountable, wins will be harder to come by.

And this Leafs team was good. Quinn understood that, and as GM made almost no changes at the March trade deadline. He trusted the group he had.

The 2002 playoffs were here. We'd face the New York Islanders in Round 1. And we were ready.

30

Pat is Here

The needle pinched as it broke the skin.

My wrist was in pain, but I was not going to sit out. A shift or two, if necessary, but not the rest of the game. Seven minutes into the first period, we were losing Game 1 of the Islanders series, 1–0. I lost a face-off in our zone, then pressed my opponent Claude Lapointe into the ice. We scrambled, and a shot from the blue line hit me in the wrist. I finished my shift, then headed to the bench and made a beeline to our athletic therapist, Chris Broadhurst, hand in the air. My language was colorful. He took me back to the locker room.

We'd started the series with several of our top guys injured, including Rob Reichel and Gary Roberts. A few more were already playing hurt. I was *not* sitting out. Broadhurst knew better than to suggest I should. We agreed to freeze it.

A few needles later, I was back on the bench. The Islanders held us scoreless until the third period, when Darcy Tucker tipped a hard shot past their goalie. Five minutes later, McCabe made a D-to-D pass to Kaberle, who faked a shot, then edged the puck forward to a waiting Domi. Tie's wrist shot hit the back of the net.

In our celebration, I nearly lifted Tie right off the ice. The fans were so loud, we couldn't hear ourselves speak on the bench. I sealed the win in the last minute with an empty-netter.

In the room, the mood was celebratory, then quickly focused on the next game. I couldn't shake the throbbing in my wrist. Normally, you get hit by the puck and it hurts like hell, but then the pain subsides. You shake it off. A bruise forms. But this pain wasn't subsiding.

We beat the Islanders, 2–0, in the second game with another empty-net goal. It was close. Intense. Chippy. The Islanders were not going to go lightly, and it was only a matter of time until their big stars like Mike Peca and Alexei Yashin found the net. When an X-ray revealed a break in my wrist, I insisted I was dressing for Game 3 anyway.

"Your wrist is *broken*," the team doctor said.

I told him to freeze it. I'd wear a cast under my glove.

I wanted to play. In hindsight, that kind of stubbornness serves no one. We lost the next game, 6–1. I didn't register a shot on net and took a big hit late in the game that pressed my casted wrist awkwardly into the boards. After the warm-up skate before Game 4, I knew I couldn't play. I could barely hold my stick. For the first time since my ankle break in 1999, I'd be sitting out. This time, I was sitting out during the Stanley Cup playoffs, and nothing was a greater torture.

The NHL playoffs are both a test of endurance and a juggling act. With the injuries, Quinn was forced to fiddle with his lineup, searching for ways to plug the holes. Over the next two games, the teams traded victories until we arrived at Game 7 in Toronto. As the captain, I was distressed at watching the guys I'd fought with all season continuing the battle while I sat on the sidelines.

We entered the third period of Game 7 with a 3–1 lead. In the first five minutes, the Islanders scored to cut the lead to 3–2. The crowd at the Air Canada Centre spent the entire period on its feet. With a minute left in the game, the Islanders pulled their goalie and pressed hard. I watched my teammates scramble, diving in front of shots, blocking, fighting. Gary Roberts caught the puck at our blue line and shoveled it forward to Alex Mogilny. Standing still on the Islanders blue line, Mogilny made a ridiculously swift move to fool the defensemen. He shot it into the open net to make it 4–2. I'd never heard the ACC crowd that loud.

There I was, the team captain, cheering with the fans. We were on to Round 2.

The doctors told me I'd likely sit out the entire series against Ottawa. Broken wrists don't heal in days, or even weeks. This would mark the third straight year of the Battle of Ontario; after getting swept last season, the Senators would be out for blood. That much was clear in the first game, when they hammered us, 5–0, in front of our home crowd. We erased a 2–0 deficit in the second game to force overtime.

After two full periods of OT, the game was still tied. In playoff hockey, you keep playing until someone scores, no matter how long it takes. After the first overtime period ends without a goal, it becomes a battle of attrition. By the end of the second overtime, guys on the ice are exhausted and the fans are hushed in their seats. A game that was supposed to end at 10 p.m. is still being played at midnight.

Less than five minutes into the third OT, Robert Reichel won the face-off and directed the puck to his winger, Gary Roberts. Roberts's shot hit the back of the net. Instantly, like a button pushed, the quiet fans erupted. The boys piled off the bench. In his perfect deadpan character, Quinn kept his arms at his side, chewing his gum, as his players celebrated. To him, this was another mile covered, but the marathon wasn't over.

Sitting out was excruciating, but I had total confidence in this group. They'd shown a lot of grit in the wins, and resilience after the losses. Guys who didn't normally score were scoring. Guys who didn't normally fight were fighting. Without me to take the face-offs, fourth-line center Alyn McCauley was getting almost twice the ice time and averaging a point a game. Wade Belak, a player Quinn picked up on waivers the season before, was switching from defense to forward and back as needed. Quinn liked his players to have roles, but if a role was vacant because of injury, another guy was finding a way to step in.

We won the series in seven games. Next up were the Carolina Hurricanes, as we made our second trip to the conference finals in four years. By Game 2 in Raleigh, I was finally cleared to play. We returned to Toronto with the series tied, 1–1. Arriving at the Air Canada Centre for Game 3, that familiar knot churned in my stomach. The players gathered, ready to start their routines. Then someone came into the room to deliver the news. That afternoon, Pat Quinn had been taken by ambulance to the hospital. The doctors were running tests and refusing to release him. Assistant coach Rick Ley would be stepping up. The room was quiet. The players trusted Rick. He was our special teams coach and we had a great power play. His messaging to us was always clear and simple. Still, of all the roles on the team, that of head coach was a tough one to fill, especially under such difficult circumstances.

We lost the game in overtime. Afterward, we were told that Quinn had been moved to the intensive care unit. For the players, there was a strange unsteadiness at the news. Hockey matters. In the conference finals, hockey matters more than anything. Then you hear that your coach, the guy you've played for all season, is in the ICU, and something shakes loose. What mattered felt murky. Pat had a wife and kids. What mattered more than that?

Our unwavering certainty around what Quinn would want us to do kept us focused. The other coaches were clear on that. He'd want us to keep the series alive until he could return, just as the team had done for me when my wrist was broken.

Game 4 was held in Toronto on an unseasonably cold Tuesday night in May. In the late afternoon, players started trickling into the rink. One of the trainers came into the dressing room.

"Pat's here," he said.

He meant Pat Quinn.

At 4 p.m., two days after entering the ICU, Quinn checked himself out of the hospital and rode the two and a half miles downtown to the Air Canada Centre. It might have unfolded like a scene from a movie: Quinn sitting in his hospital bed, mulling lines for that night's game, then deciding he can't miss it. Asking a nurse to detach any lingering wires, standing up, walking off the unit and out the hospital doors.

When he stepped into the dressing room, the guys looked around, nervous.

"I'm fine," he said.

There would be no more discussion. If Quinn said he was fine, he was fine.

We outshot the Hurricanes in that game, and arguably outplayed them. But their goalie, Artūrs Irbe, was unbeatable. Quinn was quieter than normal on the bench. Despite registering over thirty shots, we couldn't find a way to score on him. Two days later, back in Carolina, Cujo kept the series alive for us by shutting out the Hurricanes in return. We were heading back to Toronto for a must-win Game 6.

For the first two periods of that sixth game, neither team scored. Both goalies were holding strong. Halfway through the third, Jeff O'Neill broke the tie for the Hurricanes. A few minutes later, I took a shot at opponent Rod Brind'Amour, then another shot. I landed more than one punch. The referee pointed at me, and I skated to the penalty box to a chorus of fans booing at the ref. Those two minutes in the box were hell. My teammates spent the entire penalty kill in our zone, blocking shots beyond the ones Cujo saved. Back on the ice with five minutes to go, I was on a mission. My season wasn't ending on that note.

With 1:03 left in the game, Quinn called a time-out. He leaned forward on the bench, reading glasses on, play card and pen in hand. At the first opportunity, Cujo would leave the ice in exchange for the sixth attacker. With the season on the line, we knew what we needed to do to stay alive: everybody drives the net.

The next forty seconds played out in a frenzy. We kept the puck deep, cycling it. Twenty-five seconds left. When Mogilny directed the puck to Tomáš Kaberle in the slot, he faked a shot, then took one. Four Leafs descended on the net. It played out for me in slow motion: Roberts and Tucker wrestling for position, the mayhem of so many bodies in one scrum. A rebound popped loose. I tapped the puck into the net.

Twenty seconds on the clock. Tie game.

Overtime was frenetic. The team played with guts. Cujo made save after save. Carolina scored in a scramble to end the game, and the series. In hindsight, I can call up so many snapshots of the heartbreak. The sight of Cujo seated in his crease, then standing and collecting his stick as the Hurricanes celebrated next to him. A guy who had won us many games over the run, who'd shut out this team to keep us in it. The deflation on the bench. Not just the players, but the trainers, too. The equipment staff. The drop in Quinn's shoulders at the loss, when he was never one to show much emotion. And worst of all, the fans filing out of the building, dejected.

The next morning, Mike Walton showed up at my house, the house he'd recently helped me buy when I was ready to move out of the condo. Over eight years, Mike had gotten into the habit of calling me before every game to pump me up. He'd yell my nickname, Weedsy, into the phone until his voice grew hoarse. He also had a way of turning up soon after a tough loss, often with breakfast in tow. Usually, he made a point of steering the conversation away from hockey, but that morning, he knew I'd want to talk it out.

The disappointment was intense. I could feel it in my bones. My head hurt. Mike had two Stanley Cup rings, but he'd been through his share of tough losses, too. He'd spent a stint in the 1970s playing for Minnesota in the World Hockey Association before it merged with the NHL. That morning, he told me of the time his team was favored to win the playoffs, but lost the semifinal series at home. After the game, Mike couldn't get the disappointed fans out of his head, so he left the locker room without taking off his gear and walked to his car. He drove, pads and skates still on, to a sports bar nearby and walked inside. Obviously, the bar patrons took instant notice of him—that year, he'd been the highest scorer on the team, and suddenly he was standing among them at the bar like an apparition, still in his gear. Mike waved to the bartender.

"Drinks are on me," he yelled.

The crowd, he claimed, erupted.

We laughed hard at that story. I loved Mike's stories. I knew it would take a long time for this disappointment to wear off. But that morning, my disappointment was briefly replaced by gratitude for a friend and former player who showed up because he knew I could use a friendly face.

31

Locker Room

After twelve years in Canada, I'd started to feel a shift in my sense of home. When I returned to Sweden for the summer, I sometimes felt like a visitor in my birth country. I'd catch myself referring to Toronto as home. If my parents noticed, they never bothered to correct me. I loved my annual fishing trips with my brothers and cousins, my time at the cottage and my training at Bosön. Especially after a long and disappointing playoff run, it could be a relief to cross the ocean. Still, I missed Toronto.

From Sweden, I could still follow the team's summer news. In early July, Cujo signed with Detroit—given all he'd done for us in the playoffs, that was a tough one to take. Ed Belfour was coming to Toronto. It was clear Pat Quinn wasn't interested in making a ton of changes, instead trying to shore the group he had.

One contract holdout? Tie Domi.

By 2002, I was the longest-serving Maple Leaf and Tie was a very close second. We'd been teammates for eight seasons. We'd played hundreds of games and eight playoff series together. When the Carolina Hurricanes went on to lose to Detroit in the Stanley Cup Final, Tie was the first person to call me. He was a popular guy with the fans. Teams were interested, but the Leafs wanted him back. *I* wanted him back. When we met up in person in Toronto, I told him how much I wanted him to sign.

His mother had told him the same thing. So, he did. After a summer of nursing the loss to Carolina, I returned for training camp ready and optimistic. As the exhibition season started in September, Quinn hinted he was willing to try something he hadn't done the previous year: pairing Alexander Mogilny and me together on a line. Ever since he joined the team, I'd been waiting for the opportunity to play with Mogilny. I was excited to be getting the chance.

I rarely spoke up to Quinn about line combinations, and he rarely asked me. But Quinn would have known that I wanted the chance to play with Mogilny. There was mention of putting Darcy Tucker on the other wing. One afternoon, Quinn called me into his office.

"Do you really want Tie on your line?" he asked me.

I frowned, puzzled. "What?"

"Tie says you've been asking to have him moved up to play on the first line with you."

No. I hadn't suggested such a thing. I told Quinn as much. He just shook his head and put his reading glasses back on to go back to his papers. You can't blame Tie for trying.

If our first game of the season was any indication, the combination would work. With Darcy Tucker on the far wing, the three of us combined for eleven points in a 6–0 win over Pittsburgh. That offense continued through the first month, with Mogilny—Almo, as the boys called him—and me averaging over a point a game each. Yet, as Quinn was quick to point out, our offensive prowess was so aggressive that we weren't holding up on the defensive end. We might be scoring and assisting on each other's goals, but if the team is still losing, the experiment can't be declared a success.

Weeks into the season, we were near the bottom of the Eastern Conference. The team was playing scared. We lacked confidence. In late October, after tying a Saturday night game in Montreal, I hustled back to Toronto to attend an Argonauts football game where boxer Muhammad Ali was to be honored at halftime. While presenting Ali with a Leafs jersey, I felt a profound sense of honor and gratitude. It was a timely reminder of what mattered, and how lucky I was to be living my dream, playing a sport I loved.

I had a job to do. Two of the previous season's biggest character players were Curtis Joseph and Gary Roberts. Now, Cujo was a Red Wing and Gary was recovering from shoulder surgery and wasn't expected back until the new year. I saw my role as helping the new guys settle in and setting an example for them on how to train, practice and treat the team staff. I needed to double down on that.

We were in a hole, but the season was young. All we needed to do was start climbing. In November, we beat the Kings in overtime after blowing a 3–0 lead, and things eased up. We only lost a handful of games over the next six weeks. The guys gelled and settled in.

Where Cujo had been a leading presence, our new goalie, Ed Belfour, was more solitary, a great guy who happened to be ultra-competitive. Belfour was in his fifteenth season in the league and a Stanley Cup winner. It's hard to stress just how intense he was when it came to game-readiness. He was always the first guy to get to the rink and the last one to leave, sometimes staying as long as the equipment guys. Once that fall, after a loss at the Air Canada Centre, Ed asked equipment staff Brian Papineau and Scott McKay to help him take apart his glove because he felt he wasn't catching the puck as cleanly as he should. It must have been around 10:30 p.m., but Ed was ready to stay until 1 a.m. until he felt the glove had been dismantled and put back together exactly how he needed it to be. No matter how many times they had to fiddle with that glove, Pappy wasn't going to refuse Belfour's requests, even if I once caught him sneaking off to the laundry room to curse before composing himself and returning to the locker room with a smile on his face.

I loved having guys like Belfour in the room with me. Over ten years earlier, I'd learned from Guy Lafleur that, on a hockey team, traits like focus and intensity were often contagious.

By the start of 2003, we'd climbed to fifth place in the Eastern Conference, and I got a call from a familiar voice in Sweden. My coach from twenty years ago in Djurgården, Mats Hamnarbäck, would be visiting Toronto in February. Would I be okay if he came to watch a few of my games at the Air Canada Centre?

For Canadian or American NHL players, having family or former coaches attend a game wasn't unusual. Guys on my team often had loved ones in the stands. Sometimes, I'd hear of players on opposing teams, born and raised in or near Toronto, who'd had to secure a hundred tickets for everyone wanting to watch their homecoming game at the ACC. Over the years, my parents and brothers had made lots of trips to Quebec, and then to Toronto. But having Coach Mats in the stands felt like a special privilege.

The morning after he landed, Mats and I had breakfast at the King Edward Hotel. After retiring from volunteer coaching, Mats settled into life as the CEO of a major Swedish bank. He was married, with two teenagers. It seemed remarkable that I was now older than he'd been while he was my coach. During our meal, he was surprised by the number of people who stopped and waved at me. In Toronto, fans were respectful, but if they saw me, they almost always greeted me with a wave or a "Hey Mats!" The waiter knew who I was and asked for an autograph. For a reserved guy, I think Mats enjoyed the attention.

Coach Mats caught two of my games, and we won both. After

the second game, I invited him into the locker room to meet the team. The group was buoyant, especially thrilled to have Gary Roberts back in the lineup after his return from shoulder surgery. Mats made the rounds of the room. He wore the biggest smile. I gave him a signed jersey.

As we said our goodbyes, Mats looked at me squarely.

"I'm very proud of you," he said.

I nodded. I'd turned thirty-two a week earlier, but his words still meant the world.

We won the balance of our February games. Gary Roberts was a fitness nut and wanted the team dialed in on workouts and nutrition. I learned in my first two years playing with him that Gary *really* liked to work out. After being forced to retire in 1996 because of injuries, he'd resurrected his career against all odds by following a rigorous fitness and nutrition regimen. Along with the team's new strength and conditioning coach, Matt Nichol, Gary was always on hand to remind the team the value of dry-land training.

At my age, I didn't need to be reminded. I understood the need to train thanks to my intense Bosön summers with Leif Larsson. I'd already missed a few games in late 2002 when a bad hit strained my shoulder. Getting older in hockey reveals an indisputable truth: if I didn't stay strong, injuries would come more easily and linger longer.

One day, after a morning skate, I was stretching with Matt Nichol when Alex Mogilny walked by. He was showered and dressed in a suit.

"Almo," I called to him. "You should work with Nichol here. I'm telling you, ten minutes a day with Matty and you could play for another ten years."

"Why the fuck would I want to do that?" he said.

Matt and I laughed. That was Mogilny's nature. To some of

the guys on the team, he was an enigma. He was arguably the most talented guy any of us had ever played with, but he was not interested in training off-ice with us. He'd had his fair share of this as a young player in Russia. Most NHLers knew the stories of the Soviet-era Red Army team and its notorious training regimen. Kids living far away from their families, lifting weights and running six miles a day when they weren't on the ice.

Once, in the training gym, Mogilny walked by to find Roberts, Nichol and me training with some of the other guys. We were working on dead lifts and squat presses. Roberts invited him to join. Mogilny shot us an amused look.

"Boys," he said, gesturing to the weights, "I was doing this when I was fourteen."

The group started ribbing him. Enough so that Mogilny lined up under the squat press. He was wearing dress pants and shoes. Nichol had three hundred pounds on the bar.

"You might want to warm up first," Roberts suggested.

Almo didn't need a warm-up. He took position under the bar, lifted it off the rack, then proceeded to squat in perfect form, knees bent all the way—"ass to grass," as Nichol would say—then lifted it cleanly and stepped back to set it down on the rack. He wiped his hands and smiled at us.

"Satisfied?" he said.

Indeed we were. That season, for the first time since I joined the Leafs in 1994, Mogilny topped me to lead the team in scoring. Workouts or not, the team was incredibly lucky to have him, and I loved playing with him on my wing.

The older I got, the faster the game felt, too. I did a good job of adjusting my play to account for the speed and relative youth of my opponents. I could still absorb a hit and occasionally even throw a hard one. In March 2003, we set out on a three-game Western Canadian road trip that culminated in a Saturday night game in Vancouver. Halfway through the second period, with the game tied, 0–0, Canucks enforcer Brad May picked up the puck in our end and circled off the boards to the net. I lined him up for an open-ice hit. He didn't see me coming. He didn't square up or brace for impact. When my shoulder hit his shoulder, his neck snapped back and I heard a strange crunching sound.

May hit the ice and play stopped. He wasn't moving.

His teammates signaled for help. I hovered for a moment, watching him, looking for a flicker of movement. He was on his stomach, face to the side, his legs bent so that his skates pointed up. An unnatural position. When the trainers got to him, I skated to the Leafs bench and waited.

That cracking sound was not good.

More doctors arrived. The stands were quiet. Eventually, May was removed on a stretcher as the fans chanted his name. He gestured with a wave I was incredibly relieved to see. No call was made on the play.

"Clean hit, Mats," one of my teammates said. "It happens."

It *does* happen. Still, it was a terrible feeling watching that stretcher leave the ice. I figured at some point over the next few shifts, a Vancouver player would drop the gloves for a fight. That's the code when someone gets hurt. Whoever caused the injury is lined up for a fight. But that never happened. At the end of the second period, we scored the only goal of the game and finished with a 1–0 win.

In the room, a trainer told me that May had been taken to the hospital for tests. I asked someone to find me his phone number. When we got back to Toronto, I wrote him a text. He was gracious in his response and let me know he was going to be fine. I was grateful for that.

Most players with long careers will face a few close calls over the years—injuries that could have been a lot worse, given an inch or two. Dr. Leith Douglas used to joke that he was the one guy on staff everyone hoped would have little work to do.

But three weeks after that May hit, I found myself on Dr. Douglas's table again.

"Mats," he said, again chewing the gum, just like he'd done when he fished that piece of puck out of my forehead two years earlier. "Jesus, Mats. This one really is bad. Not good."

It was our next-to-last game of the season. Early in the first period, Leafs defenseman Ric Jackman picked up the puck in a scrum in front of our net and tried to clear it. I was in the way. That is, my *teeth* were in the way. The puck hit me hard in the mouth. I spun around at the impact, then dropped to my hands and knees. I spit out a mix of saliva, blood and tooth shards. I could see the alarmed look on trainer Brent Smith's face when he got to me. I skated off the ice with a hand to my mouth.

The pain was staggering.

"Not good," Dr. Douglas repeated. "Keep your girlfriend out of here, Mats. She does *not* want to see this. You're lucky I'm a plastic surgeon."

Not exactly reassuring. From the table, we could hear the roar of the home crowd.

"Goal," Dr. Douglas said, eyes focused on his task. "At least we're winning."

I could feel the tug of the stitches. The team dentist, Dr. Hawryluk, was in the room, too, taking orders from Dr. Douglas.

"Teeth are jammed right up there," Dr. Douglas continued, never at a loss for words. "Never seen the likes of it. Hammered right up into your gums. Stay still, Mats. If I don't get this just right, you'll have a harelip for the rest of your life."

No teeth and a harelip? Great.

It took two days of dental surgery and a handful of root canals to salvage what teeth they could and replace the ones they couldn't.

Two pucks to the face in my career, and both were friendly fire. By 2003, the internet was enough of a thing that my family in Sweden could access photos and even video of my games. Ever since I lost my two front teeth in the first grade, my mother had a thing about my teeth. It took more than a few phone calls to assure her I'd be fine.

I was back on the ice a few days later. A short break at season's end meant I'd be ready for the first playoff game against Philadelphia. After my first skate, Quinn called me into his office and took stock of my injury.

"The only tooth I ever lost was on the bench," he said. "In Sweden, funny enough."

He recounted a story of coaching a series of exhibition games with Team Canada in preparation for the 1986 World Championships. At a game in Stockholm, one of his players tried to clear the puck, but shot it right at the bench. The players all ducked, but Pat had his head in his notes. He needed forty stitches to repair the damage.

"I had to get a root canal, too," he added. "But mine was done in Moscow."

That year, our playoff hopes were dashed in a seven-game first-round battle against the Flyers that included three games that went into overtime. When the series ended, the media focus fell on the dynamics in the room. It was hard to face those questions. I could answer to my own performance and hold myself accountable. But team dynamics were a complicated topic. Our group had a lot of strong personalities. In a few years, we'd gone from being one of the younger teams in the league to one of the oldest. A lot of guys had long careers behind them and ideas about what worked and what didn't. Sometimes, that led to some friction in the room. In season, we might spend more time with the team than we did with our families. You're under pressure and in tight quarters for long stretches, and it can get intense. With a lot of veterans and strong personalities in the room, it was a challenging time to be captain.

It took me a few days to decide to get on a plane bound for Finland to join Team Sweden at the World Championships. I knew that the best way for me to shake off the disappointment was to play more hockey, to get back on the ice.

In the quarterfinals, we faced off against Finland, another chapter in the longstanding rivalry between neighbors. I knew my family was watching at home, grateful for a game I was playing in their own time zone.

We lost the gold medal game to Canada in overtime. Despite that loss, the week was a good reset. I flew to Stockholm to train and spend time with my family. Earlier in the year, it was announced that part of the Leafs' 2003–04 training camp and exhibition schedule would be played in Finland and Sweden, including a game in September 2003 against my old team, Djurgårdens IF. The whole Maple Leafs roster and staff would be flying to Stockholm in just a few months. I was thrilled. I'd never imagined getting the chance to play with my NHL team in front of a home crowd in Sweden. I'd need to buy a lot of tickets.

32

Norrtälje

We lined up for the pregame ceremony at Stockholm's Globen Arena. My former Swedish team faced us on the opposite blue line. When the announcer said my name, the crowd stood. On the bench, a few guys tapped me with their sticks. They knew how much it meant to me to be playing in my hometown.

We beat Djurgårdens IF, 9–2. A few days earlier, we'd played Jokerit in Helsinki, and our final game of the series would be against Färjestad, a team from central Sweden. The Leafs' strength coach, Matt Nichol, had flown across a few weeks early to train with me. I got to show him Bosön and introduce him to Leif Larsson. Matt and Leif had a lot in common. They were two guys whose life work was finding ways to diversify their training methods. Leif was still searching for the ideal workouts, and Matt was busy perfecting a magical concoction to help replenish his athletes—a potion he would eventually formulate into the popular drink BioSteel. It was fun watching them share trade secrets.

Having my Toronto teammates with me in Stockholm felt like my two faraway and cherished worlds were finally colliding. I felt humbled by the honor. A lot of the guys had never been to

Europe, or even to a country that spoke another language. My dad got a huge kick out of being around the team and watching them practice at the same rink he'd driven me to hundreds and hundreds of times. The day before our exhibition game, I went to the gym at the Hovet Arena with a few of my teammates. Wade Belak opted to work out in just shorts and running shoes. He was an incredibly strong guy, and his arms and back were covered in tattoos—the word *mayhem* down one forearm. Just as we were getting started, the Djurgårdens IF players showed up for a workout of their own. Wade greeted them warmly, then got back to lifting weights. I couldn't help but notice our opponents' eyes widen as they watched Belak in action. I knew right then we'd win the game the next day.

After one of our practices, I arranged for the team to board a bus and spend the day at my cottage in Norrtälje. Between Stockholm and the open Baltic Sea is a vast archipelago, made up of twenty-four thousand islands and inlets. The water is cold and brackish—not quite fresh, not quite salty. It looks a lot like the northern parts of Ontario where we sometimes held training camps, where some of the guys on my team would have spent parts of their summers growing up.

On the bus, the mood was happy. It felt like we were headed to summer camp together. The trip from Stockholm was only an hour, but the bus driver was too slow for a lot of the guys' tastes. Owen Nolan, my former Nordiques teammate acquired at the previous trade deadline by Quinn, made his way to the front of the bus.

"Pretty sure a dog just stopped to piss on our tire," he said, smiling.

The driver looked at him, confused. The jokes continued the entire ride. At the cottage, I'd hired a chef to prepare a lunch spread. It was mid-September and the days were cooler, but still long. We all sat on the deck as we ate lunch, looking at the sun shining off the water. After lunch, my brother Per offered to take Owen Nolan and Eddie Belfour fishing on the boat.

I have a small sauna, and we crammed more guys into it than would fit. Then we sprinted out and down the dock, leaping into the frigid Baltic Sea. I don't know if the guys were expecting the warmer lake water of Ontario, but as soon as the cannonballs landed, there was a frantic race to the ladder. Tie Domi, Gary Roberts and Wade Belak all reached it at the same time. Imagine three NHL players, about six hundred pounds of muscle combined, wrangling and splashing to climb out first. The ladder ripped right off the dock under their weight, flopping the three of them back into the sea. The guys were in tears of laughter.

I remember so many details. Per pulled the boat back up to the dock, and Nolan and Belfour showed off the pike they'd caught. Bryan Marchment took a chair and found a quiet spot to sit solo on the other side of the boathouse. He stayed there for a long time, staring out at the water, sitting in peace. After Marchment had spent fifteen years playing on several different teams, the Leafs signed him to a one-year deal that July. He was born in Toronto and played his early days in Belleville, on the shores of Lake Ontario. Now here he was, an ocean away, looking out at the Baltic Sea.

Bryan told me that the rocky landscape and blue water reminded him of home. He said it was so peaceful, and he understood why I loved it here so much. No one had iPhones then. I regret that we didn't take pictures that day, especially because Wade Belak and Bryan Marchment both died way too young in the years that followed. Two decades later, I can still stand in the same spot and see it all perfectly, a bunch of big guys leaping into the Baltic Sea like happy kids.

The bus ride home was quieter. On the flight back to Toronto, there was a real sense of hope about the upcoming season. Not just among the players, but among the coaches and management, too. John Ferguson Jr. had been hired as the new general manager. After his playoff health scares, Pat Quinn returned from summer in great shape. He'd relinquished the GM role to focus on coaching, and even proclaimed that he'd given up cigars.

For me, I was entering this new year not just as a veteran player, but as a veteran captain. This would be my seventh season with the *C* on my jersey. I felt settled in the role. I'd never morphed into a vocal or loud guy, so I wanted to continue leading by example. You can't control everything that happens in a game, so I wanted to lead in what I could control: my training regimen, my warm-up routine, my pregame focus and, as Börje had taught me, my diplomacy with the media. After our time at the cottage, I really understood that my role was also about building respect and strong bonds between the players. I wanted to ensure we spent some downtime together now and then and learned about each other's lives.

Beyond the players, some of my most important relationships were with the trainers and equipment staff. When you're lucky enough to spend several seasons on the same team, you learn that these guys are the true veterans. Brian Papineau, the head equipment manager, started with the Leafs in 1988 and continued with them for well over a decade after I eventually retired. He started his career cutting sticks for the likes of Börje Salming and ended it doing the same for Auston Matthews. These guys saw it all. You could argue that for all the scouts in the league, GMs would be better off asking a team's equipment staff if they wanted an unvarnished take on a given player.

For our home opener in October 2003, just like every other game, Brian would have been at the arena for at least eight hours by the time the players started arriving around four o'clock. Equipment staff Scott McKay and Bobby Hastings would be there, too, sharpening skates to every guy's preferred radius and edge, doing laundry, putting name bars on the jerseys, organizing the room so that everyone's stall was in perfect order. On the bench during games, they worked at lightning speed to fix broken laces or helmets. If a player cracked his stick during a shift, they'd swiftly pull his specific backup and pass it to him like a baton as he skated by the bench at full speed.

After a game, we'd peel off our gear and debrief with the coaches as the fans streamed out and the arena cleaners got to work. I would almost always take questions from the media. Then we'd retreat to the locker room for bit of quiet before showering and meeting up with any family or friends who'd attended the game.

The laundry would pile up in the bins around the room: towels, undershirts, socks. Down the hall was a laundry room where the equipment guys would stay busy for several more hours. It had two industrial washing machines and three dryers, a folding table and a hanging rack. There was a bar fridge and an old love seat jammed in the corner.

Somehow, I got in the habit of heading to the laundry room after our games. As soon as I sat on that old couch, a pressure valve seemed to release. Other players would join, sometimes trainers, too, pulling up chairs and grabbing a soda or beer from the fridge. We got to calling it the Cotton Club. It was the least fancy club on earth. Even former Leafs back in Toronto with the visiting teams would stop by to say hi before catching their bus out of the ACC. Brian would hand them a permanent marker to sign a wall that was covered in the scribbled names of Leafs old and new.

Brian, Scott and Bobby would be in and out, always working and cracking jokes. It was an unspoken rule that, while the Cotton Club was convened, we'd talk about anything else but hockey. Like I said, teammates didn't need to be best friends, but it was nice to keep track of what was going on in each other's lives. There'd be plenty of time for hockey talk after we'd showered and stepped back out into the world.

It took us a few weeks to find our footing in that 2003–04 season. Once we did, we became hard to defeat. After a short winless streak in mid-November, we beat Vancouver back to back in a home-and-home series. We just kept winning. We didn't lose a game in regulation time until after Christmas, nearly five weeks later. There was a certain magic about this group, a real sense of possibility and hope. Nearly every guy in the lineup was on track for more than twenty points.

In January, in a game against the Nashville Predators, my stick broke in the second period. Like a careless kid, I tossed the broken shaft over the boards and it landed in the stands. As soon as it left my hand, I couldn't believe what I'd done. No one was hurt, and I took the only suspension of my career over it. A couple of days later, I served that one-game suspension during a 7–1 routing by Ottawa. When Daniel Alfredsson's stick snapped partway through the game, he fake-tossed it before dropping the broken end. Quinn did not like that, and neither did Darcy Tucker. They expressed their discontent on the bench. Knowing Daniel, I thought it was kind of funny. A few months later, we returned the favor by hammering Ottawa, 6–0.

It was the perfect setup for the playoffs. We finished the season near the top of the Eastern Conference. Our first-round opponents were none other than the Ottawa Senators. For the fourth year, the Battle of Ontario was set, and for the fourth time, we won. They hated us in Ottawa. It was good to be hated. Round 2 was set. We'd get a rematch against Philadelphia.

33

Matchups

By winning their first-round series against New Jersey in five games, the Philadelphia Flyers had bought themselves three more days of rest than us. And it showed. We scored one paltry goal in each of the first two games, digging ourselves into a 2–0 series deficit. Two wins at home scrabbled us back to Philly with the series tied, where Ed Belfour paid the price for our terrible defensive effort, getting pulled in a 7–2 loss.

We flew back to Toronto for another must-win Game 6 on Tuesday, May 4. After the Monday skate, I went to Pat Quinn's office. Something had been bothering me all series. I knocked, and Pat called me in. He wore his blue coach's tracksuit, his reading glasses perched on his nose as they always were. When we first moved into the Air Canada Centre in 1999, Pat Quinn used to smoke cigars in this office. The Toronto Raptors complained the smoke was drifting into their locker room, so the arena invested in an expensive ventilation system. Now, Quinn didn't smoke anymore. Or drink much. His office smelled fresh.

I sat down.

"I'd like to talk to you about matchups," I said.

"Oh?" Quinn responded, looking up.

"You don't play me against Primeau."

I meant Keith Primeau, Philadelphia's strong center. Primeau and I had a lot in common. We were the same age. We were both centermen, both six foot five, both our team's captain. I'd played against him in dozens of games. I knew I could take him on. But every time Primeau hit the ice, Quinn pulled me off in favor of center Nik Antropov, the only player on the Leafs who was bigger than me.

"I know I can take him," I continued.

Quinn nodded. He was always willing to hear me out, even if he didn't heed my words.

Here was my logic: Despite missing four games of the Ottawa series, I was leading the Leafs in playoff points and feeling great. Flyers coach Ken Hitchcock seemed to figure out early in the series that Quinn was taking me off whenever Primeau was on. It became simple math to Hitchcock, an easy problem to solve. If he wanted me off the ice, he just had to put Primeau on.

We talked it through. In hindsight, it was a conversation I wish I'd had years earlier.

That night, in the room, we all understood the stakes. Before the warm-up, Quinn came in and circled the perimeter. Sometimes, just his presence was enough to rally us. He was an incredibly commanding guy. The best orator. He always had a whiteboard and a marker in hand. Sometimes he got so animated that the marker would end up in stains on his hands and face.

The Flyers came out too strong, and by the end of the second period, we were losing, 2–0. In the locker room, Quinn's calm, his silence, felt almost worse than anger. I was the captain and we needed a spark. If I wanted his vote of confidence, now was the time to earn it.

In the opening minute of the third period, I joined a scrum

near the boards at center ice with Flyers Branko Radivojevič and Marcus Ragnarsson. Gary Roberts was in the mix, too, the four of us jostling for control of the puck. I shoved Radivojevič. He pushed back, and I shoved some more. The puck broke free and slid to the Flyers defenseman, but Radivojevič and I were still at it. In a parting blow, I pulled his helmet off and yanked his jersey up.

We skated away. No call.

Radivojevič muttered something to me en route to the bench. I punched him in the head and he dropped a little too easily. The referee wagged a finger at me and pointed to the box. In the playoffs, referees tend to put their whistles away. But even in the third period of a do-or-die game, there were only so many sins he could overlook.

Just like in Game 6 in 2002, I spent the early minutes of the third period in the box, my heart in my throat. But my teammates handled it—Philly registered only one shot in the power play. We even got a shorthanded scoring chance. When I emerged from the box two minutes later, the game felt different.

The fans were chanting. Tentatively at first, then louder.

Go Leafs go!

We played a hard eight minutes. The refs were just watching now, too. Barring something catastrophic, there would be no more calls in the game. Around the nine-minute mark, Darcy Tucker exchanged blows and words with Philly enforcer Donald Brashear, who iced the puck. Skating back to take the face-off in their zone, I glanced up at the clock.

Eleven minutes left.

I squared up at the face-off dot against Keith Primeau. Quinn had left me on. I knew Primeau was too strong for me to sweep a clean win to my defensemen. All I needed was to create enough room. Just enough. I leaned hard into Primeau and shoveled the puck a foot or two behind me. Always ready, Mogilny stepped off the wing and picked it up, tapping it cleanly back to defenseman Karel Pilař, making his playoff debut as an injury replacement. I turned, still tangling with Primeau, and watched Pilař wind up for a slap shot.

For a split second, everything went mute. Like the fans, I could only watch. I even felt Primeau relax against me. He could only watch, too. Pilar's shot sliced through traffic and rang off the crossbar, then down. In. Goal.

The crowd exploded. The five of us gathered to celebrate. Pilař looked stunned. We patted him on the head. If you're going to score your first career playoff goal, the third period of a must-win playoff game is as good a time as any to do it.

Ten minutes left. The crowd was awake, on our side. Loud.

Momentum is a funny thing in hockey. A strange variable. It can swing on a penalty call, on the energy of the crowd, on a well-timed body check. On a goal that puts you back in contention. It can change everything, and in the dying minutes of this 2–1 game, it was now on our side.

We played hard, grinding. We exchanged chance after chance. Goalies Robert Esche and Ed Belfour made extraordinary saves. The crowd was deafening.

Five minutes left.

Mogilny and Roberts flew up the ice. I was a few strides behind them, the third man. There wasn't a lot of room; the Flyers had set a defensive box—three guys to get through. After two seasons with him on my wing, I'd learned that if a path to the net existed, Mogilny would find it. Once in the zone, Mogilny slid the puck over to Roberts, who caught it, then rammed into the Flyers defenseman and the goalie.

Four white-and-orange jerseys scrambled to protect their net. But none of them saw the puck pop out of the chaos and into the low slot. I got there first and shot it. Flyers goalie Esche hadn't recovered from the scrum. The puck sailed over his shoulder and hit the back of the net. I threw my arms up.

Tie game: 2–2.

Overtime played out in a wild blur. Chances at one end, then the other. Esche made a diving save, Belfour a swinging glove catch. The crowd was electric. Eight minutes in, Flyers forward Sami Kapanen took a monster hit on the boards from Darcy Tucker. He lay stunned, nearly out cold, but the refs didn't blow their whistles and the Flyers were all but shorthanded until Kapanen could crawl off the ice. The Flyers bench rose to their feet, screaming. Their coach, Ken Hitchcock, went red-faced with rage. No call.

I picked up the puck at the Flyers blue line and stepped into their zone. Two Flyers sandwiched me and a stick shot up and clipped me in the mouth. High stick. My head flew back at the impact, my glove up to catch the blood.

No call. Of course there was no call. In overtime, that's the game.

The puck was off my stick and over to Flyers defenseman Joni Pitkanen, who saw Jeremy Roenick racing up an open wing. Momentum can change in a split second, too. On a two-on-one, Roenick opted to shoot. The puck sailed over Belfour's shoulder. In.

The crowd deflated instantly. The Flyers collected in a wild huddle along the far boards. I skated to the bench, where my teammates sat in silence.

In that moment, you want to scream at yourself, at your teammates, at the referees, at anyone. But nothing you might say or do mattered. It washed over me that the game was over. The series was over, and so was our season.

The loss wasn't just about the overtime goal or about calls made or missed. It was about going down 2–0 in the series in the first place, about catching up by winning two games, then handing the Flyers an embarrassingly decisive 7–2 victory in Game 5. It's about every game over the course of the season that led to this playoff matchup. Every post you hit, every pass you missed and every penalty you took.

I lined up with my teammates to shake hands with the Flyers. You could feel the energy emanating from them. They were headed to Tampa to face the Lightning in the conference finals, and we were headed home.

The locker room was dead quiet. After a muted speech by Quinn, I found my way to the bathtubs. In the coming days, news headlines would be variations of the same theme. "Devastating blow to the Leafs organization." "A team built to win and still loses." I'd sit for interviews and share my thoughts on what happened. Our new GM, John Ferguson Jr., and the management would soon reconvene to start wheeling and dealing. The NHLPA—the players' union—and the NHL would continue talks to avoid another lockout like the one we endured in 1994.

I would handle all that. Face it. Show up to the media scrums. Be accountable. But right after that game, I just wanted to be alone. I sat in that bathtub, surprised at the tears welling up. I'd lost games before. I'd lost playoff series before. So, why the tears now? Why did this cut right to the bone? I guess because I was thirty-three years old. The clock on my career was ticking. I loved this city and this team with all my heart. I wanted nothing more than to win for us, for the team. But I desperately wanted to win for the fans, too. For the city. We'd come close yet again, but close wasn't good enough.

Letting them down was unbearable.

34

Superstition

It felt like I'd been hit by a train. I entered the zone at top speed and released a quick shot. I watched it sail to the net, then rebound off the goalie. Only then did I see him. A train, coming at me at full speed. Too late. I was in the air, weightless. Legs up, arms waving. Then the ice hit me. Or I hit the ice. Full speed to a dead stop in a split second. I lay on my stomach, ready to puke. My lungs couldn't pull in a breath. The whistle rang and a linesman skated over.

"Mats?"

The voice sounded far away. I rose to my knees.

"Mats. Can you hear me?"

Along the board, a fight had broken out. After the hit, my teammate Chad Kilger dropped the gloves. Kilger was about to take seventeen minutes in penalties because Atlanta Thrashers defenseman Garnet Exelby had blown me up on open ice.

My teammates helped me off the ice and the trainers took me through the tunnel to be looked over by the doctors.

"What day is it?" the doctor asked me.

"February," I said. "Seventh? Two thousand six."

He nodded. Correct.

"Where are you?"

"We're playing the Thrashers. No score." I pause. "Yet."

He checked my eyes and ears and moved my neck side to side. Once the nausea passed, I was fine. This wasn't a concussion. I'd had the wind knocked out of me, which, in the moment, as your entire body weight is crashing into the hard ice, isn't great either.

"I'm fine," I insisted.

The doctor wanted me to wait a few minutes before returning to the bench.

I hate waiting. By that Tuesday night in February 2006, nearly two years had passed since our 2004 playoff loss against Philadelphia. Not that we had played much hockey in that stretch. Shortly after the 2003–04 season ended, it was clear that the NHLPA and the league were at a total impasse. The collective bargaining agreement hammered out during the 1994 lockout was about to expire, with many of the same issues lingering, the main one being a salary cap. This time, the league had made it clear they weren't going to budge on that point.

When negotiations stalled, the NHL and its owners announced a lockout in mid-September of 2004. After a few weeks of waiting, I returned to Sweden. In December, with no end in sight, Tie called me and asked if I'd play with a team called the Worldstars. A ragtag group of NHL players was being cobbled together to face off against club teams from around Europe. We'd play ten games in two weeks, everywhere from Latvia to Norway to Russia to Poland, and of course in Sweden. It wasn't exactly well organized—more than once, we found ourselves seated on the airplane with our equipment piled up in the first few rows—but it was fun to be on the ice. During that tournament, Daniel Alfredsson and I talked about renting houses in Marbella, a beach town in the south of Spain, with his new wife and my girlfriend at the time, Tina.

That plan came together. I understood that I was lucky and extremely privileged. If the season wasn't going to happen, the south of Spain wasn't a bad place to spend the winter. Still, I missed hockey. I was anxious. Alfredsson was a hard worker and pushed me to keep up my fitness. Never one to slack, Gary Roberts even flew over to train with us for a week. On the surface, it was a good break from the ice to let my body rest. I understood that, given my salary leading up to the lockout, I was in a far better position than many of my fellow pros to withstand the strain of not getting paid for the lockout's duration. In early February 2005, league commissioner Gary Bettman announced that the season would be cancelled entirely if a deal wasn't reached by mid-month.

The final stretch of negotiations took place on the same weekend as my thirty-fourth birthday. I was now nearly a decade older than most of my teammates. A few days later, when both sides rejected the last-ditch offers, the season was cancelled.

When the lockout finally ended in July 2005 and I returned to Toronto, there were some major changes to the Leafs roster. Mogilny and Roberts were gone, to New Jersey and Florida respectively. After years of courting him, Quinn finally landed Eric Lindros on a one-year deal. But many of my longtime teammates were still in the lineup with me—Bryan McCabe, Tomáš Kaberle, Wade Belak and the guy who'd been at my side pretty much from day one, Tie Domi.

My 2005–06 season started with a break. Literally, a break. In the first two minutes of our opening game against Ottawa, a Senators player tried to clear the puck and it hit me in the face. I kneeled down on the ice and realized I had no vision in my left eye. It was black. I panicked, blinking hard to try to summon my sight back. By the time the trainer got to me, my heart was racing.

When the game ended in a tie, the teams faced off in the league's first-ever game-deciding shootout. But I wasn't there to take one of the shots. I was at the hospital, undergoing tests to ensure that my eye wasn't permanently damaged. Thankfully, it wasn't. I didn't need surgery, but my orbital bone was broken. My left eye would sit permanently lower, I'd lose 10 percent of my vision, and I'd be out for at least a month. It was the scariest injury of my career. The team fared well without me, and we played our way to Christmas with a strong winning record. While I only managed four goals in my first twenty games back, I began to find my groove in January.

In early 2006, the Leafs went on the longest winless skid we'd had in years, and by far the longest under Pat Quinn's tenure as coach. We only won one game in four weeks. By the time we got to Atlanta in early February, the winning record we'd built up in the fall had been decimated, and we were hovering around .500.

Now it was February 7, 2006, and I was in the dressing room, getting checked over by the trainers and doctor while a teammate fought on my behalf. We heard the roar of the Air Canada Centre crowd. The Leafs had just gone up 1–0 on the Thrashers.

"I'm fine," I said. "Ready to go."

In those days, there was no real concussion protocol in the league. If you seemed out of sorts after a hit or punch to the head, they'd give you a once-over, then leave it up to you to decide whether you could keep playing. The trainers and doctors were diligent and protective of their players, but the league policies were what they were. They couldn't force us to sit out. I took a seat back on the bench less than five minutes after the hit, then picked up an assist on a goal by Darcy Tucker on my first shift. Across the ice, Kilger still sat in the penalty box, where he'd spend the rest of the period as his punishment for dropping his gloves after Exelby hit me. Domi slid down the bench and edged up beside me.

"I'm good," I said to him. "I'm fine."

"He's fucking lucky I wasn't on the ice."

I nodded. A few minutes later, Tie took a roughing penalty. That hit I took from Exelby? I couldn't imagine exacting that kind of damage on my body night after night. At the time, it seemed lost on a lot of the fighting devotees that the personal and professional costs to fighting might be high. Concussions could end a player's career, and often did.

I had a lot of respect for the guys on my team who took on the enforcer role. For all his bluster, Tie was a sensitive guy. Wade Belak was famous in our group for his antics and good humor. He could deliver zingers faster than anyone else in the locker room. And he never spared himself as the target of his elaborate jokes. One training camp, he roped me into filming a spoof segment for Sportsnet where he pretended to be vying for a spot on the team's first line.

We won the game against the Thrashers that night, but then lost two in a row in a home-and-home with the Rangers. It felt like lucky timing that the league was breaking for just over two weeks so that players, including me and five of my Leaf teammates, could catch a flight to Italy for the 2006 Turin Olympic Games. Quinn was headed over, too, repeating his role as Team Canada's head coach.

The Swedish roster had a lot of the same faces that had lined our national newspapers in 2002 after the crushing loss to Belarus, including Nicklas Lidström and Daniel Alfredsson. But we had some new faces, too. Peter Forsberg was healthy. The twin phenoms Daniel and Henrik Sedin were en route from Vancouver. In 2003, at the World Championships, I'd been introduced to a young third-string goalie who'd been impenetrable in our practices. I remembered him in particular because of the tailored suits he wore. That same goalie had beaten us only a few days earlier with the Rangers, having earned the role of starter halfway through his rookie season. In Turin, Henrik Lundqvist would be Sweden's starter, too.

I hashed over the Leafs season on the flight across the Atlantic. I'd scored eleven goals, well below my usual pace. My contract had one more year left after this one, and talks were already underway about a possible extension. I loved Toronto. I wanted to win, but I specifically wanted to win in Toronto. The prospect of missing the playoffs weighed on me. I knew what happened when teams started missing the playoffs. It often led to slash and burn. I was the captain, and it was up to me to turn things around. I'd take this time in Turin to find my game again. By the time I was back in Toronto, I would need to be firing on all cylinders.

The Olympic Village in Turin was a comfortable cluster of colorful apartment buildings. My roommate was my former teammate Fredrik Modin. By then, my parents were both retired. They loved watching me play. But after flying to Nagano in 1998 and Salt Lake City in 2002, only to watch Sweden fail to make the medal round, they'd decided to skip Turin.

"I don't want to bring bad luck," my father said over the phone.

"You can fly here if we make the semifinals," I said.

"Maybe," he said. "If."

Tommy Sundin hadn't changed.

Despite my family sitting it out, I still had a bit of an entourage with me. One of the Leafs' chiropractors, Mark Scappaticci, made the trip. At thirty-five, I had every intention of visiting him daily to ensure I stayed loose. Excited for the chance to take in both an Olympic Games and some sights in Italy, and because he knew I'd need my pregame calls, Mike Walton made the trip, too. On every game day, even in Turin, I'd wake up after my nap and the phone would ring.

"Weedsy," Mike would holler. "Weedsy! Fly! Shoot the puck! Fly!"

He'd go on like that for fifteen to twenty seconds, then he'd hang up.

We won our first game against Kazakhstan handily, but then lost, 5–0, to the Russians, who themselves had lost a shocker the night before to Slovakia. After getting past Latvia and the United States, we lost, 3–0, to Slovakia, the only team in our group to emerge from the round-robin undefeated. When we beat Switzerland in the quarterfinals, and then the Czech Republic in the semis, I called my parents. In two days, we'd be facing off against the undefeated Finnish team for gold.

"You could fly here tomorrow," I said.

"Sweden is doing better with me at home," Tommy said. "I'll stay and watch from here."

You can't argue with superstition.

35

A Gold Medal

For the most part, Sweden and Finland make good neighbors. They are political friends and allies. Our languages are recognized in each other's countries. You could even argue that the Finns, given their long border with Russia, have historically offered Swedes a buffer against invasion. Our countries' bond goes way back.

That bond dies fast when it comes to sport, and especially when it comes to hockey. In my twenty years of playing with the Swedish national team, I'd faced off against Finland many times. It was always a worthy fight. We beat them in 1992 and 1998 at the World Championships, but then lost to them in the round-robin at the 1998 Nagano Olympics. I'd done my share of damage in those many games, enough so that I somehow got the nickname *Suomen kaataja*—"The Killer of Finns." One year, a Helsinki newspaper published a list of the ten most hated people in Finland. The first two on the list were murderers, and seven were a combination of war villains and criminals. I was third on the list.

My mother got hold of the clipping. She found the idea that an entire country hated her son immensely amusing. Weirdly, it made her proud. When I suggested it was a morbid thing to put in the scrapbook she kept on my career, she said she planned to keep it for as long as she lived.

For all its success in hockey, Finland had never won an Olympic gold medal. In 2006, the Finns were coming into the final game undefeated and having outscored their opponents 27–5. After our crushing loss to Belarus in 2002, we Swedes knew all too well that anything could happen in a single hockey game. In an interview before the match, our coach, Bengt-Åke Gustafsson, who'd been my linemate when Sweden won the World Championships in 1991, stated the obvious:

"All we have to do is get one goal and not allow any," he said.

Easier said than done. As we prepared for the big match, a quote by Swedish writer August Strindberg stuck with me: "By attempting the impossible, we reach the highest degree of what's possible." All we had to do was go into the game believing we could win.

The gold medal game was held on a Sunday afternoon at the Palasport Olimpico. Both teams filed to the ice through the same tunnel, shoulder to shoulder. In Italy, there was no home-crowd favorite. Each of our countries had an equal number of fans in the stands. Finland scored first. Early in the second period, we tied it up, then took a lead ten minutes later. But the Finns tied it again within less than two minutes.

Between periods, the locker room was quiet. I sat, trying to take it all in. Barely two weeks earlier, I'd turned thirty-five. I knew this was my last Olympic Games. We'd fallen short against the best in the world in Nagano and Salt Lake City. This was my last chance to win gold. I wasn't nervous, but I could feel the weight of the moment.

The Zamboni completed its laps. With a player in the box each, we would start the third period at four-on-four. Coach Gustafsson yelled out the names of the players he wanted on the ice: Forsberg and me up front, Lidström and Niklas Kronwall on defense. Lundqvist, of course, in net. The guys were calm, ready. We walked the tunnel to take the ice, and time stopped. The crowd felt far away. I knew my parents were watching at home, like millions of others. Twenty years after my first game under the lights at TV-pucken, the audience and high stakes still gave me access to strength and energy I could feel from head to toe. Hockey takes over, and I exist only in the moment. Everything else is meaningless.

I lined up against Finnish star Saku Koivu to take the third period's opening face-off. As our sticks crossed to win the draw, his snapped. He had no choice but to drop it and skate to the bench, which in a four-on-four situation gave Forsberg a bit more room on the wing. Forsberg carried the puck wide into the Finnish zone, then dropped it to me as I trailed. I took three strides, then dropped the puck again, this time to Lidström, who was just about to cross into the zone. Lidström connected on a perfect one-timer that whizzed over the goalie's shoulder. Less than ten seconds into the period, it was 3–2.

For nineteen minutes, we battled. The game went end to end and back. We'd pressure them, then the momentum would swing and they'd pressure us. With ninety seconds left, the Finns pulled their goalie.

A handful of times in my hockey career, I experienced moments of such intensity and focus, moments where I stood on the ice, or on the bench with my teammates, knowing they were feeling the same thing. The Finnish team came firing at us. With twenty seconds left, Lundqvist made a pad save that bounced the puck to the far side of the net and onto the stick of Finnish center Olli Jokinen. For a split second, a tying goal appeared a certainty. When Jokinen fired, Lundqvist did splits across his crease, catching the puck on his blocker. Everyone on our bench was convinced the puck had gone into the net. It felt like a miracle to see it pop loose. The Finns regrouped quickly and dropped the puck back to their blue line. When their defenseman released his shot, our forward Henrik Zetterberg dove sideways to block it, face-first into the line of fire. The puck bounced off him and crossed the blue line into the neutral zone.

The game was over.

This had always been the dream: winning gold while wearing the blue and yellow of my country, the *tre kronor* emblem on my chest. As we gathered in celebration at the net, I felt an overwhelming sense of pride and relief. Someone handed me a Swedish flag, and I skated a lap with it lifted over my head. We lined up to receive our medals. I kissed mine. As the anthem played, I closed my eyes to soak it in. Winning felt different than I thought it would. I was surprised at how little it was about the victory itself. It wasn't the same joy or elation I got from scoring a key goal or celebrating a big win. It was a profound sense of satisfaction and accomplishment. It was about what I now shared with the players standing next to me and the battle we'd fought as a team to get here, to secure Sweden's first-ever win in a true best-on-best tournament. I also knew, at the final whistle, that it would be the last time I'd don the *tre kronor* jersey that I'd dreamed my whole childhood of wearing.

In the hours that followed, the Swedish team had a choice to make. It was Sunday, February 26, and many of us had NHL games scheduled on the coming Tuesday. Was forty-eight hours enough time to fly to Stockholm for a celebration, then get back to North America to rejoin our teams? Probably not, but we would do it anyway. Always good for a celebration, Mike Walton planned to make the detour to Sweden, too.

The team scrambled together a chartered flight. As we crossed over the Baltic Sea into Swedish airspace, the captain came over the intercom. He told us that two JAS 39 Gripen fighter jets would soon flank the plane and guide us home. From the window seats, we could actually see the fighter pilots giving us their thumbs-up.

At Arlanda Airport, fire trucks surrounded the plane and doused us in celebration. Our family and friends awaited us at arrivals.

"I'll meet you downtown," Mike Walton said as we gathered our bags.

"No chance, Mike," I said. "You're taking the bus with the team."

We were escorted to the city center by several police cars. It finally sank in on that bus trip. This dream I'd had since I was a kid, a dream I had carried with me my whole life, had been fulfilled. I'd won a championship in the biggest best-on-best hockey tournament in the world. Years later, I'd find a photograph of that bus trip. What struck me was how happy everyone looked. I loved seeing Mike Walton in the middle of it all, smiling ear to ear, taking it all in.

We arrived at Medborgarplatsen, the square in central Stockholm, to thousands and thousands of fans. When the anthem played, we sang and swayed along. It was a magical day, a dream come true. I'd lost my grandfathers Sture in 1998 and Sven in 2002. I was grateful that my grandmothers, Marta and Elsa, were still alive to see their grandson take home the gold. My parents got to see and touch the medal, even if they hadn't been there to watch me win it.

Then, just like that, I was on an airplane with my Leafs teammate, goalie Mikael Tellqvist. We were headed straight home to face the Capitals on Tuesday. The pace of the turnaround was breakneck, but as a professional, you learn to shake off jet lag and play your game. We lost that night, and the next two games, too. After the third loss, to the Senators, I sat alone in the dressing room at the Air Canada Centre after the rest of my teammates had showered and left. Only six days earlier, I'd skated around the ice with a Swedish flag. Somehow, that high made the dejection of these losses feel especially low. Unless something changed quickly, we would miss the playoffs again. Every win mattered, and I needed to press hard to help secure them.

It was a time of change in my personal life, too. Per came from Sweden to live with me at my house in Forest Hill. I was now single, and it was too big for one person. I loved having Per around. He came to every hockey game and cheered for us with so much enthusiasm. He took English lessons and looked after the house when I was on the road. Because they didn't get to visit all the time, when they were with me in Toronto, my family served as a good reminder of how fortunate I was to have the life and career I did. Per's enthusiasm was infectious.

The end of our season was better than its start. After losing to the Senators, we only lost five games in regulation and gained real ground in the standings. There was a pattern, too. If I got a point in the game, we seemed to win. I scored twenty goals in the next twenty-two games and logged six points in an April game against the Florida Panthers. Still, we missed the playoffs by only two points. The late push didn't forgive the losses we'd racked up earlier in the season. Take back one or two of those losses along the way, and we'd have squeezed in. It wasn't enough.

The first casualty of our failure to make the playoffs was Pat Quinn. In his seven years behind the bench, the Leafs had never missed the playoffs until now. Very few coaches and captains last as long as Pat and I did. We'd had our ups and downs over the years, but I was truly sorry to see him go.

Before I left for Sweden at the end of the season, an inaccurate news story surfaced that I was planning to sell my house. Reporters started calling my agent, J. P. Barry, who had to assure them I wasn't plotting my departure. It was the opposite. My contract was for another year, and I had no intention or desire to leave Toronto.

In May 2006, a reporter from Toronto flew to Sweden to speak to me, going so far as to drive to Norrtälje and ask the locals where he might find my cottage. He never tracked me down. I wasn't avoiding him because I had something to hide; I felt no acrimony for the Toronto media. They were doing their job, and most of them clearly loved hockey. Their work fueled an interest in the team that kept the lights on at the ACC. I understood that and tried my best to be available to them. But I believed in boundaries, too. If I started speaking to reporters when they literally showed up on my front lawn, more of them would start doing the same.

36

Josephine

Even in the spring months, Sweden's win at the Olympics lingered in the air. I worked out, fished, spent time with my family and friends. In June, a group of friends made plans to attend a party for Midsommar, Sweden's most celebrated holiday after Christmas. It marks the solstice, the longest day of the year and a time for family holidays and gatherings. Even in Stockholm, the sun rises before 4 a.m. and sets sometime after 10 p.m.

Midsommar parties are all about dancing and singing. I'd been there for an hour before I spotted a beautiful woman across the room. She had flowers in her hair. Eventually, one of her friends noticed me looking at her. They pointed my way, and I could see her shaking her head. Her friend must have recognized me, but clearly she didn't.

I finally approached her and introduced myself. Her name was Josephine Johansson. The way Josephine tells it, I kissed her almost right away, but I think I was a little more reserved. She'd grown up in Nora, a small town three hours due west of Stockholm, and was studying to be a *gymnasieskola* teacher at the university in Uppsala. Josephine had an uncle who'd played Division 1 hockey in Sweden. She knew who I was, but barely. The NHL was a foreign concept to Josephine, as far away as the city of Toronto itself. She'd never been to Canada before, and only vaguely knew of the Toronto Maple Leafs.

At the end of the night, Josephine recited her number to me, then joked that I wouldn't remember it. I made sure that I did. There was no way I was going to forget it. Soon, we were together all the time. We were lucky that the early stage of our relationship was formed in a bubble of our family and friends.

Sometime in those early days, Josephine asked if I wanted to go with her to Nora to attend a birthday party and meet some of her family. Josephine's dad was named Mats, too. He and her mother, Birgïtta, were welcoming and warm. Whereas I was the middle of three brothers, Josephine was the oldest and had two sisters and one brother. Swedes are renowned for remaining reserved no matter who is in their company, so even if many at the party had surely watched the gold medal game months earlier, no one made a big deal about my presence.

One man did approach me expectantly. Josephine introduced him as Göran, her uncle, married to her mother's younger sister. He wasn't more than a decade older than me, and he looked familiar.

"We were opponents once," Göran said. "Many years ago."

I shook my head, unable to properly place him.

"I played for Tyresö when you were playing for Nacka. You slashed me hard in the arm."

Yes! Göran Lundqvist. Seventeen years ago, in the months before I was drafted, I'd slashed him in the arm and spent the rest of the game skating at top speed to avoid his retribution. At that party in Nora, we recounted the game in detail and laughed about it. He told me he'd followed my career after that, and with my successes, the slash that had riled him up in the game became a good story to tell. I could recall the scene just as clearly as he did. For all my seasons in the NHL, those formative years when I played at Djurgårdens IF and Nacka remained fresh in my memory.

At some point later that summer, a photographer snapped a picture of Josephine and me at a café, the sort of long-lens paparazzi shot you have no idea is being taken. It was printed in newspapers in Sweden and Canada, giving Josephine some taste of what life could be like when you represented the Toronto Maple Leafs. When it came time to return to Toronto in August, Josephine and I made plans for her to visit me as soon as possible. In more ways than one, it felt like a fresh start.

In October, a handful of games into the season, Josephine was in the stands at the Air Canada Centre as I squared up to take the defensive zone face-off against Calgary's captain, Jarome Iglinla. We were in overtime, and the Leafs were shorthanded on a three-on-four penalty kill. The Toronto crowd was loud and on their feet, even more so than normal for a Saturday night in October. They were cheering for a win, but also for me. I'd already scored two goals in the 4–4 tie, which happened to be the 498th and 499th of my career. For an NHL player, the five-hundred-goal milestone is one very few reach. No Maple Leaf, or Swede, had ever done it.

The puck tucked behind me on the draw and a Flames winger collected it. Calgary took their power-play formation, and my teammates Hal Gill and Tomáš Kaberle took up our kill mode. When their winger fumbled a pass on the boards, I pounced and emerged into the neutral zone with the puck. Gill, a defenseman who stood six foot nine with his skates on, joined me in the rush. He straddled the blue line to stay onside as I entered the Calgary zone. I could have dumped the puck, but I had a lane to the net. I wound up and took a slap shot that sailed over Miikka Kiprusoff's shoulder.

The Air Canada Centre goal horn started blaring and didn't stop. The crowd boomed. I could almost picture a guy somewhere in the rafters pressing that horn button as the Leafs poured off the bench to celebrate, and still holding the button down as my teammates gathered around me in a group hug. As we huddled, I could see the guys' faces beaming happy. It overwhelmed me.

In the locker room, our new coach, Paul Maurice, congratulated me, too. Someone pulled me back onto the ice to accept the crowd's applause after being named the game's first star. I stepped out to such a roar that it took me aback. I clapped up at the fans, looking toward the highest seats at all the blue and white jerseys, families and friends who'd come to this game to watch their beloved team. Somewhere in that crowd was Mike Walton. My brother Per was there, too, watching with a friend he'd made at the beer league he played in when he was in Toronto along with many other family and friends. I lingered out there longer than I normally would. By the time I stepped back onto the bench, there was no hiding the tears in my eyes.

It was October 14, 2006. Our season was off to a decent start. At training camp a month earlier, the first thing Maurice did as our new coach was call a dinner meeting with the two alternate captains, Bryan McCabe and Tomáš Kaberle, and me. It was immediately clear that Maurice was a different coach than Pat Quinn. Only four years older than me, he had young kids at home. With little penchant for oration or long speeches, he focused more on his bench and players and building accountability. Four years earlier, he'd coached the underdog Carolina Hurricanes past us to the Stanley Cup Final. At dinner, he told us that, as the team leaders, he expected us to set the tone on and off the ice. He wanted us to build a strong work ethic in the group by setting the pace in practice and during workouts.

"I want to see you fly," he said. "If you lead and work as hard as you can, the rest of the team will follow."

The Leafs had started to get younger and younger—at thirty-five, I was now the oldest player on the regular roster. Tie Domi had retired, and Ed Belfour and Eric Lindros moved on. By Christmas, injuries led to more call-ups. We reached the January 2007 All-Star break with a narrow path to a playoff berth. You could feel the pressure starting to build. The previous year, we'd missed the playoffs by only two points. No one wanted to repeat that.

Josephine was commuting between Sweden and Canada as she finished her studies. Needless to say, that's a long trip. The first time she came to visit me, I picked her up at the airport, then we drove to my house in Forest Hill. Josephine's eyes widened as we pulled into the driveway. I realized we'd never talked about my house. I had to explain to her that I didn't have an apartment in it; I lived in the whole house.

Mike Walton took Josephine under his wing. He started bringing her to games and introducing her to the players' families. She bonded with the other wives and girlfriends, so much so that they'd have dinner parties and sleepovers while we were away on road trips. Josephine was always a good antidote to the pressures of the game, too. If we lost or tied, she'd still spend the car ride home talking over her favorite plays and the fun she'd had, or what a good game I'd played. I didn't have the heart to tell her that losses are never good games.

That year, my family visited Toronto again for the holidays. Over my entire career, my parents hadn't missed a Christmas in Canada. While they were no longer in the business of smuggling contraband animal products, they did make trips to Ikea to secure large quantities of Swedish meatballs. Gone were the days of my dad scolding me for my messy apartment or poor choice of pets when I bought that fish tank. I lived in a house now, and my family could plainly see that I loved the life I'd built in Toronto.

There was the sense that my time in the NHL was winding down. Few players in the league make it to thirty-five, and it was even more rare to play until age forty. My contract was up that spring. With a team as young as ours, I wanted to stay and play that veteran role. My dad and I talked about it a lot that visit. Even in my thirties, my parents' focus remained on my well-being. Was I happy? Healthy? Did I want to stay? I felt that I did. My loyalty was to the team and to winning with them.

In early 2007, Josephine moved to Toronto. One day, I got back from a team skate around noon and found her in the living room, holding something small and furry.

"What is that?" I said. "Is that a hamster?"

"It's a dog," she said.

She set the tiny dog on the carpet. Her name was Coco, and she was small enough to fit in the cupped palms of my hands. Coco must have sensed that she had to win me over, because she worked hard at it. By spring, I went out almost every day for walks around my neighborhood with my tiny white dog. It happened often that an SUV would pull up alongside me and comment. One guy rolled down his window and slowed.

"Mats," he said, "you're the captain of the Maple Leafs. You need a bigger dog."

He was too late. Coco had already wormed her way in.

We wavered in and out of playoff contention for most of the year. We were inconsistent. In January 2007, we beat the Bruins, 10–2, in Boston on strong performances by young guys like Alex Steen and Matt Stajan in our highest-scoring game in eight years. Then, two weeks later, Leafs fans booed us when we lost at home, 6–1, to the Canucks.

Despite a strong March, by April we found ourselves in a painfully tight race for the final playoff spots. It came down to us, the

Islanders and Tampa Bay. We'd had Tampa's number all season, but the Islanders were tough. A win against them on April 5 would all but secure us that final playoff seat. We left for New York acutely aware of what was on the line.

My childhood coach, Mats Hamnarbäck, had planned a trip to New York from Sweden for his fiftieth birthday to coincide with the game. He was due to arrive the morning of, but when his flight was delayed by eight hours, he had to insist to his wife that they head straight to the arena from the airport, even if the game had already started. I'd left tickets for him in my name, and he was afforded a bit more leeway by the arena staff for showing up after puck drop with luggage.

We went into that game ahead of the Islanders in the standings, and then lost. It was an inexcusable loss. I didn't get to see Coach Mats after the game. We had our marching orders to go directly to the team bus en route to catch a flight home. Our playoff hopes now rested on winning our final game and the Islanders losing theirs. There is nothing worse than having your fate in another team's hands. We won, but so did they. For the second year in a row, we were going home in mid-April.

It was a bitter end.

In the aftermath, the team takes stock, and each player does, too. To account for the injuries to our roster, I'd played more minutes every night than I had in a decade, and I'd averaged a point per game. I felt I'd done a reasonably good job of adjusting my game to the fact that I wasn't as fast as I'd been in 1995. Still, we hadn't made the playoffs yet again. As Josephine and I readied to return to Sweden and visit our families, I was also preparing for a contract negotiation that I knew would look and feel different than it had with our winning team in 2001.

I knew I wanted to stay. I believed the team could win. We

weren't at the bottom—two years in a row, we'd missed the play-offs by one game in a close race. We were a few pieces away from being truly competitive.

That said, you could sense a tide was turning.

Near the end of April, a Toronto sports columnist published a story indicating that I'd seen a specialist and would require hip surgery. The columnist claimed to have seen my medical records. The timing of the story was very convenient, given that J. P. Barry was in tight talks to extend my contract for another season. It also wasn't true. I had seen a specialist at the team's request, which is a normal procedure if a contract is being negotiated. This doctor was considered the best orthopedic surgeon in the business, so Barry suggested I fly to connect with him in Italy while he attended a conference there. The doctor told me that he noted deterioration in line with my age, and if I continued to play hockey professionally, I might one day require hip surgery, but certainly not imminently.

On a call, J. P. and I discussed the timing of the story. When it came to signing bigger contracts, every Maple Leaf GM had to answer to the board of directors at Maple Leaf Sports & Entertainment. J. P. suggested that it certainly wasn't the first time this columnist had landed scoops about players where the calls from his anonymous source appeared to be coming from inside the house.

I wasn't a conspiracy theorist by nature, and I definitely knew better than to read the news, but here, the truth did matter to me. I was healthy. Should we sign an extension, I'd live up to my end of the bargain and arrive for camp in August in excellent shape. J. P. and I agreed that I would visit a specialist in Sweden to reinforce my health status, and back in Canada, he would talk to the media and address the rumors.

A month later, we reached an agreement on a one-year extension that lowered my earnings, with the understanding that the team would use the salary cap space we were freeing up to help bring in those missing pieces. In hindsight, I could have been more vocal earlier in my career about what the team needed, or used it as a bargaining chip with previous contracts. I did give my opinion when asked, but never believed it was my job to make personnel decisions. I wasn't the president, or the GM, or a member of the board of directors or the coach. I was—for at least one more season—the captain.

37

One More Year

I arrived at the Bosön campus in Stockholm and went straight to Leif Larsson's office. He asked me about my season and how my body had fared throughout it. Then he asked me what I wanted out of the summer of 2007.

"I want to arrive at training camp in the best shape of my life," I said.

Leif nodded. These words were music to his ears. Over the coming days and weeks, he designed a program for me that focused on strength and elasticity, on building up my speed. For two hours a day, six days a week, I was at his mercy. Mostly, I trained on my own, with a keen awareness of how much younger most of the athletes at Bosön now were. When I'd first trained here, I was half my current age. Leif pushed me to my limit, then designed a warm-up and cooldown program I could take home with me to Toronto.

In August, I returned to Toronto. At my medical screening, the team doctors called me "durable," a good word for a thirty-six-year-old. Even before the season started, some reporters were already asking questions about the contract extension. Why had

I only agreed to one year? Did I want to go play elsewhere? What about the no-trade clause?

I made it all as brief and clear as I could: I'd signed a shorter deal because I was almost thirty-seven. The no-trade clause was an extension of my contract and a show of commitment to the city even in a time of reduced certainty. What I really wanted to talk about was the upcoming season and my hopes for a turnaround, my commitment to the team and its youthful roster.

In the room, the younger guys sat next to me. That year, one of them was Alex Steen. Like me, Steen had long straddled life between Canada and Sweden. His dad was a Swedish NHL star, and Alex grew up mostly in Winnipeg. I wanted him, and the other young guys, to understand that even the longest hockey careers are ultimately short, and right from the start you need to build the routines that will maximize your time in the league. Once upon a time, I was a new player sitting close to Guy Lafleur, and now I'd been the captain of the Maple Leafs for a decade. I was the oldest guy on the team by two years. In 2007, I could in theory take face-offs against players born the year I was drafted. I was also only a handful of goals or assists away from becoming the Maple Leafs' all-time points leader. Career milestones have a way of leading you to the door. When there's no doubt that most of your career is in the rearview mirror, the stakes feel higher.

We played the Islanders in our fifth game of the season. We wanted retribution for their part in bouncing us from the playoffs the previous spring, and we got it in the form of an 8–1 win. I'd entered the game tied with Darryl Sittler for most goals and points as a Leaf. In the third period, when we were already up 6–1, I fired a pass meant for Jason Blake, but it went off an Islander's skate and into the net. The fans cheered as I skated to the bench. Brian Papineau was the first to greet me with a smile. My teammates gathered around me and patted my head. When Andy Frost's voice boomed over the public-address system to announce the goal, he announced the milestones, too. I smiled and wiped the sweat from my brow. Nine hundred and seventeen points wearing blue and white, the team's new all-time leader. It's hard to let that sink in when there's still a game to finish.

We got to the end of October with five wins in thirteen games. After a tough 7–1 Monday night loss to Washington at the ACC, I woke up groggy and was lying in bed, dwelling on the game, when I heard the ping of the security system and the opening and closing of my front door. It was 10 a.m., so Josephine had already gotten up and left to run errands.

"Weedsy!" he called from the hallway. "Get up!"

It was Mike Walton. I threw on track pants and a T-shirt and headed downstairs. He was already in the kitchen, making coffee. He wore a suit with dress shoes and no socks—never socks, no matter what time of year. He'd always had a key to my house, and he had this way of showing up the morning after tough losses. He looked around the kitchen.

"You need some flowers in this house, Mats. How many times have I told you that? Brighten the place up." He paused, pouring our coffees. "I can't believe the traffic in this city. People get their driver's licenses out of cereal boxes these days."

We laughed. I felt immediately better. Never one to show up empty-handed, Mike brought bagels. As we ate, I told him that Josephine and I were throwing a costume party for the team. Halloween was the next day, and we didn't have another game for two days after that. Sometimes, when the rink becomes a stressful place to be, the team needs to let loose together. Anytime I brought up team antics, Mike had a story from his playing days that bested anything our group would do.

"Make sure no one goes near the pool in their costumes," he said.

I smiled and waited for more. When he played for the Leafs, there was one practice arena out of town where they'd have to change in a room shared with the facility's swimming pool. Still fully dressed in their hockey gear, the Leafs team ended up on the pool deck. Someone dared Mike to jump in.

"I'll do one better," he said.

As Mike told it, he climbed to a higher diving board and leapt into the pool. When he surfaced, his teammates cheered wildly. But Mike hadn't accounted for how heavy his hockey equipment would get when wet, and he had to be fished out before he sank to the bottom.

"Moral of the story," Mike said, "no jumping in the pool."

I laughed again. Mike tidied up, then got organized to leave. He had real estate showings that day. He reminded me that he planned to take Josephine to dinner before our next game and asked about my family's visit at Christmas. I'm not sure if I ever took the time to tell Mike just how much it meant to me that he showed up like that, as if some sixth sense was telling him I could use a friend. On his way out the door, he'd always holler one more command my way.

"Go outside, Mats!" he'd scream. "Get some fresh air."

Josephine and I spent the next day getting organized for the party. Times were different in 2007. The iPhone had just been introduced, and social media was not much of a thing. It was a time when two-hundred-pound NHL players could put on a French maid's costume or a blond Dolly Parton wig and not worry about the pictures showing up online. Darcy Tucker dressed up as a surgeon and Tomáš Kaberle as a pilot. The trainers and equipment guys all came, too. Wade Belak brought a beer bong to that Halloween party that, two years later, I would ship home to Sweden and send to my cottage, where I still have it.

The morning after the Halloween party, I came downstairs to

find the hardwood floor covered in strange dots, like little pock-marks. I bent to run my finger over one of them, scratching my head. Josephine was the one to point out the culprit.

"High heels," she said.

I had to have the floors entirely redone. It was a great team party, but an expensive one in the end.

By Christmas, we were two points out of a playoff spot in a tight four-way race. You could feel the tension growing and the specula-tion starting. Was it time to clean house and start a rebuild? I didn't think so, and neither did Paul Maurice. There was talent in our group. We had the ability to win. I was on track for a one-hundred-point season and working harder off the ice than I ever had.

In early January of 2008, we boarded a plane for a three-game West Coast road trip. MLSE president Richard Peddie was on the trip with us, which was unusual. The president almost never traveled with the team. It was clear to us that we needed to col-lect at least three points on the road trip to stay in contention. Since Anaheim and San Jose were two of the best teams in the league, they would be a tough go, but the LA Kings were at the very bottom of the standings. In the first game, Anaheim beat us, 5–0.

For Toronto players, the once-a-year trip to California was always a highlight. Most hockey players grew up in small towns and always spent a lot of time at the rink. Very few had been to places like Los Angeles before making the NHL. Toronto had a lot of famous fans who liked to attend our games against the Kings wearing their retro Leafs jerseys.

Before the game, I sat in my stall. The guys were focused, but as I looked around, I wondered if they had a similar sense of urgency. It was as though I could see dark clouds in the distance, and they nudged a little closer every time we lost a game. A few more losses and they'd be right overhead.

No matter how much we needed the win, by the end of the first period, we were losing, 4–0.

In hockey, a team might surmount a 4–0 deficit once in a season. As the buzzer went, I was the last guy off the ice. Something bubbled up inside of me as I walked the tunnel to the dressing room. I heard chatter. Given our terrible performance, I'd have expected rage and swearing, or frustrated silence. My entire career, I'd prided myself on being the calm and stoic player and leader. But now I was enraged.

The trainers had set up a folding table in the middle of the room. As I stepped in, Matt Nichol was busy lining up cups of his custom sports drink, along with gum and tape, mindful of staying out of our way as we started to hash out the period.

He didn't see me coming when I marched into the room, lifted my stick over my head and brought it down full force onto the table. Matt jumped out of the way as cups and tape flew everywhere. I hit the table again and it buckled. *Now* you could hear a pin drop.

Whatever I said next came from the gut. I can't remember my exact words. I was angrier than I'd ever been. Not just about this must-win game we were now poised to lose. I went on about the privilege of wearing the Leafs jersey, how lucky we were to be sitting in that room, dressed in blue and white. I was disgusted by our lack of effort and character. We needed to do better and earn the logo on our chests.

No one could look me in the eye. My voice even cracked a few times. It wasn't a performance, though.

We came out stronger in the second period, but the lead was insurmountable. Two nights later, we lost to San Jose. The rumblings were getting louder. Reporters started asking me more bluntly. I had a no-trade clause and had been vehement that I would never waive it, but that didn't stop my name from coming up. Over the next week, we cobbled together a three-game winning streak to keep our playoff hopes alive. I still believed in our team, for better or for worse. All we needed to do was make the playoffs; then we could go on a run as the underdogs. But my belief alone wasn't enough.

At the end of January, John Ferguson Jr. was fired as GM and replaced in the interim by a familiar face known for his willingness to make the toughest calls: Cliff Fletcher.

38

The No-Trade Clause

The bus pulled up to the hotel in Raleigh, North Carolina. It was cool and rainy out. As I walked into the hotel lobby, Cliff Fletcher intercepted me.

"Do you have a minute, Mats?"

I told him that I'd check in and get settled, then come find him in his room. On the elevator, a bad feeling started creeping in. I unlocked my room, set my suitcase on the floor and hung my suit in the closet. I stood there for a moment, taking a deep breath.

Cliff's room was down the hall. I knocked and he opened the door right away. Cliff was always so well put together, older of course than he'd been when he picked me up at the Toronto airport nearly fourteen years earlier, but his silver hair was still perfect, and he was still dressed in an impeccable suit and tie. He was a consummate professional, too. Even in moments of tension like this one, he could lead with humor. His hotel room had a seating area. We sat facing each other.

"Do you want a drink?" he asked me.

"No, thanks, I'm good."

Cliff leaned back and paused, eyes out the window.

"Tell me, Mats. Do you want to be traded to another team?"

As soon as he said the words, I had to stop myself from standing up and walking out the door. Slamming it behind me. Instead, I just looked at him.

"I think we can still make the playoffs, Cliff. We aren't that far out."

He nodded, but said nothing.

"I don't want to play for another team," I continued. "My job is here. I want to finish it here."

Cliff's expression was serious.

"You could win a Stanley Cup," he said. "There are contenders that want you."

He kept talking, bringing up teams who'd shown interest, but I couldn't focus on his words. My mind raced. Of course I wanted to win a Stanley Cup. I could have screamed: *I want to win the Stanley Cup in Toronto! What part of that don't you understand?* I wanted to build, not destroy. I believed we had the chance. I was having my best season in years. I didn't want it wasted. Cliff was still talking.

"In the end, Mats, it's up to you."

"I've said it for months, Cliff. I want to stay here."

He was gracious. I stood and we shook hands. As I walked the hall back to my room, I was hit with a profound wave of emptiness. I really did believe this team had a chance. But if the management didn't and were set on starting over, I wanted to be the one to lead the rebuild. No one except the equipment guys had been around as long as me. I'd outlived many GMs and coaches. I understood what it took to play in a market like Toronto. I'd been loyal, even in the best years of my career, when the team was faltering. I knew hockey was a business and it was naive to expect loyalty in return, but when I got back to my room, I sat on the bed and put my head in my hands.

Over the coming days, it emerged in the news that I'd been asked to waive my no-trade clause and refused. Fletcher took a lot of questions and repeated every time that I was within my rights to do so. Still, it seemed that the narrative in the media was being shaped in a certain way: that I was too comfortable in Toronto, too selfish to put my team before myself.

By then, I had a cordial and respectful relationship with many of the Toronto reporters. A few days after my meeting with Cliff, a scrum formed around me as I left the rink after a morning skate. Usually, my answers were stock and simple. That day, I struggled to make sense of their questions.

"Does it bother you that some people might blame you for holding the Leafs back?" one reporter asked. "Or say that you're too comfortable here?"

My no-trade clause wasn't about being comfortable. In February 2008, Toronto was not a comfortable place for me to be. The stress was waking me up at night. Yes, I loved Toronto and didn't want to leave. But uprooting would have been relatively simple for Josephine and me. While we had just become engaged, we weren't married yet and didn't have kids.

Even as the weight of the scrutiny bore down on me, I maintained that it was not the time to throw in the towel and begin a rebuild. All we had to do was make the playoffs. As I'd learned so many times in my career, as I'd come to believe many years earlier, the NHL playoffs are a reset button. The variables change. It becomes more about grit and injuries and timing. It becomes about team chemistry and selflessness. About playing for the guy sitting next to you in the room. Not many fans know that NHL players stop getting paid in the middle of April, whether their team makes the playoffs or not. At that point, the only reward is the grind, the climb to the ultimate prize. Players put their bodies on the line in bigger ways. The teams that finish at the top of the standings in the regular season almost never survive the climb and win the Cup. Why couldn't that be us?

In early February, as we were set to face off against the Detroit Red Wings in Toronto, my friend Nicklas Lidström, now the Wings' captain, told the media that he would love to see me traded to his team. It was a conversation Nicklas and I had had behind closed doors, too. By then, Lidström had won the Cup three times and had never missed the playoffs in his seventeen-year career with Detroit. He understood better than anyone what it takes to win, and he believed I could be part of another winning Red Wings effort. Just like I told Cliff, and the media, I told Lidström I didn't want to be a rental player. I didn't want to devote my season to one team, then leave it for another. Maybe that loyalty was misplaced, but as the captain, it was how I truly felt.

All the talk of rebuilding took the wind out of our sails, and our playoff hopes began to fade. I was waking up at night more and more frequently. I felt betrayed by the narrative. I know it was naive to believe, as I did, that the strength of my season to date might translate into management wanting to keep me around. They were clearly focused instead on my value in the trade market. As the player with the longest tenure and the team's all-time leading scorer, I also believed that I'd earned the right to have the no-trade clause we'd agreed on honored. It was one thing for us to revisit it behind closed doors once management felt the season was not salvageable. The reports in the media so closely resembled their talking points that it was clear those doors weren't closed very tightly.

At one point, I joked to the media that they should ask Cliff Fletcher to call off the moving trucks he had lined up at my house. Given Cliff's rousing speech to us in 1996, it felt like a full-circle moment. In the end, I understood that management were only doing their job. In late February, I released a statement to the media that I hoped would end the conversation once and for all. I reiterated that I'd never believed in the concept of a rental player, and that my commitment was to the Maple Leafs.

Despite all this, my on-ice production increased. I had something to prove. The 2007–08 season was shaping up to be one of the best of my career. After a morning skate in Philadelphia in early March, just as the focus appeared to finally be waning, I asked trainer Matt Nichol to skip the bus and walk with me from the training rink to the hotel.

"That's four miles," Matt said.

But he agreed, and we walked. I think I just needed to vent. Matt was always a good listener. We talked about the past few months. I truly believed that my experience and leadership would have value in the rebuild, and felt let down at being portrayed as selfish. Matt expressed frustration at how I'd been treated. He understood that trying to fight a narrative built up by the Toronto media was a losing battle. All you could do was stay true to what you believed in.

"I love this city and this team," I told him. "I want to win here. Why does that make me the bad guy?"

"It doesn't," Matt said.

I was grateful he was willing to hear me out. It's what I needed in that moment. We didn't make the playoffs that year, and a groin injury kept me from playing the team's final games. On July 1, I would become a free agent. As I packed my stall at the Air Canada Centre, it felt impossible that my fourteen years in Toronto would end there, just like that. I believed that my career was over. The circus around the trade deadline and our disappointing finish had been painful. I wasn't sure I could come back from it and find the will to play again. Years later, Matt reminded me what I'd said to him on our walk in Philadelphia.

"I'm the captain," I'd said. "And the captain is supposed to go down with the ship."

39

Vancouver

I pulled into the driveway of my cottage in Norrtälje, then wandered to the dock. For May, it was a warm and sunny day, and the Baltic Sea was calm. I needed the solitude and the silence. When Josephine and I first landed in Stockholm after the end of the 2007–08 season, I'd been wracked with anxiety. Back in Canada, I knew that my agent, J. P. Barry, was working hard on my behalf to secure options for the upcoming season, but at that point, I couldn't imagine playing again.

The dock still reminded me of my teammates and our visit in September 2003. It had been a time of such hope for the Leafs and for me. Sitting there, I couldn't begin to reconcile that memory against the hell of my last few months in Toronto. I believed in my heart that I'd been the one fighting for the team. I believed I was the one with tenure, with the respect and ear of the team staff, and, if a rebuild was all we had left, the ability to help usher in that new era. I believed with all my heart that I wanted what was best for the team, and that a slash-and-burn approach would set the Leafs on a path that might take many years to steer back from. In the end, my decision was framed as a selfish one: I was worth the most money, and had refused to let them cash in that value. There was nothing I could do about that perception. I should have known better than to take it personally, but it wrecked me. I sat on that dock for a long while, trying to steady my thoughts. My body was tired.

A few weeks later, my brothers and I set out on our fishing trip. In the far north of Sweden, I found some space and time. I returned to Stockholm and visited Leif Larsson at Bosön, but told him I needed more rest than heavy training. I didn't see myself back on the ice in two months. He was surprised.

"You have good years left, Mats," he said.

In our regular calls, J. P. Barry insisted that I was still a player of interest. He'd held talks with Toronto. I'd made it clear that I'd accept a discount to stay, but every conversation still returned to the need to trade me for value in March. On every call where that was raised, I felt the same swell of anger I'd felt when Cliff and I met in Raleigh. How many times would I have to repeat the same refrain?

On July 1, the day I became an unrestricted free agent, J. P. called me in Stockholm.

"A big offer has come in from Vancouver," he said.

"Okay," I said.

"Two years, twenty million," he said. "Ten million a year."

That *was* a big offer. Far more money than I'd made in Toronto, and far more money than Toronto was offering. Still, I wasn't ready to make the decision. Even as the strain of the past few months started to wane, I still wasn't sure I would be ready to lace up my skates again in September. I thanked J. P., but insisted I couldn't say yes right away.

"I think I'm done, J. P.," I told him. "I haven't trained and I'm not sure I can find the motivation. I have to think about it."

"Think about it?" he said.

"Listen, J. P.," I said. "I—"

But the line was dead. J. P. had hung up on me. I understood his frustration. He was calling me with an offer he'd surely spent months negotiating. He'd no doubt held dozens of meetings and dinners with GMs, hammering out details on my behalf. J. P. was a good friend and an excellent agent. He knew I liked living in Canada, that I had a good relationship with the Sedin brothers in Vancouver. He also understood, in a way I wasn't yet fully willing to accept, that a comparable deal with Toronto was not going to happen. He understood that I still had life in me yet. With that in mind, he'd done his job very well and had a huge offer on the table from a competitive team.

And here I was, wavering. He had every right to be mad.

He called me back the next day, calmer. I joked that years later we'd probably laugh about all this. All J. P. wanted was for me to think seriously about it and not let my judgment be too clouded by the way things had unfolded in Toronto.

August came and went, and training camps began. I was still in Stockholm. It wasn't until the regular season began that some kind of instinct set in, a voice telling me it was time to get going, a gut desire to be on the ice. I *wasn't* done. I called J. P. and told him to restart the conversations. Josephine and I left Sweden and rented a house in Los Angeles. We wanted a warm and neutral place to be, somewhere I could complete on-ice training and work to get back into shape without attracting too much attention. J. P. and I met with the management team in Toronto again, but it was clear to everyone that it wasn't going to work. Montreal's GM, Bob Gainey, flew out to take me to dinner. In the end, J. P. was right: Vancouver was the fit. For all my heartache at not returning to Toronto, I was grateful for the chance to play again.

I landed in Vancouver in early January 2009. After my first practice, the coaches implied that I'd spend another week or so finding my legs with the team before lacing up to play. Then, after only two skates, it was decided that I would dress for a Wednesday night game in Edmonton. I hadn't played an NHL game in 285 days. I played fifteen minutes in that 4–2 win, but didn't register a shot on net. I understood then what it meant, at thirty-seven years old, to be joining a top team like the Canucks mid-season. It was a humbling night.

The Canucks' coaching system was different. I learned quickly that they used a "scoring" system of their own that had nothing to do with how many goals or assists you got. They had an entire staff dedicated to tracking hypercomplex analytics before the practice became common among NHL teams. Their focus had more to do with battles and chances won or lost. They were looking to quantify aspects of the game you could argue are too nuanced to quantify. It was new to me, but I appreciated all the work going into measuring accountability, even if my numbers weren't all that impressive at the start.

Over my career, I've had a few periods where timing felt fateful, either for better or for worse. After my first game in Edmonton, the team embarked on its worst losing streak of the season. I was getting a few points, but also penalties I'd never normally take. After the losses, the biggest media scrums were reserved for me. I knew it was going to be hard to find my legs, but I'd underestimated just how tough it would be to hit the ground running mid-season. NHL hockey is fast at the best of times, but the Canucks were a top team. I wasn't coming off a summer of training with Leif at Bosön; I'd worked out and prepared, but still, I was now climbing a steep hill. On a California road trip weeks later, an assistant coach approached me at the game-day skate in Anaheim.

"Mats," he said, "I was thinking. You should shoot the puck more."

It had been eighteen years and well over five hundred goals since Guy Lafleur had said the same to me, along with my grandfather Sture. I wasn't terribly gracious in my response to that coach. I might have even bitten his head off as my new teammates hovered nearby. He was well-meaning, and I felt bad.

After the February night in Toronto where I scored the shootout winner, my luck changed bit by bit. I learned about my new teammates and started finding the net. Josephine and I started building a little life in our new city. We settled into an apartment overlooking the water in Yaletown. Our dog, Coco, loved to sit at the window and watch floatplanes landing and tugboats passing on the Burrard Inlet. We got into the habit of taking long walks in Stanley Park. I'd never lived among mountains before, and I loved spotting them in the distance. Vancouver was a beautiful city with a landscape so different from both Stockholm and Toronto.

One difference that surprised me involved the Canuck fans. Over my fourteen years in Toronto, fans called out to me all the time on the street. Toronto fans are known for their bluster when it comes to their beloved team, but remarkably, never—not once over all those years—did a Leafs fan stop me in public to comment on my play or taunt me for a scoring drought. In Vancouver, it happened more than once. Still, my guess is they probably left the Sedin brothers alone. As a new face attached to high expectations, I was an easier target.

By the time the playoffs rolled around, my game was where it needed to be. We swept St. Louis in the first round, then moved on to play Chicago. We knew it would be a hard-fought series. And it was. After taking a series lead twice, the Canucks fell behind, three games to two. If we won Game 6, at the United Center in Chicago, the series would return to Vancouver for a deciding seventh game. If we lost, our season was over. Quite possibly, my career as well.

Of course, nothing was that clear-cut in the moment. I didn't arrive at the United Center thinking about my retirement. I showed up ready to win and to continue our playoff run.

Just like the guys in Toronto always did, the Canucks' equipment crew made every away arena feel like home. While the players slept, they were at the rink, sometimes all night, unpacking, cleaning, hanging, tightening, ironing, sharpening, taping.

I walked into the visitors' dressing room to the sight of Canucks jerseys lining each stall: Roberto Luongo, our goalie and captain, in his usual spot at the end. Ryan Kesler, Pavol Demitra. Kevin Bieksa. Three of my 2006 Olympic teammates: the Sedin brothers, Henrik and Daniel, and defenseman Mattias Öhlund. In nineteen years, I never tired of entering the room before a game and finding the jerseys crisp and ready and the early-bird players already locked into their routines. In my short time with the Canucks, in the forty-eight games I'd played with them, I'd come to really respect this group. I wanted more.

We went into the third period tied, 3–3, and confident we could secure the lead. Three minutes into the period, Kesler won a clean face-off. A rebound off Alex Edler's shot bounced to Öhlund, who tapped it over to me. I had a clean shot from the high slot.

Goal. We were up 4–3.

The lead evaporated when Chicago scored two minutes later. Shortly after that, Daniel Sedin scored. With barely eight minutes left in the game, we were ahead, 5–4. But in hockey, especially playoff hockey, eight minutes is a lifetime. Chicago scored less than a minute later, then again less than a minute after that. With six minutes left, we were losing, 6–5.

Chicago had a very distinct goal song: "Chelsea Dagger" by a Scottish band called the Fratellis. I didn't know the band's name at the time. All I knew was that this fast, drumming song—DE de de DE de de DE de de DE—blared every time they scored. It was the worst kind of earworm. When Chicago scored again with four minutes left in the game, the crowd was deafening. You could barely hear the coaches trying to give us instructions.

A hockey game isn't over until the final buzzer goes. We played hard as the clock wound down. But in the dying seconds of that game, on the bench, this sense of finality came over me. I was dripping with sweat, catching my breath after a shift as I'd done thousands and thousands of times. I looked up into the crowd, focusing on random faces. I rarely took note of fans while I was playing.

It felt absurd to be sitting there, listening to the opponents' victory song as the clock ticked to zero and the game ended. We'd just been knocked out. It wasn't how I'd wanted this season to end at all. Yet as the players lined up to shake hands, I was overtaken by a surprising feeling—gratitude.

I was no longer the same person I'd been when I started my career so many years ago. All I wanted in those early years was to be the guy who scored the big goals and saved the day. Over time, it became more about the team. Even if you're lucky enough to have a long career like mine, the journey from rookie to veteran is still short. I shook hands with our Chicago opponents and hugged my Canucks teammates. The room was quiet. It was a devastating loss, and I felt that with them. I also believed that these guys would go on to do great things. Many of them had long careers still ahead of them. I couldn't wait to watch them make their mark with their incredible talent and skill.

The Canucks management wanted me to play another year. It would be another four months before I'd officially retire, but in my heart, as we left the rink to fly home to Vancouver, I knew that I'd just played my last game. I knew it on the ice as the clock wound down. I'd never pull on an NHL jersey again.

Very few of us are lucky enough to write the precise happy

ending we want. I'd always imagined the glory of the Stanley Cup parade in Toronto. Even the most illustrious hockey careers often end with a whimper; an injury, a contract not re-signed, or, like tonight, a playoff loss. It wasn't the perfect ending, but it was mine nonetheless.

40

Home and Home

The lights in the arena lowered, and players from Toronto and Montreal lined up on the blue lines. I stood at center ice. On the blue carpet with me were Josephine and my parents, Tommy and Gunilla. Almost three years to the day after scoring the shootout goal for the Canucks, I was back at the Air Canada Centre.

Tonight, the Maple Leafs were raising my banner to the rafters.

The arena fell silent when the familiar voice of announcer Andy Frost filled the air. He spoke about my time as a Leaf, about the nearly 1,000 games I played in blue and white, 840 of them as captain. Thirteen seasons. Leading scorer in the franchise's ninety-five-year history. Most goals, most assists, most overtime goals. It was surreal to hear it laid out like that. When you're playing the game, you aren't focused on milestones. Only in hindsight does their significance come into focus.

When Frost stopped speaking, a violin version of U2's "With or Without You" started playing as scenes from my time as a Leaf played on the Jumbotron overhead. They aired clips of me scoring goals, but also of me celebrating and laughing with my teammates. I heard the familiar voices of Bob Cole and Joe Bowen announcing some of my highlight plays. As I watched, my love for the game washed over me.

I played so many games as a Leaf over fourteen years, with hundreds of different teammates. In that moment, I could have named every one of them, from the guys who played with me for years to the call-ups who came along for one road trip. Many of them, along with family and friends from Toronto and Sweden, were in the stands that night.

When the montage was over, Frost introduced us. I approached the podium as Josephine and my parents stood by. I wasn't sure I'd get through my speech. When my voice cracked at my first words, the crowd roared.

That's the thing about Toronto fans. They truly were—and are—the best in the world. They cheered as I pulled myself together. When I started to speak again, a guy in the nosebleeds hollered my name so loudly, it pierced through the entire arena. I laughed. I began by telling the fans what I missed the most about playing hockey. I missed that knot in my stomach on the way to the rink and practicing and playing with the best hockey players in the world. But mostly, I missed Toronto and its passion. I missed the best fans in the world.

When it came time to thank my former teammates, I had to pause to catch my breath at the mention of Wade Belak. My teammate for seven years, Wade died in 2010 when he was only thirty-five. His tragic death started some difficult conversations around the implications of the enforcer role, a conversation that comes up more and more often now. I spoke of Igor Korolev and Alexander Karpovtsev, two former teammates killed when the plane carrying the Russian hockey team they were both coaching crashed on September 7, 2011. These were all good men who devoted their lives to hockey and were lost way too soon.

My final words were to the players now sitting on the bench.

In the four years since I left the Maple Leafs, the entire roster had turned over and not a single player from my time remained. This 2012 squad was the youngest group in many years.

I finished speaking then lined up next to Josephine and we watched the banner rise to the rafters of the Air Canada Centre. I looked over at my parents. Both had eyes full of tears. That was happening more and more with Tommy lately, now that he had a few grandchildren and, as Josephine and I had recently learned, one more on the way that summer.

Josephine and I were married in August 2009 in Stockholm. Many of my former teammates attended the wedding, along with former coaches, trainers, equipment staff and, of course, Mike Walton. I wanted to celebrate with everyone who'd been such a big part of my life for so many years. A few weeks after the wedding, I officially announced my retirement, and Josephine and I made the decision to settle in Stockholm.

It took time for me to adjust to life back in Sweden. In 2010, I participated in a radio show called *Sommar i P1*, where the featured person tells stories about their life and picks music that matches those stories. It took three months for the producer and me to put it together. I spoke a lot about my childhood, but as we made the show, I noticed how much of my adult life was set in Toronto. For nearly fifteen years, it was my home. I left Sweden at nineteen; I'd lived in Canada for as many years. For a boy nervous about his Swedish accent at the draft, I was reading and even dreaming in English by the time my career ended.

There was a sacrifice in leaving Sweden in 1990, too. Without cell phones and email, it was hard to keep in touch with my friends. My parents and brothers and grandparents, and eventually my nieces and nephews, were always two plane rides away. It was time to settle closer to them. The way I saw it, I was lucky to have two homes: one where I happened to be, and one far away, awaiting my return. In that same spirit, I started a foundation and partnered the University of Toronto with Stockholm's Karolinska Institutet to create fellowships in support of early childhood research. Stockholm and Toronto would always both be home, and I wanted to give back to both cities in equal measure.

After the banner-raising ceremony, we returned to Sweden and readied for our expanding family. That June, my cell phone rang with a call from a Canadian number.

"Mats?"

I recognized his gruff voice right away. It was Pat Quinn.

"Hello, Pat," I said.

Nerves immediately got the best of me. Retired NHL players become eligible for induction into the Hockey Hall of Fame three years after they retire. I'd retired three years before, and Quinn was on the HHOF selection committee. I knew it was a possibility, but the 2012 class had many great eligible candidates, and I wondered if my difficult ending with the Leafs might affect my chances.

We exchanged quick pleasantries, and then Quinn got to the point.

"I wanted to be the one to call you," he said. "Congratulations, Mats. You've been elected to the Hockey Hall of Fame."

For a moment I couldn't speak.

"Thank you," I said finally. "Thank you, Pat."

He must have heard the waver in my voice. Pat filled the silence by listing my three fellow inductees: Joe Sakic, my first-ever captain from the Nordiques; Pavel Bure, the Soviet star whom Pat Quinn had craftily selected in the sixth round the year I was drafted; and Adam Oates, the Canadian superstar who played an astonishing twenty-two seasons in the league.

"I'm honored," I said.

"It's an honor to make this call," Quinn said. "We had a lot of good years together, Mats."

"We did."

I could tell he was getting choked up, too. We stayed on the phone for a while. He told me about his family. I told him about my life in Stockholm and the house Josephine and I were planning to build close to the Baltic Sea. Our first baby was due in August—a girl.

"You can bring her to the ceremony in November," he said.

"We will," I said. "Thank you, Pat."

For a long time after we parted ways in 2006, I thought of Pat Quinn only in terms of our years together on the Leafs. There were always going to be ups and downs in a coach–captain relationship as longstanding as ours, especially under a spotlight like Toronto's. Sometimes, I tended to focus on our differences, as I'm sure Pat did, too.

But with time, Pat Quinn's impact on my life came into clearer focus. When I was still just a boy, a Canadian guy in a fedora handed me a Vancouver Canucks pin and told me I had a future in the NHL. Two years after that, he shook my hand after I was drafted. Ten years later, he became my coach. We were part of a team that went to the conference finals twice. We faced off against each other at the Olympics. Together, we pulled out huge wins and endured the toughest losses. No one could command a room like Quinn could. Even when we disagreed, the mutual respect between us was always profound.

Before we hung up, I told him I was grateful for everything he'd done for me. True to his character, he brushed it off. He wasn't about to take credit for anything. But I did have many reasons to be grateful; twenty-five years after handing me that Canucks pin, Pat Quinn had successfully made the case for my induction into the Hockey Hall of Fame.

We parted with the promise to see each other in November. Three months after our daughter, Bonnie, was born, my family traveled to Toronto for the ceremony: my parents, Josephine, Bonnie and my brothers, Patrick and Per. Josephine's mother, Birgitta, even came to stay with little Bonnie while we attended the ceremony.

As I took the stage to make my speech, I looked out at my family and the many of my former teammates and friends who'd made the trip. My love for this game sent my life in a direction I never could have dreamed of when I was growing up in Sollentuna. My favorite hobby became my profession. It afforded me the opportunity to travel the world and meet so many wonderful people along the way. The most frequent question I get since retiring is whether I regret that I never won a Stanley Cup. The truth is, I regret not being able to win a Cup for the fans of Toronto. I wish I could have done that for the city. But at the same time, I wouldn't trade my years in Toronto for the world. I'm profoundly grateful for my career and all that it gave me.

On that Hockey Hall of Fame stage, I thanked as many people as I could for getting me that far. It felt fateful to have Joe Sakic inducted at the same time, a guy only two years older than me who served as my mentor, captain and linemate when I arrived in Quebec so many years ago. I was only the second Swede to be inducted after my dear friend Börje Salming, who was on hand to celebrate with me. I was really glad that Pat Quinn was there, too, one of the few who witnessed the beginnings of my career who was still with me to honor its end.

41

A Circle Closing

The Nobel Prize ceremony is held at Stockholm's Konserthuset Hall each winter and attended by the highest-ranking political figures and members of the royal family. In 2015, after learning he'd been awarded the Nobel Prize for Physics, Canadian scientist Dr. Arthur McDonald spoke with a Swedish colleague about his historic win. Never mind his Nobel Prize; the conversation turned almost immediately to hockey, with Dr. McDonald musing that he wished I still played for the Leafs.

Börje Salming and I were invited to a formal luncheon at the Canadian Embassy to meet him. After we shook hands, Dr. McDonald opened his suit jacket to reveal a Leafs logo pinned inside. Apparently he'd asked the embassy staff if it was acceptable to wear a Leafs jersey to the luncheon, and they'd suggested a suit might be a better choice, so he'd settled for the pin.

At the luncheon, a member of the prize committee asked Dr. McDonald to outline the discovery that led to this honor. He offered to explain it in hockey terms, and proceeded to illustrate his groundbreaking research on the movement of neutrinos by referencing goaltending and goalie cameras. Imagine you are

Henrik Lundqvist, he said. You save almost every puck fired at you. But what if the puck was the size of a pea?

As he spoke about mass neutrinos, Börje and I could not stop smiling. Everyone else in the room seemed baffled. After his talk, Dr. McDonald and I were interviewed together. He told the reporter stories of listening to Leaf games on the radio sixty years ago at his childhood home in Nova Scotia. I presented him with a signed jersey. At the formal ceremony a few days later, another reporter asked Dr. McDonald's son about their time in Sweden. Though he was there to collect a Nobel Prize, his son joked to the reporter that meeting Börje and me was the highlight of his father's trip.

The Swedes around us seemed to find this enthusiasm for his favorite hockey team amusing and strange. But Börje and I weren't surprised at all. Dr. McDonald was part of Leafs Nation. In the six years since moving back to Sweden, I was often stumped when I tried to explain Leafs Nation to outsiders, or to describe what it was like to play for a team as storied as the Maple Leafs. I couldn't articulate the privilege of being their captain or what it meant to play in front of fans as devoted as those in Toronto. In every country, in many cities around the world, people love sports. Swedes love sports. But Maple Leaf fans are die-hard in the best possible way. So much so that a Nobel laureate's love for his team would shine through even in the biggest moment of his life and career. When someone does greet me on the streets in Stockholm or calls out, "Mats!" from afar, my odds are on them being a tourist from Toronto.

Sometimes, though, they aren't just tourists. In early May of 2017, I got a 6 p.m. call from my friend Kristoffer Ahlbom, who asked if I could attend a concert that very night at the Globen Arena. The Swedish CEO of Spotify, Daniel Ek, would be there, and the performer was from Toronto and a fan of mine. We had a newborn at home, so getting out on short notice was tough. I told him I was exhausted and was planning on an early night.

"It's Drake, Mats," my friend said. "Your fan is Drake. You should try to make it work."

Needless to say, I did. Josephine and I scrambled together a babysitter and put on some nice clothes. We arrived at the arena and were ushered into a special section to watch the show. Onstage, Drake gave me shout-out, telling the crowd that he'd had my poster on his wall as a kid. After the concert, we waited backstage until Drake and someone from his entourage came to find us.

"I can finally check meeting you off my bucket list," Drake said as we shook hands.

Josephine took a few selfies of the three of us. It was surreal and humbling to meet him, a Toronto kid who'd followed my career as a fan and then gone on to do great things. Even the biggest stars don't outgrow Leafs Nation.

• • •

Since 2012, Josephine and I have been busy building our family life and traditions. After Bonnie was born, we welcomed Nathanael in 2014 and Julian in 2017. In many ways, I find it a blessing that my kids weren't born until after I retired, because I'm not on the road all the time as they grow up. I'm at home with them, doing school drop-offs and pickups, immersed in their lives just as my parents were in mine. My brothers and I still make our annual trip up north to fish. My father attends his grandchildren's sporting events now. He's not the main driver, but he's happy to be called on when needed. We live close to the water, just outside of central Stockholm. Coco the dog is still remarkably frisky at eighteen years old. While she transitioned well to life in Stockholm, she's a Toronto dog at heart.

In 2015, we traveled to Toronto as a family for my induction into Legends Row with Börje Salming. I loved watching Bonnie and Börje's grandchildren climbing on our bronze figures. We had dinner with Börje and his family. Seeing our statues side-by-side was very emotional for us both.

Fifty years after my father built it, my parents still live in that house in Sollentuna. There have been some minor renovations, but it's held up remarkably well. My kids pick apples from the trees my mother planted the summer after we moved in. My old bedroom is now full of Leafs memorabilia and medals from international play with Team Sweden that my dad proudly shows to visitors. Last summer, I took my children to the cabin by the Voxnan River so they could see where I spent much of my childhood. Decades after my grandfather sold it, it looked the same.

In September 2023, our extended family traveled to Kainulasjärvi to celebrate my mother Gunilla's eightieth birthday on the land where she grew up. Josephine and I take the kids up there several times a year, passing on the same traditions that were gifted to my brothers and me. Even though all four of my grandparents—Sture, Marta, Sven and Elsa—are gone, their legacy is strong.

The one downside to having my kids later is that they have little sense of my status as an NHL player, no matter how hard I try to convince them I was once pretty good. It took my father fifty years to produce actual proof that he'd attended the Swedish junior team's camp. He did eventually dig up a photo. There's plenty of evidence of my career online, but my kids aren't that interested in watching grainy videos of me scoring goals in 1991 or 2009. They're keener on the game's young stars.

Understandably, when the Toronto Maple Leafs announced they'd be playing in Stockholm for the NHL's 2023 Global Series, my kids were thrilled. When the team arrived on Swedish soil that November, we were swept right into their fold. I brought my kids and their cousins to Leaf practices at Hovet Arena and skills events throughout the city. Max Domi, Tie's son, now a forward on the team, joined my family for dinner at home. I'd gone with Tie to watch Max play hockey when he was a little kid in Toronto, and he'd taken to calling me Uncle Mats. I'm so proud to see him thriving in his own career. We made a video call to Tie from the table.

That week, the Maple Leafs held a special event to honor our beloved Börje Salming, whom we lost in 2022 to amyotrophic lateral sclerosis, or ALS. Losing Börje caused me to reflect on the fateful ways our paths intertwined. How amazing it was that two guys from Sweden would end up so deeply tied to the same NHL team nearly four thousand miles away from home. How he assured me in 1994 that I would love it in Toronto, then convinced me in 1997 to take the captaincy. He was a hero to me, then a mentor and dear friend.

On the last day of the Global Series, the Leafs played the Minnesota Wild.

When the captains were called to line up for the ceremonial face-off, I approached and smiled for the cameras. Of course, I'm not an NHL captain anymore. That day, my job was to drop the puck. My three kids stood nervously at my side in their blue Sundin jerseys. My parents and family were in the stands. Brothers, nieces, nephews, friends. So was Mats Hamnarbäck, my childhood coach.

I dropped the puck and shook the captains' hands. On the bench, the young Leaf players tapped their sticks for me. Max gave me a wave. I gathered my kids and ushered them off the ice as the crowd called my name. Even in Sweden, the stands were full of blue and white. When we got to our seats, my dad was choked up. He wanted everyone to text him photos of his three grandkids standing with me at center ice.

The Leafs won the game in overtime when Swedish star William Nylander scored the winning goal in front of his own hometown crowd. It made me feel old to think I played with his father, Michael, on the national team before William was born. After the game, my kids and I visited the Leafs dressing room. I got to speak with the young stars, like Auston Matthews, and connect with my former opponent and now Leafs president, Brendan Shanahan.

As we left the rink, I thought of the Leafs equipment guys who'd pack everything up for the flight to Toronto, then unpack it all on the other side. Bobby Hastings, who'd been on staff in my era, was still with the team. There were trainers who'd check in on the players. The coaches who'd move on from this win, their sights already on the next opponent. The families who awaited the players back home in Toronto. The players who'd do their best to sleep on the plane but might opt instead to play cards or video games, to enjoy the camaraderie they've built over the first few months of the season.

Four months later, in March 2024, I again found myself at Hovet Arena. That night, Djurgårdens IF was set to play Östersund in HockeyAllsvenskan, Sweden's second-tier league. But I was not there as a fan or a retired player. I was there as a dad. The league had invited a team of nine- and ten-year-olds to play a quick game during the first intermission in front of the sold-out crowd. My son Nathanael would be on the ice.

The night before, Nate had a hard time falling asleep. He was nervous. We talked about the knot in his stomach. I explained that it was a good thing. It meant he cared.

After school, Nate and I organized his equipment, taped up his stick and threw everything in the trunk of the car. I don't live in Sollentuna anymore, but as we crossed through Stockholm, our route to Hovet Arena merged into the same route I took with my father. It all felt so familiar—the drive, the anticipation, the knot in the stomach. But this time, I was in the driver's seat and my son was the passenger. He was the one fidgeting, his thoughts on the game. The hair on my arms and neck stood up at the symmetry of it all. How time flies.

We entered the rink using the same door as the players. I dropped Nate off at his locker room and took my seat to watch the first period of the game. As the clock wound down, I found I was nervous, too.

Finally, Nate and his teammates took to the ice. Nate is easy to pick out, but it was still shocking how small he and his teammates look out on the big ice surface. Music played as they chased the puck. The game flowed from end to end.

Nate's team gained the zone. One of his teammates circled behind the net with the puck. He released a perfect pass into the slot, where Nate waited. Nate caught the pass and fired the puck at the top corner, over the goalie's shoulder.

Goal. The crowd roared.

Nate raised his hands in muted celebration, looking for a team-mate to hug. I couldn't wait to tell Josephine. She'd want a video, which I didn't think to take. Luckily, a mom on the team caught it all on her phone and promised to send it to me.

We returned to the locker rooms to collect them. Nate was breathless, smiling.

"Did you see my goal?" he asked.

"Of course I did. It was incredible."

After the game, Nate and I carried his equipment to the car, then pulled out of the parking lot in silence. I imagined Nate re-living his moment of glory, that sensation of the pass landing on his stick, leaning forward to shoot, then watching the puck hit the back of the net. It's the best feeling.

"I was a teenager when I scored my first goal at Hovet Arena," I said. "You are only nine."

He didn't respond. He just squinted and smiled. Like my parents, I will never press my kids or impose my ambitions on them.

It's too early to know what Nate's dreams will be, what Bonnie or Julian will dream of for their lives. Whether it's sport, or science, or art, they will have our time and support in pursuing it. Josephine and I want them to work hard, stay active and be happy. To be good citizens.

As we drove, I felt an overwhelming sense of gratitude and peace. For a guy who wore the number 13 on his back his entire career, I was—and am—incredibly fortunate. I collected so many memories along the way, a list too long of people who guided and supported me, of teammates I was honored to sit next to on the bench. It was a wonderful ride. Fifteen years later, I have my beautiful family and two places to call home. One here in Sweden, and one across the ocean in Toronto.

Now it was my turn to be the driver. The parent in the stands. The equipment manager, the support person. To take on all those roles that people took on for me, in hockey and in everything else. It's a privilege.

We took a ramp onto the highway, cutting north through the brightly lit city of Stockholm. The road home was familiar, and my son sat happy next to me.

It felt like a circle closing.

Acknowledgments

Both Mats Sundin and Amy Stuart would like to thank the team at Simon & Schuster Canada for all their work in bringing *Home and Away* to readers, especially Jim Gifford for his guidance and editorial eye, as well as Nicole Winstanley, Rita Silva, Mackenzie Croft, Mike Turnbull, Dan French, Michael Guy-Haddock, Muna Hussein, Hunter Sleeth, Cali Platek, Kaycee Chapman and everyone in sales, publicity and marketing. Thank you also to Kevin Hanson and Nita Pronovost for believing in this project from the start, and to copyeditor Lloyd Davis and production editor Amy Medeiros for ensuring the manuscript was in top form.

We are grateful to Ulf Töregård and the team at Bookmark for bringing *Home and Away* to readers in Sweden, especially Claes Ericson, Stephanie Demmler, Frida Påhlsson, translator Cecilia Berglund Barklem and the sales, marketing and PR teams of Kristoffer Stjernberg, Fanny Wetterdal, Katja Lindgren Anttila and Lili Assefa.

From Mats

Ever since I was a kid, hockey was my vocation. With this book, I wanted to answer the most common question I get: How did I become a hockey player? My story has been full of ups and downs, but my love for the game was always the foundation, together with the support of my family, coaches and friends. I loved nothing more than being part of a team. Thank you to the NHL for bringing the best game in the world to fans, to Larry Tanenbaum and the entire Maple Leafs organization and to the city of Toronto and Leafs Nation for the fourteen fantastic years I spent with you. Thanks to the teammates whom I played with during my career; every single one of you made me a better player and person. To J. P. Barry: you are a true professional and the best at what you do, and most importantly a great man and friend. To Mike Walton, thank you for being a true friend to me for so many years. Thank you as well to my coaches with Djurgårdens IF, the Nordiques, Maple Leafs, Canucks and Swedish National teams who pushed me to be better, and especially to all the equipment managers, trainers and support staff who made it possible for me to play and perform, game after game, especially Brian Papineau and Scott McKay, who remain great friends of mine.

As I got older and especially after I retired, I realized that the best part of the game was the journey, and I remember everyone who was along for mine with fondness and gratitude. To every hockey fan out there in Canada, Sweden and around the world, I say: thank you. Being a parent has taught me that the most important things in my life are my family and health. I believe we need to let our kids play as many different sports for as long as possible, and to let them dream big. We don't need to get serious about sports early, because life gets serious quickly enough. Being physically active is the big win. Not everyone plays in the big leagues. Being part of a team is what matters the most.

Special thanks to Amy Stuart for being patient and down to earth, and for sharing your passion for writing. Thanks to Simon & Schuster for giving us a chance—this book would have been impossible without your team. Thank you to my parents, Tommy and Gunilla, my brothers, Patrick and Per, and their families, for everything.

To my kids, Bonnie, Nate and Julian, I am so proud of you. Most importantly, thank you to my wife and best friend, Josephine, for encouraging me to tell my story and for being patient with me as I did. You gave me the most important thing in our life, our kids. This book is for you. I love you.

From Amy

Working on *Home and Away* has been a dream come true for me as a hockey fan, player and coach. Mats has often joked that I didn't know him before we started working on this book, even if, as a lifelong Leafs fan, I thought I did. He is right—the player I figured to be quiet and reserved turned out to be a funny, thoughtful, intelligent guy with a passion for history, the outdoors and his family. I'm grateful to Mats for giving me the chance to help him tell his story. Many thanks also to Josephine Sundin and their three amazing kids, Bonnie, Nate and Julian, for welcoming me into their home and enthusiastically helping me piece together Mats's story. To Tommy and Gunilla Sundin, thank you for inviting me to Sollentuna, filling in the childhood years, showing me albums upon albums and allowing me to fawn over all your Maple Leafs and hockey memorabilia. To Mats's brothers, Per Sundin and Patrick Sundin, and their families, in particular to Per, Jenny, Stella and Frank Sundin, thank you for allowing me to tag along to local hockey arenas and hosting me for dinner. When I traveled to Stockholm in November to watch the Leafs play in the Global Series, the entire Sundin family was generously tolerant of my unbridled cheering as I sat among them in the stands.

In Sweden, I was so fortunate to meet many people who had a big impact on Mats's life. I got to visit arenas where Mats played as a boy and reminisce with his friend and former coach Mats Hamnarbäck. I toured Bosön athletic complex with the wonderful Leif Larsson, and spent an afternoon talking about Mats's draft year with Bengt Lundholm. It was a true honor to meet the legendary Nicklas Lidström and hear stories of their time together playing for Sweden. In Toronto, I got to meet Matt Nichol at his training facility, Paragenix Systems. I spoke at length with longtime Leafs equipment manager Brian Papineau, who even connected with the youth team I coach at a tournament and taped my players' sticks for them. Agent extraordinaire J. P. Barry took the time to answer many questions for me. As the book took shape, I need to doubly thank Matt Nichol, Brian Papineau and Per Sundin for patiently answering my text messages with questions on everything from Swedish meat cuts to brands of hockey tape. I'm incredibly grateful to everyone who so generously gave me their time and stories.

Thank you always to the team at Transatlantic Agency, especially my agent, Sam Haywood, for advocating for me and insisting that a novelist hockey fan might be the right fit for this job.

Thank you to my beloved Ian, Flynn, Joey and Leo, for your love and support and wildly good humor. To the Flynns, McQuillans, Van Dykes and Boydens for cheering me on from start to finish. I'm thankful always to my mom, Marilyn Flynn, to my extended family, and to my friends, hockey family and writing peers for upholding the community that surrounds me.

Above all, I want to thank my dad, Richard "Dick" Flynn. Nearly forty years ago, he listened when I begged to play hockey like him over taking figure skating lessons, as was the standard for girls my age. In 1987, he took me to my first game at Maple Leaf Gardens, begrudgingly cheering for the Leafs with his hockey-crazed daughter despite growing up a Habs fan himself. Decades later, when my sons started playing hockey, he became their number one driver and cheerleader, ready at any hour to be called to duty. As his Alzheimer's disease progresses, I feel a deep sense of loss that he can't quite marvel in all this, as I know he'd have done. I'm forever grateful to him, and I hope I've made him proud.

Career Statistics

NHL Regular Season					
GP	**G**	**A**	**TP**	**PIM**	**+/-**
1346	564	785	1349	1093	73
NHL Playoffs					
GP	**G**	**A**	**TP**	**PIM**	**+/-**
91	38	44	82	74	2
Olympic Games					
GP	**G**	**A**	**TP**	**PIM**	**+/-**
16	11	9	20	18	6
World Championships					
GP	**G**	**A**	**TP**	**PIM**	**+/-**
49	25	31	56	42	36
Canada Cup / World Cup					
GP	**G**	**A**	**TP**	**PIM**	**+/-**
14	7	11	18	20	5

Career Milestones

- First European-born player drafted to the NHL #1 overall: 1989
- Second in points on the Quebec Nordiques: 1990–1991, 1991–1992
- World Championship Gold Medalist: 1991, 1992, 1998
- Leading tournament points, World Championship: 1991, 1994
- Leading points and only season with 100+ points (114), Quebec Nordiques: 1992–1993

- Leading points for Toronto Maple Leafs for 12 of 13 seasons: 1995, 1996, 1997, 1998, 1999, 2000, 2001, 2002, 2004, 2006, 2007, 2008
- Leading playoff points for Toronto Maple Leafs for 5 seasons: 1995, 1999, 2000, 2001, 2004
- Sweden Olympic Team: 1998, 2002, 2006
- Overall leading scorer, Salt Lake City Olympics: 2002
- NHL Second All-Star Team: 2002, 2004
- Played in NHL All-Star Game: 1996, 1997, 1998, 1999, 2000, 2001, 2002, 2004
- Inducted into the Hockey Hall of Fame in first year of eligibility: 2012

Career Records

- 4th longest point streak of all time, behind only Wayne Gretzky and Mario Lemieux, 30 games: 1992–1993 season
- Ranked 30 all-time leading points in NHL
- Tied 23rd in career NHL goals: 564, shared with Joe Nieuwendyk
- Ranked 35th in NHL career assists: 785
- 28th all-time in career points: 1,349
- Only Swedish player to reach the 500-goal milestone: 564
- Most career points and goals by a Swedish hockey player
- First Swedish player to reach 1,000 points

Maple Leafs

- All-time points leader: 987
- All-time goals leader: 420
- Second all-time in assists, behind only Börje Salming: 567
- All-time game-winning goals: 79
- All-time game-winning assists: 101
- All-time leader, power-play goals: 124

About the Authors

Mats Sundin is the longest-serving captain not born in North America in NHL history. He enjoyed a prolific eighteen-season NHL career as well as a superb international career playing for Sweden, his homeland. When he was selected by the Quebec Nordiques in the 1989 NHL Entry Draft, he became the first European-born player ever drafted first overall. The Nordiques traded him to the Toronto Maple Leafs, and the rest is hockey history. At the time of his retirement, Sundin stood as the Toronto Maple Leafs' all-time franchise leader in goals and points. A quiet leader, the durable Sundin is regarded as one of the finest Swedes to have played in the National Hockey League, and one of the greatest Toronto Maple Leafs of all time. He lives in Sweden and visits Toronto often.

Amy Stuart's fourth novel, *A Death at the Party*, emerged as a long-standing #1 bestseller. She is the author of three other bestselling novels—*Still Mine, Still Water,* and *Still Here*—and all of her books have been optioned for film/television. Amy's other love is hockey. She is one of only a handful of women head coaches in the Greater Toronto Hockey League, the world's largest youth competitive hockey league. She was born in Toronto, where she still lives with her husband and their three sons. They also spend much of their time on Prince Edward Island, where Amy's family is originally from. Visit her website at www.AmyStuart.ca or find her on Instagram and Facebook @AmyStuartWriter.